AMERICAN MELODRAMA

THE AMERICAN DRAMA LIBRARY

The American Drama Library is an ongoing series of American plays in anthology format, in which we plan to emphasize nineteenth and early twentieth century plays. Each volume will be edited by a specialist in the field, with the purpose of revisioning a particular genre, historical perspective, or individual playwright. The greater portion of the plays will be those which are previously unpublished, out-of-print, or difficult to find.

Much of our dramatic past has been ignored, belittled, or misunderstood, with the result that dramatic literature as a genre has not taken its rightful place in American letters. A serious loss in the study of American drama is the unavailability of published plays, and the commentary on them by which an art form and its audience interrogates itself and its responses to social and artistic change, from an historical point of view. This is the all-important process by which a field of study matures in relationship to the new ideas of any age. It is also the basis from which a dramatic repertoire grows.

The American Drama Library will, we believe, bring many more plays, new interpretations of dramatic form and cultural history, and reconsideration of literary reputations to our readers. Perhaps in the reflection of American experience this new material gives back to us, we may see in greater detail how, as a society, we give form to our feelings in the art of drama.

The Publishers

AMERICAN MELODRAMA

THE POOR OF NEW YORK
Dion Boucicault

UNCLE TOM'S CABIN
George Aiken/Harriet Beecher Stowe

UNDER THE GASLIGHT
Augustin Daly

THE GIRL OF THE GOLDEN WEST
David Belasco

Edited, with an Introduction, by
Daniel C. Gerould

PERFORMING ARTS JOURNAL PUBLICATIONS
NEW YORK CITY

General Editors of The American Drama Library series:
Bonnie Marranca and Gautam Dasgupta

Library of Congress Cataloging in Publication Data
American Melodrama
CONTENTS: *The Poor of New York, Uncle Tom's Cabin, Under the Gaslight, The Girl of the Golden West.*
Library of Congress Catalog Card No.: 82-62096
ISBN: 0-933826-20-6 (cloth)
ISBN: 0-933826-21-4 (paper)

Graphic Design: Gautam Dasgupta

Printed in the United States of America

Publication of this book has been made possible in part by grants received from the National Endowment for the Arts, Washington, D.C., a federal agency, and the New York State Council on the Arts.

Contents

The Americanization of Melodrama

Daniel C. Gerould

The United States and melodrama came into existence at almost the same time—the late eighteenth century—and for much the same reason—the democratic revolution in thought and feeling. Crude, violent, dynamic in action, psychologically and morally simplistic, reliant on machinery and technological know-how for its powerful effects, melodrama became a direct expression of American society and national character. Originally a foreign import from Europe, the genre grew acclimatized on American soil during the nineteenth century. And by the mid-twentieth century, American melodrama—particularly film—would be exported throughout the world, viewed on a global scale, and widely imitated.

What seems to me the most significant thread to follow in this story is the way in which melodrama has shaped the American popular imagination, molding our perceptions of self and country. My intention is not to give a history of melodrama or to define the formal characteristics of the genre (others have dealt with these issues), but rather to explore its Americanization, to look at the picture that it paints of nineteenth-century American society and values and the heritage that it leaves to modern American popular culture.

Addressing the same broad public as contemporary cinema and televison, the melodramatic stage offered the citizens of the new nation the first "moving" pictures of their lives. In so doing, the theatre determined to a large degree how Americans saw their world and imagined their place in it.

My vocation is simply that of a *painter* . . . There is no arguing with pictures, and everybody is impressed by them, whether they mean to be or not.

So wrote the greatest of American melodramatists, Harriet Beecher Stowe, of her pictorial method in writing *Uncle Tom's Cabin* and its effect on our consciousness. In the inscrutably baroque prose of his autobiographical *A Small Boy and Others* (1913), the seventy-year-old Henry James looks back and remembers how as an eleven-year-old he was enthralled by *Uncle Tom's Cabin* at Barnum's American Museum, finding in its blatant tinsel "the flower of the ideal" and signs of "our earliest aesthetic seeds." Although James, in later years much given to the royal we, probably used "our" in a purely personal sense, the remark can just as well be construed in a wider fashion to apply to the country as a whole. For, out of the aesthetic seeds of melodrama grew the main stream of serious American drama, reaching its apex in O'Neill and continuing to the present, in affectionately ironic forms, in Richard Foreman and Sam Shepard. A mixture of reality and romance that embodies "the flower of the ideal," melodrama was and still is a major art form in America. Despite this striking pre-eminence, theatre—particularly nineteenth-century theatre—has not been regarded as part of our high culture, and the names of Boucicault, Daly, and Belasco rarely appear in histories of American literature (at best they get a passing reference), while the stage version of *Uncle Tom's Cabin* is patronized with a superior smile. I should like to adopt a more sympathetic attitude towards these popular melodramatic entertainments and consider them as cultural artifacts, expressing the American temperament, preaching American ideologies, embodying American aesthetic principles.

A new form of theatre that arose in Europe a decade after the French Revolution and reflected the progressive social ideals of the time (Rousseauism and the Rights of Man), melodrama is above all a democratic genre of popular art, designed for large mass audiences ignorant of artistic tradition and indiscriminating in matters of culture, but avid for robust entertainment and rudimentary moral instruction. Little wonder that this unabashedly plebeian dramatic mode—eclectic, vulgar, impure—found a receptive home in nineteenth-century America, flourished in the vast metropolitan theatres of New York and Philadelphia as well as on make-shift frontier stages in California and the West, and has remained to this day the most enduring species of "serious" (as opposed to comic) drama, film, and televison in the United States.

A saleable commodity, manufactured first in France, then perfected in England, melodrama was a product well-suited to export to the New World, where it could be easily adjusted to the rough and ready ethos of nineteenth-century Americans. From the start a penchant for innovation and quick acceptance of the new have been characteristic of American civilization, and the very nature of the melodramatic stage invited uninhibited search for novelty and sensation, rapid exploitation of topical subjects and trends, and venturesome ingenuity in pursuit of commercial success. For a pragmatic nation that preferred action to contemplation, here was a practical, non-elite art form—unhallowed by Aristotle, Horace, the Renaissance, or any theory—that obtained instant results from audiences.

And melodrama could be fabricated by almost any one—in no time at all (one week seems to have been the average time required to turn out a play). No need to be acquainted with the classics or the rules of literature, no need to know how to write verse, no need even to be creative. French or British dramas could be adapted in a few days, stories could be appropriated from dime novels. Quantity, not quality, was the measure of success. Boucicault and Belasco went over the hundred mark; Daly was not far behind. Non-verbal skills counted for more than literary mastery. The ability to stage strong situations and convey powerful emotion theatrically was the melodramatist's prime weapon.

Whatever melodrama lacked in psychological insight and artistic depth, it made up for by sheer technological skill. If its style and thought were primitive, the special effects of melodrama were sophisticated products of the latest advances in applied science. American materialism and entrepreneurial capitalism found in melodrama a congenial art. Intensely competitive and responsive to market conditions, theatres deployed battalions of stage hands to reproduce ever more faithfully trainwrecks, fires, snow-storms, steamship explosions, and avalanches (known as sensation scenes).

The melodramatic *Weltanschauung* could not fail to appeal to a new civilization, still in the process of expansive evolution, founded on a belief in opportunity for all, and dedicated to getting ahead and making money. For, the universe of melodrama is totally devoid of fatality and inevitability. Contingency rules; things can and will be otherwise. The individual can make of himself what he will. Naively optimistic, unscarred by any tragic awareness of man's limitations, the melodramatist nurtures a faith in human equality, the power of innocence, the triumph of justice (often outside social institutions and their imperfect structures).

Heroes and heroines of melodrama make their own destiny and forge their own morality. Good and evil are diametrically opposed in melodrama, but far from immutable; the absolutes are only provisional. The Russian playwright, Greek scholar, and film theorist, Adrian Piotrovsky, grasped this truth in 1924, when he declared, thinking of the recent Revolution and Civil War in his country:

Melodrama is the child of transitional epochs. Chance and relative morality, these are its driving forces. Melodrama by its very nature is individualistic.

On the melodramatic stage mute peasants, blind orphans, destitute pariahs are made whole again, receive inheritances, find ideal mates, discover better parents, acquire new identities, become rich and happy. Everything is possible: undergo a change of heart, start life anew, reform, move on, escape, be someone else. Even the villain may be offered these options. Social background, genes, wealth, talent are not major determinants in melodrama. All empathy goes to long-shots who come from behind, to triumphant underdogs, to lucky lottery ticket holders. If not *every one* can win, *each* human being has the chance in a society unfettered by Old World hierarchies of class and profession.

From the early days of the republic American audiences responded enthusiastically to the democratic sentiments with which melodrama overflowed. But there had been no declaration of independence in the realm of playwriting. Here the United States remained very much a colony of Great Britain for more than one hundred years after 1776. By a characteristic form of American anti-American snobbery (by no means extinct today), playgoers in the United States preferred European to native American melodramas, which won slow and grudging acceptance only in the second half of the nineteenth century. In his *History of the American Theatre* (1832), the early American playwright William Dunlap observes that audiences wanted plays that "had been sanctioned by a London audience." How like the present day! Because a prior British production guaranteed success in New York, Dunlap and other American writers of the time were pleased to have it thought that their plays were written by Englishmen.

Up to the Civil War, the repertory of the Chestnut Theatre in Philadelphia and the Park in New York—the country's two leading houses—dutifully repeated the offerings of Drury Lane and Covent Garden in London. American playwrights were reduced to imitating the works of European writers. David Belasco began his career as a play hack in California dramatizing the novels of Dickens, Collins, and Reade and adapting by the dozens hits from London and Paris. As a theatre manager, Augustin Daly was himself guilty of anti-American prejudice, producing almost exclusively foreign dramas.

It was only with the international success of *Uncle Tom's Cabin* (1852) and *The Poor of New York* (1857) that native American melodrama acquired prestige and impetus. Now for the first time in the 1850s first-rate melodramas on distinctively American themes, with colorful regional settings, started to be written, produced, and even exported. Given its chance, American melodrama quickly developed its own national flavor, colloquial idiom, hectic tempo, and special geographic structure.

From the days of Guilbert de Pixérécourt, the French father of the new form, melodrama has always been an art of wholesale borrowing. Unhampered by international copyright laws (which until 1875 lacked any teeth as far as adaptations and imitations were concerned), the nineteenth-century melodramatists took material where they could find it. Most adaptations were unacknowledged and unauthorized, and often three or four different pirated versions of a French melodrama currently in vogue would play in rival theatres at the same time.

The great master of adaptation was Dionysius Boucicault, a chameleon of a playwright who could take on the coloration of his habitat and, depending on his country of residence, write dramas that were typically British, Irish, or American. This Anglo-Irishman of French ancestry spent four years in Paris, from 1844 to 1848, learning the tricks of the melodramatic trade, and then during his first extended visit to the United States from 1853 to 1860 created three of the best American dramas of the 1850s: *The Poor of New York*, *The Octoroon*, and *Belle Lamar*.

THE POOR OF NEW YORK

The Poor of New York is an interesting case of partial Americanization, a hybrid work that still shows its European upbringing while already talking with an American accent. The French original—*Les Pauvres de Paris* by Brisebarre and Nus—was the hit of the 1856 season in Paris, and when the British novelist and playwright Charles Reade went to France that year looking for a new property to adapt for the London stage, he immediately settled on *Les Pauvres de Paris*, publishing his adaptation, *Poverty and Pride*, in 1856. But before he could get it produced, two pirated versions appeared on stage: *Fraud and its Victims*, and *The Pride of Poverty, or the Real Poor of London*. While Reade became involved in futile lawsuits and never succeeded in getting his adaptation staged, Boucicault quickly prepared his multi-titled version, which first appeared in America as *The Poor of New York* and *The Streets of Philadelphia*, then was exported as *The Poor of Liverpool*, *The Streets of London*, and *The Streets of Dublin*, and later revived as *The Streets of New York*.

"I localize it for each town, and hit the public between the eyes," the playwright asserted aggressively. Recognizing that what audiences now wanted was "the actual, the contemporaneous, the photographic," Boucicault in *The Poor of New York* supplies a wealth of authentic local details, mentioning real places, people, institutions, and events, with actual addresses and dates, such as Union Square, Fifth Avenue, Five Points, Brooklyn Heights, the Astors, the Livingstones, the Academy of Music, the Union Club, the Herald, and the Panics of 1837 and 1857.

But in adapting *Les Pauvres de Paris*, Boucicault did more than cleverly change street signs; he drastically shifted the focus of the drama, constantly adding topical references where no French equivalent exists in the original and supplanting sentiment by observation of national character and regional custom. *Les Pauvres de Paris* has the elegant plot architectonics characteristic of mid-century French melodrama. Effects are carefully calculated, and scenes neatly constructed to produce maximum emotional impact. The sociology of poverty and suicide is explored and exploited to elicit compassionate tears for the downtrodden. Boucicault, on the other hand, is more concerned with what the audience sees than with what it feels; he aims for the eyes, not the heart. New and unique to his American version is the equation of poor with streets and the stress on setting, urban dynamics, topography, the city as colorful spectacle, and citizens as undaunted performers. Instead of pathos, Boucicault gives us place; rather than maudlin, he prizes the histrionic. By simplifying the lengthy, tear-stained narrations of *Les Pauvres de Paris* and making the characters more vivid and amusing, the Anglo-Irish dramatist not only found the proper rhythms for a melodrama about fast-paced New York, but he also established what were to be the outstanding virtues of American melodramatic playwriting: speed and precision of tempo, and attention to comic detail—qualities, incidentally, that would be carried over into early American silent film.

From the point of view of the sociology and the iconography of the popular arts, the scene in *Les Pauvres de Paris* in which mother and daughter at first attempt suicide separately, then agree to die together, is fascinating. It shows to what degree popular nineteeth-century melodrama often reflected actual social problems. In mid-century France, particularly in Paris, the number of suicides by members of the lower classes, who often preferred death to slow starvation, rose to alarming proportions—a grim fact of life widely acknowledged in France at the time, as witness the frequent appearance of the motif in the serious literature of the period as well as in the serialized novels of Eugène Sue, melodramas, street ballads, and the graphic arts. Brisebarre and Nus were inspired by a popular narrative painting of the time, Octave Tassaert's "An Unfortunate Family, or the Suicide," showing a destitute mother and daughter in a miserable garret awaiting death from the carbon monoxide fumes of a charcoal heater.

The interconnection of poverty and suicide, a major French social issue, becomes an alien theme once the characters and plot are transferred to American soil. Confronted with extreme misfortune, American melodramatic heroes and heroines do not contemplate suicide—they fight back, get to work, start a new life, unrestrained by the passive gentility that holds back the Fairweathers, who remain unassimilated transplants from a European dramatic context. In *The Poor of New York*, Boucicault simply reduces the scene of the attempted suicides to a few short exchanges and downplays both sentiment and religion; nor is there any mention of the economic pressures forcing poor girls like Lucy to embark on a life of prostitution. Moreover, Boucicault downgrades the importance of the suicide scene in the structure of his adaptation; it is no longer the climax, but only a prelude to the true climax of *The Poor of New York*, the fire set by Bloodgood in the tenement at Five Points, which follows immediately in the next act. For the high point of his drama, Boucicault preferred a larger blaze, something more theatrically visible and exciting than a few pieces of glowing charcoal.

Ideologies of poverty differ radically in the New World and the Old. Act VII of *Les Pauvres de Paris*, set in the Townhall of the Twelfth Arrondissement, presents the thesis that the French authors are arguing: the "honest poor" must swallow their pride, seek help from the authorities, and accept public assistance. Boucicault discards this act and its message of social welfare—even in the face of overwhelmingly hostile odds, native American characters are self-reliant and eternally optimistic.

To give a realistic picture of contemporary life in New York, Boucicault studied the newspapers, searched the *Illustrated Journal* for scenes to dramatize, observed closely the world around him. Mid-nineteenth-century New York was famous for both its conflagrations and its fire-fighting. It was, in the words of one of its early chroniclers—Asa Green in *A Glance at New York* (1837)—"a very full-of-fires city." By making the sensation scene of *The Poor of New York* a spectacular blaze in a tenement house, Boucicault put on stage one of the most typical and theatrical sights of the city, characteristic of its wild energy and near anarchy. Fire was the best show in town, the city's most dependable spectacle, an integral part of New York's entertainment scene, always able to draw a sizeable crowd.

Until 1865, when a Paid Fire Department was first established, fire fighting in New York was done entirely by unpaid volunteers who served for love of the excitement, noise, and opportunities for fun and mischief. Youths engaged in the handicrafts and mechanical trades, Bowery Boys, and roughnecks made volunteer fire-fighting into a glamorous way of life and turned the firehouses into clubhouses, sumptuously furnished by local businessmen. The fireboys lounged about on the sidewalk, insulting passers-by and getting into fights, and those who were single—and sometimes even the married—lived at the engine houses (young Dan Puffy in *The Poor of New York* is proud and happy to be able to sleep at George Washington No. 4, his company). The colorful costumes—which the boys paid for themselves—consisted of dark pantaloons with a leather belt around the waist, large boots, a thick red shirt without coat or vest, and a helmet. Followed by hosts of screaming children, the fireboys raced along the streets at breakneck speed to the conflagration, pulling the huge lavishly ornamented engines by ropes (horses were not used until some years later) ringing alarm bells, blowing horns, and yelling as loud as they could.

Fireboy Dan—originally played by an actress—was a role particularly appreciated by audiences. Since the 1840s dramas about firemen and fire-fighting had been a distinctive American genre with no parallel whatsoever in British or French theatre, and Boucicault drew upon this tradition and the great popularity of Mose, the volunteer fireman who had first appeared in Benjamin Barker's *A Glance at New York* (1848) and then been taken up in many later comedies.

Extremely sensitive to the social and political climate in mid-century America, Boucicault correctly gauged the power of a crowd gathering in the streets of New York. A fire or a speech in the park could draw a crowd and quickly become a political—and theatrical—event. Brilliantly characteristic of Boucicault's dramaturgy is the way in which he transforms a high-pitched rhetorical speech in *Les Pauvres de Paris*—Livingstone's disquisition to Paul on the poor in Act II ("The poor!—whom do you call the poor?")—into a piece of street theatre simply by cutting the flow of words and adding a crowd of responsive spectators. In Boucicault's hands, a typical bit of French verbal gymnastics becomes an American street scene; the crowd in the Park near Tammany Hall interprets Livingstone's speech as a political oration and is broken up by the police who fear riots by the unemployed.

The melodramatic comic man who becomes the guardian angel and savior of the Fairweathers, Tom Badger (for whom only a pallid original existed in *Les Pauvres de Paris*) is the mainspring of the play, the embodiment of Boucicault's dramatic vision, and the quintessential New Yorker. It is easy to see why the actor-manager Lester Wallack, then known as Mr. Lester (himself a British transplant to the United States), became the toast of the town for his performance of the role. Brash, opportunisitic, wise-cracking, full of get-rich-quick schemes, garrulous, and softhearted, Tom Badger is a mid-ninenteenth-century prototype of the colorful New Yorkers popularized many years later by O. Henry and Damon Runyon.

By changing the dates of the action in the prologue and the main body of *Les Pauvres de Paris* from 1840 and 1855 to 1837 and 1857, Boucicault anchors his drama to the two great financial crises—or panics as they were then called—that hit New York, twenty years apart, in the mid-century. These panics gave *The Poor of New York* not only topical interest and authentic local color, but also its true theme: the pursuit of wealth in the Great City, the struggle for financial survival, the scramble for jobs, housing, and security. Boucicault views New York as an arena for fast and feverish speculation, as a theatre where the most amazing—and amusing—reversals of fortune can occur overnight. Poverty itself is but transient, a temporary offshoot of money-making and its sudden ups and downs. In such a volatile plutocracy, where business, politics, real estate, journalism, and fire-fighting are all intertwined, and nothing rules but wealth, surprising recoveries are always possible; one may lose a fortune, but an enterprising New Yorker never loses heart.

Changes in profession and place of residence mark one's fluctuating fortune in the Great City. Ups and downs on the ladder of success are accompanied by a constant moving to more or less fashionable or undesirable districts. The Fairweathers go from prosperous Brooklyn Heights to Five Points—the present Chinatown, the most dangerous and disreputable section of New York in the 1850s—and back again. Bloodgood has recently acquired his house on Madison Square, the new home of the rich as fashion gradually moves uptown. Real estate is on the mind of every New Yorker, as Puffy indicates when he observes to Livingstone, "You, poor, who own a square mile of New York?" A man's address and style of living (not the source of his income) defines his position in the Great City.

The Poor of New York came over from Europe, underwent naturalization on this side of the Atlantic, then traveled back to London, Liverpool, Dublin, Edinburgh. No matter how cleverly it was rendered topographically authentic in atmosphere and detail, the play remained derivative of its French original. Like its author-adaptor Boucicault, this relocatable theatrical commodity could find a home in diverse cultural contexts. The villainous banker was an international figure: Villebrun in a Parisian salon, Bloodgood in a mansion on Fifth Avenue, Crawley in a villa on Regent's Park, and the ubiquitous urban "Poor" were cosmopolitan, able to shiver in snow-storms or garrets in any great metropolis. It is for these reasons that I have dealt first with *The Poor of New York,* as a transitional work whose Americanization is a matter of conscious artistry and whose national identity cannot be more than partial.

UNCLE TOM'S CABIN

Now we must go back a little. Five years before Boucicault's transatlantic transplant opened in New York at Wallack's Theatre, American melodrama came of age with a purely native-born triumph, *Uncle Tom's Cabin.* In writing her novel, Harriet Beecher Stowe used only the most deeply indigenous material—Southern planters, Blacks, Yankees. Here was a story that could never be transferred to a foreign setting and that owed its fascination to its unique national flavor! There was no European model or precedent for such a radically American work. If there was another author, who served as a source for *Uncle Tom,* it was no one less than God himself who—Mrs. Stowe claimed—actually dictated the book to her. No ordinary nineteenth-century melodramatist would acknowledge as co-author the Almighty! But this tale of "Life Among the Lowly," as it was subtitled, was an altogether exceptional example of popular literature, expressing the "heart's indignant cry for justice," spiritual in intention and not authorized for adaptation to the stage.

Similar scruples did not hold back the world of commercial enterprise, which discovered in the dramatized *Uncle Tom's Cabin*—for which Mrs. Stowe never received any payment whatsoever—America's first long-running hit, the greatest success in the history of the American theatre. By the end of the century five hundred Tom companies were touring the United States; many actors spent their entire professional lives playing in *Uncle Tom.* As in the *commedia dell'arte,* performers became known by the roles they played: a Tom, a St. Clare, a Legree. Starting as a five-hundred-page novel in 1851, Mrs. Stowe's *Cabin* has existed in innumerable different scale replicas, both small and large. In its theatrical form, it has varied from a short one-act miniature with a handful of actors to five-hour six-act spectaculars with live animals—dogs, donkeys, horses, even alligators—two hundred jubilee singers, and real cotton ginned on stage.

The pandemic craze for *Uncle Tom*—first as a novel, then as a play—was extraordinary, giving rise to what we would call spin-off industries: dozens of songs, such as "Eliza's Flight" ("The ice is floating in the stream, / The wintry day is wild"), Uncle Tom dishes and crockery, restaurants, and even a board game called "Uncle Tom and Little Eva." Abroad the response was no less impassioned. Count Leo Tolstoi placed Mrs. Stowe's novel in the highest ranks of universal art, and Vincent van Gogh read and reread it with deep emotion. An *Oncle Tom Strasse* was named in Berlin, and *l'oncletomerie* became a French word.

Those two special melodramatic pleasures—excitation at flight and pursuit, and moral outrage at the victimization of innocence—find their highest expression in *Uncle Tom's Cabin,* particularly in those many scenes where mother love comes into play. For, as Mrs. Stowe wrote of Eliza's miraculous escape from her pursuers, "Stronger than all was maternal love." Melodrama lives, first and foremost, by its powerful appeal to the feelings, and herein lies what the Russian formalist critic Sergei Balukhatyi calls the emotional teleology of the genre. Since children torn forcibly from their mother's arms have always elicited the maximum of fearful empathy and tears, stolen babies were among the big weapons in the nineteenth-century melodramatic arsenal. But under a system where slave families could be violently sundered at any moment, every black child was potentially an orphan. Slavery was the great child-snatcher.

Harriet Beecher Stowe's most telling indictment of slavery was its destruction of the integrity of the Christian family, its ripping of husbands from wives, brothers from sisters, sons and daughters from parents. It constantly violated mother love. What all the most pernicious villains of nineteenth-century melodrama could accomplish only on a small personal scale in the way of assaults on virgins and mothers, the legal institution of slavery in the United States perpetrated every day against an entire race.

In *Uncle Tom's Cabin* traditional melodramatic character types and attitudes become infused with new social meanings. Harriet Beecher Stowe put the old formulas in the service of social criticism of the status quo. In an economic system supported by the state and its laws, whereby human beings become property bought and sold for profit, Mrs. Stowe unmasked a super melodramatic villain—the slave-owner, the slave-driver, the slave-dealer—abetted by legions of accomplices, both vocal and silent, who victimized the poor and defenseless on a mass scale. For the first, and perhaps only time, nineteeth-century melodrama found both a serious cause and an uncompromising author willing to treat the subject of social oppression without the evasions by which melodramatists from Pixérécourt to Boucicault had undercut their own championship of the downtrodden.

In the second half of the nineteeth century there appeared at least twelve different English-language stage versions of *Uncle Tom*, and uncounted foreign adaptations. George Aiken's dramatization was one of the very first and certainly the most successful and enduring. The twenty-two-year-old Aiken was the juvenile lead and journeyman playwright of the company led by his cousin, George C. Howard, who asked the young actor to do an adaptation of *Uncle Tom* in one week—for which he received forty dollars and a gold watch. In an expanded six-act form revised by Howard himself, Aiken's *Uncle Tom's Cabin*, starring the four-year-old Cordelia Howard as Little Eva, played for an unprecedented one hundred performances at the Troy Museum Theatre in Troy, New York—and Howard and family continued presenting it for the next thirty-five years until the actor-manager's death in 1887.

Aiken should in no way be blamed for later degenerate versions, such as the Double Mammoth Uncle Tom Shows, with two Uncle Toms and two Topsies, minstrel interludes, animal acts, cakewalk contests, and song and dance routines. Rather than a desecration, Aiken's stage version is in several ways an improvement on Mrs. Stowe's novel, to which it is for the most part remarkably faithful. Mrs. Stowe wrote her novel largely in dialogue form, making adaptation that much easier, and much of the time Aiken's lines are taken verbatim from the book. As Edmund Wilson pointed out, Harriet Beecher Stowe's dialogue was better than her narrative prose (she was a clever mimic and could imitate the way people actually talked), and the play version draws upon the strength of the original. But even the conversations in the novel become boring because they go on too long; here the condensation required for dramatizing *Uncle Tom* could not but help in reducing the verbosity.

Aiken understood that his primary task was to achieve "melodramatic intensities," and he did not hesitate to cut through the novel's leisurely exposition and garrulous explanations to do so. Quite instinctively, the young apprentice playwright made all the right choices about what to include and what to omit from his source.

Aiken retained all the major scenes in the novel which have become a part of American folklore: Eliza crossing the ice, Tom and Eva, Little Eva's death, Simon Legree torturing Tom to death—characters and events unwisely discarded by some of the other adaptors.

Having chosen to stress the relentless unfolding of events, Aiken has no time for the comic Senator Bird, or for Mrs. Stowe's facetious ethnic humor about Uncle Tom's "woolly-pated" brood of children, Aunt Chloe, Sam and Andy (comic slaves on Shelby's estate who help thwart Haley's attempts to catch Eliza), and the cook Dinah, Adolph the coachman, and other "amusing" blacks at St. Claire's mansion in New Orleans. Dropped too is the long sequence in which Cassy and Emmeline hide in Legree's attic and pretend to be ghosts. Except for Topsy (who, as we shall see a bit later, quite transcends the purely comic), Aiken reserved all the comedy in the play for the white characters, especially the Yankees—Gumption Cute and Deacon Perry, his own inventions. For modern readers, Mrs. Stowe's attempts at black folkloristic humor are unpalatable; for Aiken, they were simply detrimental to the singleness of melodramatic effect that he sought. Accordingly, in the stage version there is only one very brief scene set in Uncle Tom's famous cabin, and it is entirely devoted to Eliza's flight.

Slavery in Aiken's *Uncle Tom's Cabin* is an unmitigatedly grim business, without the palliative of black local color. By leaving out the cosy and comical domestic scenes that Harriet Beecher Stowe gave her black heroes and heroines, the young playwright isolates characters like George and Eliza Harris and renders their situation stark and desperate at all times. In Aiken's dramatization Eliza's plight is more extreme, and her daring greater, since she must stand totally alone and defend herself unaided, whereas in Mrs. Stowe's novel she is abetted by Mrs. Shelby and Shelby's other slaves, all of whom deliberately mislead Haley and impede his pursuit.

Aiken gives us the highlights of the novel, its key images, best scenes, major characters—all in précis. And he does this through a spatial unfolding of the action—continuous physical movement in scenically differentiated place—that anticipates the techniques of film. Eliza's flight is a good illustration of the pre-cinematography that melodrama pioneered. Eliza first appears in her unadorned room in Shelby's mansion where she learns from her husband George that he plans to flee to Canada; then, having overheard that she and her son will be sold, Eliza suddenly bursts into the elegantly furnished dining room where over dessert wine Shelby and Haley are deciding her fate, and retrieves little Harry. Next, in rapid succession, she visits Uncle Tom's cabin to announce her flight, reaches the tavern by the riverside, escapes through the window pursued by Haley, Marks, and Loker, flees across the snowy countryside, and crosses the Ohio River on cakes of ice. A camera seems to track Eliza; the dynamic spatial progression of a film scenario has replaced the fixed perspective of old-fashioned verbal dramaturgy.

Melodrama is place-oriented; the titles, or sub-titles, of most melodramas specify a location. *Uncle Tom's Cabin* is organized topographically, on a scale commensurate with the new nation. In such a vast country, characters appear and disappear, never to return; the black protagonists move in opposite directions, from state to state. George and Eliza cross from Kentucky into Ohio, then Pennsylvania on their way up to Canada—by the end of Act II they are gone forever. Tom goes down river to New Orleans and then to Legree's "dark places" in Louisiana—the evil slave-driver enters for the first time in Act V—while Topsy goes up to Vermont with the New England spinster, Miss Ophelia. Northern and Southern polarities increase throughout *Uncle Tom's Cabin* and threaten to pull it apart—as happened to the two sections of the United States in the 1850s prior to the outbreak of the Civil War.

The supremacy of image over word in melodrama is illustrated by the use of tableaux, accompanied by music, to end many scenes and all acts in a wordless picture encapsulating the import and impact of an entire episode. Sometimes, as in Eliza's floating slowly across the river on a cake of ice, these tableaux were "moving" pictures, or they might be motionless poses held for a few instants, forerunners of the filmic freeze frame. The most famous tableau in all of American drama is the final scene of Aiken's *Uncle Tom*.

Frequently ridiculed and parodied, this ultimate apotheosis boils down many pages of treacle in the novel (where Tom dreams of Eva rising from the ground to the heavens, a golden halo around her head) into one lusciously syrupy visual image of the purest kitsch. Vision scenes were popular in mid-century melodrama, and such a gaudy triumph in the sky was perhaps the only way to bring to a rapid and happy conclusion a drama that ended badly here on earth. In the final chapters of the novel, Harriet Beecher Stowe has recourse to the last-minute discoveries of Roman comedy for her denouement. George Harris is re-united to his long-lost sister, and Eliza finds her mother in Cassy, whose shattered faith in mankind is promptly restored. Such a providential happy end can only weaken Mrs. Stowe's outraged protest against the barbarities of slavery. Aiken's use of the beatific tableau, immediately following Tom's harrowing death, provides powerful dramatic foreshortening and contrast, theatrically preferable to Harriet Beecher Stowe's tying up of loose ends through long-winded revelations of identity.

Within one hundred years of the publication of Mrs. Stowe's novel, this same Uncle Tom—instead of exemplifying the highest virtues—had become for black Americans the very symbol of all that was to be despised: an "Uncle Tom" was a byword for a servile, truckling coward and traitor to his race. Although in the text of *Uncle Tom's Cabin* black characters had enjoyed for the first time central roles as heroes and heroines (an equality that they would not achieve again in American drama until the twentieth century), such desegregation never existed in the theatre. On stage *Uncle Tom* was always a demeaning "black-face" show, with white actors aping the supposed shuffling gait and ludicrous diction of plantation "darkies." Only George and Eliza, Cassy and Emmeline—who looked white and could pass—were played without burnt cork or dialect. It was not until 1914 that Sam Lucas became the first black actor to play the part of Uncle Tom.

By the late 1940s—as the civil rights movement and struggle for racial integration gained momentum—*Uncle Tom's Cabin* seemed a grotesque reminder of a shameful past, something almost obscene, that was best buried and forgotten. Due to protests by liberals, both black and white, the novel was kept out of school curricula, and the play was banished from the stage. *Uncle Tom's Cabin*, once held responsible for starting the Civil War, was now branded as racist in its stereotypes and became unperformed and unperformable.

But this controversial work has proved hardy, and its meanings have shifted with historical change. Pride in blackness, renewal of interest in the American past, exploration of early American theatre, and simple nostalgia have combined to open new perspectives on Mrs. Stowe's novel and its stage versions. For the first time *Uncle Tom's Cabin* can be viewed dispassionately—although still with emotion—as an integral part of our cultural and social history. When in 1978 the Trinity Square

Repertory Theatre in Providence, Rhode Island, staged *Uncle Tom* in a new version by Adrian Hall and Richard Cumming, the production was called "A History" and included both the drama itself and extensive commentary on it by Harriet Beecher Stowe, George Aiken, and Frederick Douglass, among others, who discussed the history of the theatre and American prejudices against the actor and his art.

Above and beyond these embellishments (the high point being Wolcott Gibbs's hilarious parody of Little Eva's death), most of the old drama proved theatrically exciting and valid in itself. Nothing added to *Uncle Tom* could improve on its powerful images. In the case of the tragicomic Topsy, the critics were agreed that not only did the vitality and humor of the role come alive in performance, but also the dreadful sense of wasted human ability in this bright, but neglected and abused child, who—lonely and unloved by any one—was consumed by feelings of worthlessness and self-hatred. Here was the tragedy of slavery, and the rehabilitation of *Uncle Tom's Cabin.*

UNDER THE GASLIGHT

"It is the desire of every American to see New York, the largest and most wonderful city in the Union." So opens the Preface to *Lights and Shadows of New York; or, the Sights and Sensations of the Great City* (1872), one of the many journalisitic exposés appearing in the second half of the nineteenth century designed to satisfy the ever-growing curiosity of the entire nation about the metropolis and "its splendors and wretchedness, its high and low life, its marble palaces and dark dens, its attractions and dangers." By the end of the Civil War, New York had become transformed from a bustling town to a huge modern metropolis of nearly one million. Describing the extreme contrasts of urban existence, James McCabe, author of *Lights and Shadows*, quite naturally falls into the hyperoblic and emotionally overwrought language of the stage—an indication of the extent to which reality was then perceived in melodramatic terms. In grandeur and depravity New York could now compete with the capitals of Europe. "Though this city is not so large as London," Matthew Hale Smith boasts in *Sunshine and Shadow in New York* (1868), "life here is more intense, crime is move vivid and daring; the votaries of fashion and pleasure are more passionate and open." Augustin Daly's *Under the Gaslight* is a dramatic version of these handbooks and offers much the same thrills. Mid-century American melodramas like *Under the Gaslight* gave the public an opportunity to visit, with complete immunity, the most terrifying and fascinating sites of the urban landscape. With its extremes of wealth and poverty, its stark contrasts of virtue and vice, the metropolis itself became the great world theatre of melodrama.

The craze for lurid city dramas was created by the French novelist Eugène Sue, with his eight-volume serial, *Les Mystères de Paris*, published in 1843 and adapted for the stage the following year. Probing, in a sensationalistic fashion, the misery of the poor laboring classes, exploited by society and victimized by criminal elements, Sue's Parisian epic popularized the image of the teeming metropolitan labyrinth with its shameful secrets and hidden iniquities. Imitations were quickly concocted by authors anxious to cash in on the extraordinary success of Sue's mysteries. Grangé and Dennery's *The Bohemians of Paris* in 1843, Félix Pyat's *The Ragpicker of Paris* in 1847, and Paul Féval's *The Mysteries of London, or The Gentlemen of the Night*, dramatized from his own novel in 1848, continued the vogue for realistic urban scenes featuring derelicts and vagabonds and helped to establish the melodrama of low life as a successful formula. In Britain off-shoots such as *Lost in London* (1867), *London by Night* (1868), *After Dark* (1868), *The Great City* (1867), *The Lights o' London* (1882), and *The Great World of London* (1898) reflect the limitless curiosity of audiences to see portrayed on stage the fearful and distressing aspects of city life.

In America, dramas about New York—along with the Wild West shows—represent one of the earliest forms of native theatre, but for many years these plays were farcical in tone and played only at the low-class Bowery theatres. Boucicault's *The Poor of New York*—given uptown at Wallack's Theatre on Broadway and Thirteenth Street—marked a turning point in Great City drama and served as a model and inspiration to native American playwrights desirous of painting a serious picture of contemporary urban life. The most thoroughly indigenous of such plays is Augustin Daly's *Under the Gaslight*, presented on August 12, 1867, at the New York Theatre where it ran for over one hundred performances during its initial season.

At first glance, Daly's melodrama—subtitled *Life and Love in These Times*—may strike us as a rather loose stringing together of picturesque episodes of urban life that take the spectator from the elegant blue ballroom of Delmonico's new restaurant on Fifth Avenue and Fourteenth Street to Pier 30 on the Hudson, and from the Tombs Police Court at Leonard and Centre Streets to a fashionable resort home on the beach at Long Branch, New Jersey. In such a city travelogue, the notorious railroad sensation scene—the villain ties a one-armed Civil War veteran to the tracks—seems almost an afterthought, and at the end the whole implausible story is hastily tied together with that old piece of frayed twine, babies changed in cradles.

What gives *Under the Gaslight* its magical power lies beneath its haphazard plot and thread-bare devices. Daly's melodrama of the Great City speaks directly to the spectator's primitive fears and longings. In the young heroine's sudden dispossession and last-minute restitution, we experience dream terrors and fantasies of wish-fulfillment. With the precise details and real settings of a nightmare, a world of night-time obsession and childish dread is called up from the depths. Menacing figures lurk in the shadows. Old Judas looms at the basement window, and when least expected, Byke pushes the door open—try as we may, we cannot hold the door shut against the pressure from the outside. The dark, subterranean forces will not be gainsaid.

Whereas *Uncle Tom's Cabin* presents the pain of enforced separation between parents and children from the adult point of view of the mother, *Under the Gaslight* dramatizes the same anxiety as seen through the eyes of the child. In the perilous ordeal of the classic fairy tale, as described by Bruno Bettelheim in *The Uses of Enchantment*, the hero or heroine undergoes a process of psychic maturation through deprivation. Such is also the case in *Under the Gaslight*. Already bereaved of her adoptive mother when the play opens, Laura is quickly divested of the love and protection of sweetheart and family, cast out by society, brutally abandoned and left alone to suffer the severest trials. The world of melodrama—with its radical polarities and colorful simplifications—is in many respects akin to that of the fairy tale.

Bereft of her accustomed supporting cast of upper-class characters, Laura discovers kind-hearted and loyal comic helpers among the poor, including Peachblossom, who has a brush and broom and a Shakespearian fairy name, and Snorkey, Bermudas, and Peanuts, who have comic-strip names and professions (messenger boy, street vendor, newspaper boy). In her underground dungeon-basement, Laura learns to fend for herself, to overcome dangers, even to protect her protectors. Once her sheltered and privileged self has been rudely dislodged, the heroine can grow up in the real world and be independent, until at last she learns her true identity and can be re-integrated into the old society that had cast her out.

On the social level *Under the Gaslight* contains still deeper and less re-assuring implications. (Why should we always assume that the psychological level is the deepest?) For nineteenth-century Americans the truth about poverty and crime was repressed. These social sores were visible enough, but so familiar that few actually saw them or were willing to search out the causes of haggard poverty amid colossal wealth.

Squalor and ugliness, washed clean from Boucicault's tidy *The Poor of New York*, surface as the tip of the iceberg in *Under the Gaslight*. The huge, lumbering, shabbily-dressed, drunken villain Byke and his filthy female accomplice Old Judas are hideous figures from what was then called "The Nether Side of New York," to use the title of yet another journalistic exposé of the period. Coming up out of the slums into the light of Fifth Avenue, these two slugs from the under-classes keep crawling onto the doorsteps of the rich, forcing their way into elegant salons, corrupting the courts of justice.

Former commanders of a juvenile army of beggars and pickpockets, Byke and Old Judas draw Laura back into what she imagines to be her inescapable past. Laura was one of this vast horde of shivering, ill-clothed, half-starved paupers—there were at least ten thousand such waifs under the age of fourteen adrift in the streets of New York at the time.

Dickens's *Oliver Twist* left a deep impress on the melodramatic stage, and Laura's experiences as a child owe something to those of Oliver and the other boys schooled in crime by Fagan. And Laura, like Oliver, is pursued by the criminals and kidnapped on the hypocritical pretense of returning the child to her rightful family. In one case, the kidnapper is Fagan's sinister henchman Sykes; in the other, it is Byke—even the name is Dickens-derived, as this juxtaposition reveals. Daly remained under the spell of Dickens; he later adapted *Oliver Twist* and presented it at the Fifth Avenue Theatre in 1874.

Just as *Uncle Tom's Cabin* had offered white audiences a glimpse of what it felt like to be a slave, so *Under the Gaslight* gave the public a taste of poverty. Melodrama has always sought out new areas of experience, capable of shocking and titillating. The same technique was used later in American novels probing racial prejudice, such as *Gentleman's Agreement* and *Black Like Me* (both subsequently made into films), where the hero conducts a conscious experiment by changing his identity or the pigment of his skin in order to discover what Jews and blacks suffer because of discrimination. In *Under the Gaslight* Daly sets up a similar test case: a rich girl suddenly finds herself displaced and forced to confront the horrors of poverty. Of course, given her character and upbringing, Laura quickly becomes self-sufficient, earning her living by retouching photographs in her scrupulously clean and neat basement apartment. No victim of grim determinism, she triumphs over circumstance through an exemplary display of industry and good humor. But another fate could have overtaken any one with less resolution, as Daly is at pains to make clear.

In the most surprising reversal of what we might expect in the melodramatic ethos, Daly makes his heroine not the saved, but the saver. The poor working girl chops her way out of the shed and pulls the one-armed veteran from the tracks at the very last moment. Thrust out from her world of privilege, Laura has learned to use her hands and to handle tools—kitchen utensils for cooking her own meals, re-touching instruments for her work with photographs. Now she takes up the axe. Her presence of mind and heroism lead Snorkey to comment, "And these are the women who ain't to have a vote!" This topical reference to the unsuccessful activity of American suffragists helps to place *Under the Gaslight* in the larger cultural context of the time.

Although Daly argues no thesis in his play and concludes *Under the Gaslight* with an old-fashioned "babies-and-cradles" denouement that dissolves in wish-ful-filling euphoria the initial class conflicts of the drama, we are still left with sharp, bright images of, on the one hand, an effete, self-indulgent upper class, shallow and egotistical in Pearl, weak and cowardly in Ray, who had obtained a commission during the Civil War, but who left when the fighting began in earnest (much as he abandoned Laura), and, on the other hand, a picturesque, self-reliant under-class, criminal and dangerous in Byke and Old Judas, good-humored and eager to work in Snorkey, Peachblossom, Peanuts, and Bermudas. The social elite of New York are explicitly characterized as a pack of wolves. Byke—as Snorkey explains—was at least "hard up" and without hypocritical pretense, unlike a good many Christians. Laura bridges both worlds, experiencing the hard lot of the poor and returning to a life of ease only after developing her own sense of worth and independence.

In *Under the Gaslight* Daly created the most memorable of all sensation scenes: helpless victim bound hand and foot by the villain and placed in the path of an oncoming train. The American playwright invented the victim-on-the-track effect, but he was not the first to put a train on stage. This had been done the preceding year, in 1866, in the unsuccessful British drama, *The Engineer*, given at London's Victoria Theatre, and Daly was accused of stealing the idea.

If *Under the Gaslight* can be considered a fairy tale, then the train is its giant, dragon, or monster, over which the heroine achieves victory. And I think it likely that Daly remembered the personification of the railroad in Dickens's *Dombey and Son* as a remorseless giant, a fiery devil that with "a shriek, and a roar, and a rattle" rips through the countryside, fearsome and death-bringing. In nineteenth-century literature the railroad often played a sinister role.

Seen in the social history of the period, Daly's train represents change. It is a sign of the transformations that were rapidly obliterating the old rural America and ushering in the age of bigness, technology, depersonalization, financial manipulation. The expanding railroad industry was the source of many New York fortunes and made accessible to the rich luxurious out-of-town residences, such as the Court-lands' in Long Branch. But while the railroad increased the wealth of the few, it produced slums and urban blight wherever it went, making the life of the poor still grimmer and grimier, placing the dispossessed forever on the wrong side of its tracks. With its deafening noise and blinding light and speed, the train bearing down on Snorkey and threatening to dismember his already maimed body becomes the fearful onrush of modern urban life, the very embodiment of the oppressive Great City.

On opening night the terrifying effect of the sensation scene in *Under the Gas-*

light was spoiled by a technical mishap: the train fell apart immediately after its climactic appearance on stage. From contemporary accounts we know that sensation scenes in nineteenth-century melodrama (like their counterparts in our modern disaster films) could have a staggering impact on audiences. During the explosion of the dynamited steamship in *The World*, a spectacular British drama of 1880, "women shrieked, and men got up from their seats to flee the theatre." Technical know-how quickly improved, leaving far behind the crudely simulated train that split in two on opening night, and whereas a single sensation had once sufficed to make a play a success, within a few years there had to be a spectacular effect in each act in order to attract the public.

As soon as it first rushed on stage, other melodramatists clambered to get aboard Daly's train, and several of them successfully commandeered it. The most celebrated train theft was the work of that master adapter, Dionysius Boucicault, who put a comparable scene in his "Drama of London Life," *After Dark*, which opened on August 12, 1868, in London, where *Under the Gaslight* had already been playing since July. To make it as contemporaneous and topical as possible, Boucicault placed his sensation in the subway; the London Metropolitan Underground Railway had opened in 1863 and was still a great novelty, and the playwright sensed that the tube could be a striking symbol of urban peril. In *After Dark*, as the train roars down an adjacent tunnel, where the hero Gordon Chumley lies unconscious on the tracks, we watch Old Tom frantically dig his way through a brick wall.

Daly, who regarded the rescue from the tracks as his private property and therefore patentable, brought suit against Boucicault, but existing copyright laws made no provision for international rights. But when *After Dark* was announced for production in New York, Daly brought an injunction against Boucicault for infringement of his copyright, starting a series of lawsuits and legal battles that went on for the next twenty-six years, from 1868 to 1894, finally reaching the Supreme Court. The first ruling had been that Boucicault must pay royalties to Daly on every American performance, but subsequently *After Dark* was staged in slightly altered form to circumvent the law. Evidence at the new trial became incredibly complex as various witnesses described the precise staging of the train scene at different performances in different cities, while the defense attempted to prove that the railroad episode was not original with Daly but came from an earlier play *London by Night* (which in actual fact in its revised form plagiarized the famous scene from *Under the Gaslight*). In 1889 Daly's injunction against Boucicault was denied on the technicality that there was a verbal difference between the registered and the published subtitle of *Under the Gaslight*, the one being "A Drama of Love and Life in These Times," the other being "A Romantic Panorama of Streets and Homes in New York."

So Daly lost the battle of the railroads. In the meantime, not only had *After Dark* proved an immense success, but *Under the Gaslight* was also a hit in England, both under its own title and in disguised forms, such as *London by Gaslight*, without Daly's receiving any royalties. American melodrama now had the distinction of being pillaged by British writers; the process of adaptation moves back across the Atlantic.

THE GIRL OF THE GOLDEN WEST

By the early twentieth century attendance at the popular melodrama houses had drastically fallen off. Managers, critics, and playwrights speculated as to the cause of the crisis. Was it the competition from the new five-cent moving pictures that had sprung up everywhere? Or were vaudeville and burlesque theatres, where seats were also fifty cents, offering better entertainment? Or had audiences simply grown tired of the old rapid-fire melodrama with its devilish villains, breakneck thrills, and endless sensations? Whatever the reasons for the decline in popularity, the solution—all agreed—was to provide "higher class" melodrama.

The classiest purveyor of the new sophisticated melodrama was the great American theatre impresario, David Belasco. Actor, adapter, playwright, director, manager, Belasco—who became known as the "Bishop of Broadway" because of his penchant for wearing reversed collars—had served his apprenticeship in the old school of rough and ready melodrama while in his native California where by the time he was twenty-five he had turned out more than one hundred plays and acted in many West Coast theatres (he appeared in a San Francisco production of *Under the Gaslight*).

The Girl of the Golden West—generally regarded as Belasco's finest play and the best melodrama of the West—was produced at the New Belasco Theatre in Pittsburgh on October 3, 1905, and at the Belasco Theatre in New York on November 14, 1905, a late point in the history of melodrama by which time the now venerable genre was in its dotage and being challenged on all sides: by the silent cinema (already a major entertainment industry), by realism and naturalism in the theatre, and by newer, more tolerant attitudes to matters of sexual and social morality.

We are now in the twentieth century, and many changes have taken place in the fifty years since *The Poor of New York* and *Uncle Tom's Cabin* first broke new ground. The crude devices, informational asides, and stereotyped characters of the mid-century melodramas were no longer acceptable in the 1890s. At a time when all but the worst hack British playwrights had already given up the genre as hopelessly old-fashioned, Belasco—along with two other American playwrights, William Gillette (*Secret Service*, 1895, and *Sherlock Holmes*, 1899) and Augustus Thomas (*Arizona*, 1899)—modernized melodrama by reducing its sentimentality and wooden rhetoric, limiting its violence (chiefly to act endings), and making its plots more coherent and its characters and themes more serious and intellectually respectable. Intended for literate Broadway audiences, the new wave of melodramas showed the impact of realism and its more rigorous standards of verisimilitude. In fact, in the period between 1900 and 1910 there was a complete separation effected between serious middle-class melodrama and the cheap proletarian variety—known as "10, 20, 30" because of its low-priced tickets—which became an independent industry with its own repertory (plays such as *The Chinatown Trunk Mystery* and *Bertha, the Sewing Machine Girl*), companies, and theatres (in the Bowery as well as in the provinces).

Three characteristics of the new melodrama are well illustrated in *The Girl of the Golden West*. First, discarding the episodic form with its many, small contrastive units used by Boucicault and Daly, Belasco in *The Girl* aims at greater structural unity and simplicity of action. There is a single plot line, fully developed and coherent, to which all else is integrated, and each act has a single, scrupulously realistic setting that represents an authentic milieu. Second, instead of stilted declamation, Belasco writes dialogue that is colloquial, off-hand, ironic, and closer to the tone, syntax, and rhythms of regional American speech. Third, gesture has grown smaller and effect subtler in *The Girl* than in the earlier school. Belasco's goal is to diminish acting extravagances, downplay the obviously melodramatic in melodrama, and seek concentrated impact through small lifelike details. An example of such a powerful effect achieved by minimal means is the drops of blood falling on the Sheriff's handkerchief, alerting Rance to the presence of Johnson in the loft. How much simpler than the fires, express trains, and flights across frozen rivers of the earlier melodramas! Belasco even specifies that the second act is to be played "easily and naturally" with no suggestion of dramatic emphasis.

Naturalness, attention to detail, verisimilitude were the hallmarks of Belasco's technique. When in 1980 the American Conservatory Theatre in San Francisco revived *The Girl of the Golden West* as a tribute to the city's famous native son born in the gold rush days, the production was undertaken in the same spirit of fidelity to the environment, local color, and atmosphere. Members of the company visited gold rush territory, went through the old mining towns of Columbia and Central City, studied contemporary accounts, read letters by eyewitnesses.

At first the nascent cinema had imitated stage melodrama, but by 1905 Belasco in *The Girl* found himself already competing with film and its new pictorial techniques. He created a visual prologue to the play through the use of a painted canvas rolled vertically on drums across the proscenium opening; the scenes depicted on it gave a moving, map-like panorama of the entire setting of the drama, showing Cloudy Mountain, the Girl's Cabin, and the Polka Saloon, much in the same way that a motion picture could present the full sweep of a locale by means of a long panning shot. Then, after seeing the outside of the saloon and hearing the music coming from it, the audience is taken inside when the curtain rises on the first act.

Belasco's new style of sensation scene—the meticulously realistic snowstorm in Act II of *The Girl*—was designed to equal or surpass the veristic thrills achieved by cinema. By sparing neither effort nor expense, Belasco demonstrated that nature could be copied in the theatre with great exactitude. For the blizzard scene, the impresario used thirty-two highly trained special effects men (the cast of the play had only twenty-three speaking roles) led by a conductor who directed this mechanical orchestra from a podium in full view of all the technicians. The storm, an active expression of the natural environment, became a living character in the play and the antagonist of the hero and heroine.

In his quest for perfection in mechanical reproduction and technical detail, Belasco devised batteries of lights as sensitive as the palette of colors commanded by a master painter.

The lighting effects on my stages have been secured only after years of experiment and at an expense which many other producers would consider ridiculous. Sometimes I have spent five thousand dollars attempting to reproduce the delicate hues of a sunset and then have thrown the scene away altogether. I recall that when I produced *The Girl of the Golden West,* I experimented three months to secure exactly the soft colors of a Californian sunset over the Sierra Nevada, and then turned to another method. It was a good sunset, but it was not Californian. Afterward I sold it to the producers of *Salomy Jane,* and it proved very effective and perfectly adjusted to the needs of that play.

Here we have a fine illustration of American ingenuity and enterprise in the fabrication of melodramatic illusion. Every sunset has its price tag! And geographical coloration is the key to authenticity. If the final product fails to match the precise hues of the sun as it sinks below the Sierra Nevadas, it can be sold to a competitor for use in another play. Belasco's theatre of technological know-how represents the apogee of American melodrama and its picturesque and largely external view of reality.

As melodrama grew sophisticated and was cross-fertilized by other genres and currents, the old character stereotypes became more flexible or eroded completely. In particular, the villain—that indispensable driving force of earlier melodrama—fades away. Belasco wrought changes in the simple classifications of hero, heroine, villain and in the moral underpinnings of these types.

The Girl of the Golden West is one of the new villainless melodramas. The cynical, cigar-smoking, card-playing Sheriff, Rance, is but a vestigial villain, eager to get his hands on the heroine and willing to bet freedom for the hero against possession of the Girl in one fatal hand of poker—yet for all that, a man of honor who keeps his word when he loses (due to deceit by the heroine). The Sheriff represents no force of evil. In fact, the old polarity of good and evil has been replaced by more modern psychological and social discriminations. A divided hero with a dual name and identity assumes the functions of villain and generates the conflict. As Johnson, he is the suave gentlemanly suitor of the Girl; as Ramerrez, he is the bandit come to rob her.

The drama centers around the redemptive power of love to heal the rift within Johnson/Ramerrez and to lead him safely from his lawless present (Spanish vendetta against the United States) to a reclaimed American future (wife and job). The epigraph to Act III, "We always may be what we might have been," expresses Belasco's romantic conception of character, and the Girl's innocence and belief in the power of self-transformation are the motive forces behind the struggle. For if melodrama can dispense with the villain, it cannot do without innocence, no matter how disguised this absence of sin and cynicism may be under a tough-talking, gun-toting exterior.

The Girl was, in Belasco's view, "a new and unique type" of distinctly American heroine—frank, open, unconventional, quite unlike the tradition-bound European women of the period. As described by the author in the novelized version of the play, the Girl is "a child of nature, spontaneous and untrammelled by the dictates of society, and normally and healthily at home in the company of the opposite sex." Minnie Smith—or is it Falconer? she is not quite sure what her last name really is—can serve as another example of a strong-minded American woman who performs heroic feats to save the one she loves. A product of the frontier and gold rush, the Girl is naturally independent and self-reliant, with a strong sense of her own worth as a human being. Innocent but not ignorant, Minnie is quite aware of the physical side of love and knows exactly what the men who pursue her are after, but she makes them respect her because she esteems herself. And for protection of both her person and her property, she carries a gun and is ready to use it if necessary. Capitalist entrepreneur and saloon-keeper, she can ride a horse, swear, drink, shoot, play poker (and win by cheating). A talent for business and money-making is eminently compatible with the virtues of a nineteenth-century American heroine, or hero, of melodrama.

Place is central to American melodrama, its geography is more important than its plot, and a map or street plan of where the action unfolds has been essential to understanding *The Poor of New York*, *Uncle Tom's Cabin*, and *Under the Gaslight*. It is all the more true of *The Girl of the Golden West*, which opposes the freedom and naturalness of the West to the traditional order of settled society in the genteel East.

In opposing West to East, Belasco drew upon an already vast American literature of the frontier. In his tales of the California gold fields (written in the 1870s), such as "The Luck of Roaring Camp," "The Outcasts of Poker Flat," and "Miggles" (about a woman bartender), Bret Harte explored the power of love to transform rough mining camp characters for all the sentiment and local color that he could extract from such a theme. And in Frank H. Murdoch's frontier drama, *Davy Crockett* (1874), where the hero saves the heroine by holding the cabin door shut all night long against the ravening wolves, the theme is no longer the old contrast of American and European, but rather the opposition between Western American and Eastern American.

Characters in melodrama constantly remember their dead mothers. *The Girl of the Golden West* is no exception to the rule that melodrama is matriarchal in its pieties (the *drame bourgeois* from Lillo to Arthur Miller has, on the other hand, been notably father-ridden), but the Girl's memories of mother are connected not with high moral principles or self-sacrifice, but with a paradigm of love—wedded, to be sure—but no less physical and therefore exceptional in melodrama even though legally sanctioned. We have left far behind such pallid and asexual heroines as the Fairweathers, mother and daughter, in *The Poor and New York*, and Laura in *Under the Gaslight*. In mid-century melodrama, sexual activity was left to the villain as something inherently nasty. In *Uncle Tom's Cabin*, for example, except for blonde Eva's infantile infatuation for black Tom, the only erotic vitality was shown by Legree in his sadistic debauching of his female slaves.

This re-interpretation of the melodramatic heroine, seen in *The Girl of the Golden West* as a woman of action uninhibited by customary taboos and unafraid of men or sexuality, is a reflection of widespread changes in attitude that have already made themselves felt in popular American fiction towards the end of the nineteenth century. Instead of the old ideal of female submissiveness, we now find sympathetic portraits of self-reliant heroines who manage to combine wildness and femininity.

Belasco's Girl owes something to the gun-slinging dime novel heroines of the 1870s and 1880s, such as Hurricane Nell who can "outrun, out-ride, out-shoot, out-lasso, and out-yell" any man in town. A somewhat more plausible version of the dime novel heroine, the Girl in Belasco's drama has been freed from the code of gentility to which earlier American melodramatic heroines had been more or less tightly bound. "I can look after myself," Minnie tells the solicitous Johnson, worried about her safety, " I carry my little wepping—(*Touching her pocket to show that she has a pistol*.) I'm independent—I'm happy." Like most of her fellow Americans, then and now, she believes strongly in self-defense and goes about armed. The Girl is a specifically American version of the New Woman who appeared in life as in literature around the turn of the century.

Frank, innocent, and open, this new American heroine fascinated Europeans and Europeanized Americans who were accustomed to the intricate repressions of over-civilized sexual mores. It was precisely these qualities of freshness and unconventionality in the Girl's nature that captivated the suave, Eastern-educated, European-travelled hero of the play, Johnson/Ramerrez, whose notions of women derive in part from his Spanish father. Another gentleman of European culture was also intrigued by the Girl and succumbed to her wild charm. Giacomo Puccini was his name.

Puccini, who had already used one of Belasco's plays as the libretto for *Madama Butterfly*, was looking for a new subject for an opera when in 1907 he passed through New York and went to see *The Girl of the Golden West*. Although he understood hardly a word because of his meager English, the Italian composer was attracted by the novelty of the setting and the exotic atmosphere. Three years later Puccini completed *La Fanciulla del West*, which he always referred to affectionately as *La Girl* or *mia Girl* and which has also been called "Uncle Giacomo's Cabin." The first grand opera on an American theme and the first world premiere ever given in the United States, *La Fanciulla del West* opened at the Metropolitan Opera House on December 10, 1910, with Enrico Caruso as Johnson, the Czech singer Emmy Destin as the Girl, the orchestra conducted by Arturo Toscanini, and Belasco himself as stage manager. With such fanfare, it is little wonder that the fame of the opera soon eclipsed that of Belasco's original play.

American melodrama had become European grand opera! Puccini's *La Fanciulla* is evidence that by the early twentieth century the American popular arts were a cultural export to Europe. But just as fifty years before French and British melodramas had been adapted to American taste, so Belasco's *Girl* in becoming La Fanciulla underwent a metamorphosis that illuminates the specifically American qualities of the original. Not only did Puccini's *mia Girl* now speak a different language, but she also expressed sentiments compatible with European cultural values and European perceptions of the American frontier and American women.

The Italianization of *The Girl of the Golden West* resulted in the re-imposition of traditional hierarchies, transforming Belasco's modern heroine into a more conventional figure who is all passion and palpitation and restoring the crude violence and excitement that Belasco had deliberately eliminated. Puccini turned the clock back. Uncle Giacomo's Cabin is an old-fashioned melodrama—in fact, it is quite literally a horse opera, featuring, in keeping with Italian taste and the composer's express wishes, some eight or ten horses on stage.

In *The Girl of the Golden West*, nineteenth-century American melodrama reaches its terminus. We experience a sense of the limitations of human life, the necessity of making painful choices, an end to the dream of infinite possibilities. For Belasco, who was born in San Francisco during the gold rush years but went East to make his fortune, this frontier drama written long after there was no more frontier is an exercise in nostalgia, a fond looking back at an imagined promised land, a farewell not only to the mythic West but also to the naive and touching simplicities of nineteenth-century melodrama.

The world of nineteenth-century American melodrama, like that of the frontier, was egalitarian: every one had the opportunity to strike gold, but only a few would actually do so. There was no expectation of a just or equal distribution of riches, although sentimental philanthropy was practiced to benefit the needy.

Whether it was gold rush California of 1848 and '49, New York of the panics of 1837 and '57, or the slave plantation South, the basic facts of existence were much the same: economic instability, constant fear of financial ruin, hectic scrambling to make money. *The Lottery of Life*—the title of a play of the period—aptly describes the melodramatic perception of human destiny as an arbitrary process dominated by chance and circumstance. Fortunes were quickly made and as quickly lost. Bloodgood rises and falls, while the Fairweathers fall and rise. Laura is plunged from riches to rags, then bobs to the top again. The slave-owners Shelby and St. Clare sink into debt and insolvency (slavery is not an economically sound institution), whereas the nouveau riche slave-trader Haley is climbing up and the fugitive slave-catchers Loker and Marks line their pockets. Johnson's aristocratic Spanish father has been financially destroyed by statehood for California and is reduced to banditry, a career which his son must pursue—until he goes East to seek a job.

"In this broad, free air," writes Junius Henri Browne, the author of *The Great Metropolis: A Mirror of New York* (1869), "there is hope for all. [The rich and the poor] . . . may change positions in a few years. The lowly strive to climb, and the lofty are likely to fall." Despite the glaring extremes of wealth and poverty, the egalitarianism of American society always impressed European visitors, as witness the comments of the British journalist Edward Dicey in 1863:

> Undoubtedly, out of doors, you see evidence of a public equality, or rather absence of inequality, among all classes, which cannot fail to strike an inhabitant of the Old World. In the streets, the man in the hat and broadcloth coat and the man in corduroys and fustian jacket never get out of each other's way or expect the other to make way for him. . . . There is a great deal of poverty in New York, and the Five Points—the Seven Dials of the City—is, especially on a bitter winter's day, as miserable a haunt of vice and misery as it was ever my lot to witness in Europe. Still, compared with the size of New York, this quarter is a very small one; and poverty there, bad as it is, is not helpless poverty. The fleeting population of the Five Points is composed of the lowest and most shiftless of the recent emigrants; and in the course of a few years they, or at any rate their children, move to other quarters, and become prosperous and respectable.

The reference to low and shiftless emigrants calls to mind the derogatory epithets used for racial minorites in nineteenth-century American melodramas. The one group relegated to the bottom of the heap in the egalitarian society was the cast (or is it caste?) of ethnic characters assigned only minor and menial comic roles: Chinese, Blacks, Mexicans, Indians, disparagingly called chinamen, niggers, greasers. They occupy the lowest rung in a highly mobile society dedicated to money-making, do much of the dirty work, get nothing but abuse in return. Only Harriet Beecher Stowe, who used melodrama as a protest against the existing order, objected to excluding ethnic Americans from the lottery of life—on the interesting grounds that such exclusion was wasteful since, as she argued, blacks were potential money-makers (George Harris's inventions, Tom's managerial abilities) and their talents would be more profitable free than slave. For the most part, melodrama accepted the status quo and gave a cruel, but accurate picture of how Americans felt about racial minorities, from whom they did not welcome any competition.

Popular American melodrama of the past century gave an optimistic reading of reality. Undoubtedly, such an idealization of American life offered audiences a perception of self that corresponded to powerful longings and imaginings about country and national character. If the rich and powerful are taken down a peg or two, poverty in melodrama is sentimentalized: the poor are uncomplaining, kind-hearted, generous, high-spirited—as opposed to the harsher pictures of squalor and degradation found in Crane's *Maggie* or Jacob Riis's photographic essay, *How the Other Half Lives.*

And yet there is truth to be found in the melodramatists' depiction of American society as a colorful, dynamic lottery, a great gamble, for this is how our ancestors chose to see themselves and their nation. The risks seemed worth running. The chance was always there.

The nineteenth century American melodramatists are our theatrical primitives. They paint magical, child-like pictures of rushing trains, snowstorms, fires, frozen rivers; they offer dreamscapes of the Great City, the Wild West, the Old South, mixing realism and romance in broad patches of bright primary colors. They present stereoscopic view cards of the opportunities for success or calamity that a new mass society opened for its citizens.

THE POOR OF NEW YORK

Dion Boucicault

THE CAST:

Captain Fairweather
Gideon Bloodgood
Badger
Mark Livingstone
Paul
Puffy
Dan
Daniels
Edwards
Mrs. Fairweather
Mrs. Puffy
Alida
Lucy

The first act occurs during the Commercial Panic of 1837. The remainder of the drama takes place during the Panic of 1857.

ACT I

The Panic of 1837

The private office of a banking house in New York; door at back, leading to the Bank; Door leading to a side street; Gideon Bloodgood seated, at desk.

(Enter Edwards, with a sheet of paper.)

EDWARDS: The stock list, sir;—second board of brokers.
BLOODGOOD: *(Rising eagerly.)* Let me see it. Tell the cashier to close the Bank on the stroke of three, and dismiss the clerks. *(Reads.)*

(Exit Edwards.)

So—as I expected, every stock is down further still, and my last effort to retrieve my fortune has plunged me into utter ruin? *(Crushes up the paper.)* To-morrow, my drafts to the amount of eighty thousand dollars will be protested. Tomorrow, yonder street, now so still, will be filled with a howling multitude, for the house of Bloodgood, the Banker, will fail, and in its fall will crush hundreds, thousands, who have their fortunes laid up here.

(Re-enter Edwards.)

EDWARDS: Here are the keys of the safe sir, and the vault. *(Leaves keys on desk and shows a check to Bloodgood.)* The building committee of St. Peter's new church have applied for your donation. It is a thousand dollars.
BLOODGOOD: Pay it. *(Exit Edwards.)* To-morrow, New York will ring from Union Square to the Battery with the news—"Bloodgood has absconded"—but to-morrow I shall be safe on board the packet for Liverpool—all is prepared for my flight with my only care in life, my only hope—my darling child—her fortune is secure—*(Rises.)* The affair will blow over; Bloodgood's bankruptcy will

soon be forgotten in the whirl of New York trade, but Alida, my dear Alida will be safe from want.

(Re-enter Edwards.)

EDWARDS: Here, sir, are the drafts on the Bank of England, 70,000 dollars. *(Hands papers to Bloodgood, who places them in his pocketbook.)*
BLOODGOOD: Are the clerks all gone?
EDWARDS: All, sir, except Mr. Badger.
BLOODGOOD: Badger! the most negligent of all! That is strange.
EDWARDS: His entries are behindhand, he says, and he is balancing his books.
BLOODGOOD: Desire him to come to me. *(Sits. Exit Edwards.)*

(Enter Badger, smoking cigar.)

BADGER: You have asked for me.
BLOODGOOD: Yes; you are strangely attentive to business to-day, Mr. Badger.
BADGER: Everything has a beginning.
BLOODGOOD: Then you will please begin to-morrow.
BADGER: To-morrow! no sir, my business must be done to-day. *Carpe diem*—make most of to-day—that's my philosophy.
BLOODGOOD: Mr. Badger, Philosophy is not a virtue in a banker's clerk.
BADGER: Think not?
BLOODGOOD: *(Impatiently.)* Neither philosophy nor impertinence. You are discharged from my employment.
BADGER: Pardon me! I do not catch the precise word.
BLOODGOOD: *(Sternly.)* Go, sir, go! I discharge you.
BADGER: Go!—discharge me? I am still more in the dark, I can understand my services not being required in a house that goes on, but where the house is ready to burst up the formality of telling a clerk he is discharged, does seem to me an unnecessary luxury.
BLOODGOOD: *(Troubled.)* I do not understand you, sir.
BADGER: *(Seating himself on a desk, deliberately dangling his legs.)* No! well I'll dot my i's and cross my t's and make myself plain to the meanest capacity. In business there are two ways of getting rich, one hard, slow and troublous: this is called labor;—
BLOODGOOD: Sir!
BADGER: Allow me to finish. The other easy, quick and demanding nothing but a pliant conscience and a daring mind—is now pleasantly denominated financiering—but when New York was honest, it was called fraudulent bankruptcy, that was before you and I were born.
BLOODGOOD: What do you mean?
BADGER: I mean that for more than two years I have watched your business transactions; when you thought me idle, my eyes were everywhere: in your books, in your safe, in your vaults; if you doubt me question me about your operations for the last three months.
BLOODGOOD: This is infamous!
BADGER: That is precisely the word I used when I came to the end of your books.
EDWARDS: *(Outside.)* This way, sir.

(*Enter Edwards, with Captain Fairweather.*)

BLOODGOOD: (*To Badger, in alarm.*) Not a word.
BADGER: All right.
EDWARDS: (*Introducing Captain Fairweather.*) This is Mr. Bloodgood.
CAPTAIN: Glad to see you, sir. You will pardon my intruding at an hour when the bank, I am told, is closed.
BLOODGOOD: I am at your service, sir.

(*He makes a sign for Badger to retire, but the latter remains.*)

BADGER: (*To Captain.*) You may speak, sir; Mr. Bloodgood has no secrets from me. I am in his confidence.
CAPTAIN: (*Sits.*) I am a sea-captain, in the India Trade. My voyages are of the longest and thus I am obliged to leave my wife and two children almost at the mercy of circumstances. I was spending a happy month with my darlings at a little cozy place I have at Yonkers while my ship was loading, when this infernal commercial squall set in—all my fortune, 100,000 dollars, the fruits of thirty years' hard toil—was invested in the United States Bank—it was the livelihood of my wife—the food of my little children—I hurried to my brokers and sold out. I saved myself just in time.
BLOODGOOD: I admire your promptitude.
CAPTAIN: To-morrow I sail for China; for the last three weeks I have worried my brains to think how I should bestow my money—to-day I bethought me of your house—the oldest in New York—your name stands beyond suspicion, and if I leave this money in your hands, I can sleep nightly with the happy assurance that whatever happens to me, my dearest ones are safe.
BADGER: You may pull your nightcap over your ears with that established conviction.
CAPTAIN: Now, I know your bank is closed, but if you will accept this money as a special deposit, I will write to you how I desire it to be invested hereafter.
BLOODGOOD: (*Pensive.*) You have a family?
CAPTAIN: Don't talk of them—tears of joy come into my eyes whenever I think of those children—and my dear wife, the patient, devoted companion of the old sailor, whose loving voice murmurs each evening a prayer for those who are on the sea; and my children, sir, two little angels; one a fair little thing—we call her Lucy—she is the youngest—all red and white like a little bundle of flowers; and my eldest—my son Paul—we named him after Paul Jones—a sailor's whim; well, sir, when the ship is creaking and groaning under my feet, when the squall drives the hail and sleet across my face, amidst the thunder, I only hear three voices—through the gloom I can see only three faces, pressed together like three angels waiting for me in heaven, and that heaven is my home. But, how I do talk, sir—forgetting that these things can't interest you.
BLOODGOOD: They do, more than you imagine. I, too, have a child—only one—a motherless child!
CAPTAIN: Ain't it good to speak of the little beings? Don't it fill the heart like a draught of sweet water? My darling torments, here is their fortune—I have it in my hand—it is here—I have snatched it from the waves; I have won it across the tempest; I have labored, wrestled, and suffered for it; but it seemed nothing, for

it was for them. Take it, sir. (*He hands a pocketbook.*) In this pocketbook you will find one hundred thousand dollars. May I take your receipt and at once depart for my vessel?

BADGER: (*Aside.*) This is getting positively interesting.

BLOODGOOD: Your confidence flatters me. You desire to place this money with me as a special deposit?

CAPTAIN: If you please. Will you see that the amount is correct?

BLOODGOOD: (*Counting.*) Mr. Badger, prepare the receipt.

BADGER: (*Writing.*) "New York, 13th of December, 1837. Received, on special deposit, from ———" (*To Captain.*) Your name, sir?

CAPTAIN: Captain Fairweather, of the ship Paul and Lucy, of New York.

BADGER: (*Writing.*) Captain Fairweather, of the ship—

BLOODGOOD: One hundred thousand dollars—quite correct.

BADGER: (*Handing receipt to Bloodgood, and watching him closely as he takes the pen.*) Please sign the receipt. (*Aside.*) His hand does not tremble, not a muscle moves. What a magnificent robber!

BLOODGOOD: (*To Captain.*) Here is your receipt.

CAPTAIN: A thousand thanks. Now I am relieved of all trouble.

BADGER: (*Aside.*) That's true.

CAPTAIN: I must return in haste to the Astor House, where I dine with my owners at four—I fear I am late. Good-day, Mr. Bloodgood.

BLOODGOOD: Good-day Captain, and a prosperous voyage to you. (*Exit Captain Fairweather. Badger opens ledger.*) What are you doing, Mr. Badger?

BADGER: I am going to enter that special deposit in the ledger.

BLOODGOOD: Mr. Badger!

BADGER: Mr. Bloodgood!

BLOODGOOD: (*Brings him down.*) I have been deceived in you. I confess I did not know your value.

BADGER: (*Modestly.*) Patience and perseverance, sir, tells in the long run.

BLOODGOOD: Here are one thousand dollars—I present them to you for your past services.

BADGER: (*Takes the money, and walks over to the ledger on the desk which he closes significantly.*) And for the present service?

BLOODGOOD: What do you mean?

BADGER: My meaning is as clear as Croton. I thought you were going to fail—I see I was wrong—you are going to abscond.

BLOODGOOD: Mr. Badger! this language—

BADGER: This deposit is special; you dare not use it in your business; your creditors cannot touch it—ergo, you mean to make a raise, and there's but one way—absconsion! absquatulation.

BLOODGOOD: (*Smiling.*) It is possible that this evening I may take a little walk out of town.

BADGER: In a steamboat?

BLOODGOOD: Meet me at Peck Slip, at five o'clock, and I will hand you double the sum I gave you.

BADGER: (*Aside.*) In all three thousand dollars.

(*Re-enter Edwards.*)

EDWARDS: Your daughter, sir; Miss Alida is in the carriage at the door and is screaming to be admitted.

BLOODGOOD: Tell the nurse to pacify her for a few moments.

EDWARDS: She dare not, sir; Miss Alida has torn nurse's face in a fearful manner already. (*Exit.*)

BADGER: Dear, high-spirited child! If she is so gentle now, what will she be when she is twenty, and her nails are fully developed?

BLOODGOOD: (*Takes hat.*) I will return immediately. (*Exit.*)

BADGER: (*Following Bloodgood with his eyes.*) Oh, nature, wonderful mistress! Keep close to your daughter, Bloodgood, for she is your master! Ruin, pillage, rob fifty families to make her rich with their misery, happy in their tears. I watched him as he received the fortune of that noble old sailor—not a blink—his heart of iron never quailed, but in this heart of iron there is a straw, a weakness by which it may be cracked, and that weakness is his own child—children! They are the devil in disguise. I have not got any except my passions, my vices—a large family of spoilt and ungrateful little devils, who threaten their loving father with a prison.

EDWARDS: (*Outside.*) I tell you, sir, he is not in.

CAPTAIN: (*Outside.*) Let me pass I say. (*He enters very much agitated.*) Where is he? Where is he?

BADGER: (*Surprised.*) What is the matter, sir?

CAPTAIN: Mr. Bloodgood—I must see him—speak to him this instant. Do you not hear me?

BADGER: But—

CAPTAIN: He has not gone.

BADGER: Sir—

CAPTAIN: Ah! he is here!

(*Re-enter Bloodgood.*)

BLOODGOOD: What is the meaning of this.

CAPTAIN: Ah! you—it is you—(*Trying to restrain his emotion.*) Sir, I have changed my mind; here is your receipt; have the goodness to return me the deposit I—I—left with you.

BLOODGOOD: Sir!

CAPTAIN: I have another investment for this sum, and I—beg you to restore it to me.

BLOODGOOD: Restore it! you have a very strange way, sir, of demanding what is due to you.

CAPTAIN: It is true; pardon me but I have told you it is all I possess. It is the fortune of my wife, of my children, of my brave Paul, and my dear little Lucy. It is their future happiness, their life! Listen, sir; I will be frank with you. Just now, on returning to my hotel, I found the owners of my ship waiting dinner for me, well, they were speaking as merchants will speak of each other—your name was mentioned—I listened—and they said—It makes me tremble even now—they said there were rumors abroad to-day that your house was in peril.

BLOODGOOD: I attach no importance, sir, to idle talk.

CAPTAIN: But I attach importance to it, sir. How can I leave the city with this suspicion on my mind that perhaps I have compromised the future of my family.

BLOODGOOD: Sir!

CAPTAIN: Take back your receipt, and return me my money.

BLOODGOOD: You know sir, that it is after banking hours. Return to-morrow.
CAPTAIN: No. You received my deposit after banking hours.
BLOODGOOD: I am not a paying teller, to count out money.
CAPTAIN: You did not say so, when you counted it in.

(*Enter Edwards.*)

EDWARDS: The driver says you will be late for the—
BLOODGOOD: (*Trying to stop him.*) That will do. (*Exit Edwards.*)
CAPTAIN: What did he say? (*Runs to the window.*) A carriage at the door—
BADGER: (*Aside.*) Things are getting complicated here.
CAPTAIN: Yes—I see it all. He is going to fly with the fortunes and savings of his
    dupes! (*Tearing his cravat.*) Ah! I shall choke! (*Furiously to Bloodgood.*) But I
    am here, villain, I am here in time.
BLOODGOOD: Sir.
CAPTAIN: To-morrow, you said—return to-morrow—but to-morrow you will be
    gone. (*Precipitates himself on Bloodgood.*) My money, my money. I will have it
    this instant! Do not speak a word, it is useless, I will not listen to you. My
    money, or I will kill you as a coward should be killed, Robber! Thief!
BADGER: (*Aside.*) Hi!hi! This is worth fifty cents—reserved seats extra.
BLOODGOOD: (*Disengaging himself.*) Enough of this scandal. You shall have your
    money back again.
CAPTAIN: Give it me—ah!—(*In pain.*) My head! (*To Bloodgood.*) Be quick,
    give it to me, and let me go. (*Staggering and putting his hands to face.*) My God!
    what is this strange feeling which overcomes me.
BADGER: He is falling, what's the matter of him?

(*Captain falls in chair.*)

BLOODGOOD: His face is purple. (*Takes pocketbook and commences to count out
    money.*)

(*Soft music to end of act.*)

CAPTAIN: I am suffocating; some air. I cannot see; everything is black before my
    eyes. Am I dying? O, no, no! it cannot be, I will not die. I must see them again.
    Some water—quick! Come to me—my wife—my children! Where are they that
    I cannot fold them in my arms! (*He looks strangely and fearfully into the face of
    Bloodgood for an instant, and then breaks into a loud sob.*) Oh, my chil-
    dren—my poor, poor, little children! (*After some convulsive efforts to speak his
    eyes become fixed.*)
BLOODGOOD: (*Distracted.*) Some one run for help. Badger, a doctor quick.
BADGER: (*Standing over Captain.*) All right, sir, I have studied medicine—that is
    how I learned most of my loose habits. (*Examines the Captain's pulse and eyes.*)
    It is useless sir. He is dead.
BLOODGOOD: (*Horrified.*) Dead! (*Bloodgood's attitude is one of extreme hor-
    ror. This position gradually relaxes as he begins to see the advantages that will
    result from the Captain's death.*) Can it be possible?
BADGER: (*Tearing open the Captain's vest. The receipt falls on the ground.*) His
    heart has ceased to beat—congestion in all its diagnostics.

BLOODGOOD: Dead!

BADGER: Apoplexy—the symptoms well developed—the causes natural, over-excitement and sudden emotion.

BLOODGOOD: (*Relaxing into an attitude of cunning.*) Dead!

BADGER: You are spared the agony of counting out his money.

BLOODGOOD: Dead!

BADGER: (*Sees receipt on ground.*) Ha! here is the receipt! Signed by Bloodgood. As a general rule never destroy a receipt—there is no knowing when it may yet prove useful. (*Picks it up, and puts it in his pocket.*)

Tableau.

END OF ACT I

(*A lapse of twenty years is supposed to intervene between the First and Second Acts.*)

ACT II

The Panic of 1857

SCENE I

The Park, near Tammany Hall.

(Enter Livingstone.)

LIVINGSTONE: Eight o'clock in the morning! For the last hour I have been hovering round Chatham street—I wanted to sell my overcoat to some enterprising Israelite, but I could not muster the courage to enter one of those dens. Can I realize the fact? Three months ago, I stood there the fashionable Mark Livingstone, owner of the Waterwitch yacht, one of the original stock-holders in the Academy of Music, and now, burst up, sold out, and reduced to breakfast off this coat. *(Feels in pocket.)* What do I feel? a gold dollar—undiscovered in the Raglan of other days! *(Withdraws his hand.)* No; 'tis a five-cent piece!

(Enter Puffy, with a hot-potato arrangement.)

PUFFY: Past eight o'clock! I am late this morning.
LIVINGSTONE: I wonder what that fellow has in his tin volcano—it smells well. Ha! what are those funny things? Ah!
PUFFY: Sweet potatoes, sir.
LIVINGSTONE: Indeed! *(Aside.)* If the Union Club saw me—*(Looks around.)* No; I am incog—hunger cries aloud. Here goes.
PUFFY: Why, bless me, if it ain't Mr. Livingstone!
LIVINSTONE: The devil! He knows me—I dare not eat a morsel.
PUFFY: I'm Puffy, sir; the baker that was—in Broadway—served you sir, and your good father afore you.
LIVINSTONE: Oh, Puffy—ah, true. *(Aside.)* I wonder if I owe him anything.
PUFFY: Down in the world now, sir—over speculated like the rest on 'em. I expanded on a new-fangled oven, that was to bake enough bread in six hours to supply to the whole United States—got done brown in it myself—subsided into

Bowery—expanded again on woffles, caught a second time—obliged to contract into a twelve foot front on Division street. Mrs. P. tends the indoor trade—I do a locomotive business in potatoes, and we let our second floor. My son Dan sleeps with George Washington No. 4, while Mrs. P. and I make out under the counter; Mrs. P., bein' wide, objects some, but I says—says I, "My dear, everybody must contract themselves in these here hard times."

LIVINSTONE: So you are poor now, are you? (*Takes a potato, playfully.*)

PUFFY: Yes sir; I ain't ashamed to own it—for I hurt nobody but myself. Take a little salt, sir. But, Lord bless you, sir, poverty don't come amiss to me—I've got no pride to support. Now, there's my lodgers—

LIVINGSTONE: Ah, your second floor.

PUFFY: A widow lady and her two grown children—poor as mice, but proud, sir— they was grand folks once; you can see that by the way they try to hide it. Mrs. Fairweather is a—

LIVINGSTONE: Fairweather—the widow of a sea captain, who died here in New York twenty years ago.

PUFFY: Do you know my lodgers?

LIVINGSTONE: Three months ago, they lived in Brooklyn—Paul had a clerkship in the Navy Yard.

PUFFY: But when the panic set in, the United States government contracted—it paid off a number of employees, and Mr. Paul was discharged.

LIVINGSTONE: They are reduced to poverty and I did not know it.—No, how could I. (*Aside.*) Since my ruin I have avoided them. (*Aloud.*) And Lucy—I mean Miss Fairweather?—

PUFFY: She works at a milliner's in Broadway—bless her sweet face and kind smile—me and my wife, we could bake ourselves into bread afore she and they should come to want; and as for my boy Dan—talk of going through fire and water for her—he does that every night for nothing. Why, sir, you can't say "Lucy," but a big tear will come up in his eye as big as a cartwheel, and then he'll let out an almighty cuss, that sounds like a thousand o' brick.

(*Enter Paul and Mrs. Fairweather, dressed in black.*)

LIVINGSTONE: Oh! (*In confusion, hides the potato in his pocket, and hums an air as he walks away. Aside.*) I wonder if they know me.

MRS. FAIRWEATHER: Ah, Mr. Puffy.

PUFFY: What, my second floor. Mrs. Fairweather—good morning, Mr. Paul; I hope no misfortune has happened—you are dressed in mourning.

MRS. FAIRWEATHER: This is the anniversary of my poor husband's death; this day, twenty years ago, he was taken away from us—we keep it sacred to his memory.

PAUL: It was a fatal day for us. When my father left home he had 100,000 dollars on his person—when he was found lying dead on the sidewalk of Liberty street, he was robbed of all.

MRS. FAIRWEATHER: From that hour misfortune has tracked us—we have lost our friends.

PUFFY: Friends—that reminds me—why where is Mr. Livingstone—there's his coat—

PAUL: Livingstone!

PUFFY: We were talking of you, when you came up. He slipped away.

(*Re-enter Livingstone.*)

LIVINGSTONE: I think I dropped my coat. (*Recognizing them.*) Paul—am I mistaken?

MRS. FAIRWEATHER: No, Mr. Livingstone.

PAUL: Good morning, sir.

LIVINGSTONE: Sir!—Mr. Livingstone!—have I offended you?

PAUL: We could not expect you to descend to visit us in our poor lodging.

MRS. FAIRWEATHER: We cannot afford the pleasure of your society.

LIVINGSTONE: Let me assure you that I was ignorant of your misfortune—and if I have not called—it was because—a—because—(*Aside.*) What shall I say. (*Aloud.*)—I have been absent from the city;—may I ask how is your sister?

PAUL: My sister Lucy is now employed in a millinery store in Broadway—she sees you pass the door every day.

LIVINGSTONE: (*Aside.*) The devil—I must confess my ruin, or appear a contemptible scoundrel.

PAUL: Livingstone—I cannot conceal my feelings, we were schoolmates together—and I must speak out.

LIVINGSTONE: (*Aside.*) I know what's coming.

PAUL: I'm a blunt New York boy, and have something of the old bluff sailor's blood in my veins—so pardon me if I tell you that you have behaved badly to my sister Lucy.

LIVINGSTONE: For many months I was a daily visitor at your house—I loved your sister.

PAUL: You asked me for Lucy's hand—I gave it, because I loved you as a brother—not because you were rich.

LIVINGSTONE: (*Aside.*) To retrieve my fortunes so that I might marry—I speculated in stocks and lost all I possessed. To enrich Lucy and her family, I involved myself in utter ruin.

PAUL: The next day I lost my clerkship—we were reduced to poverty, and you disappeared.

LIVINGSTONE: I can't stand it—I will confess all—let me sacrifice every feeling but Lucy's love and your esteem—

MRS. FAIRWEATHER: Beware, Mr. Livingstone, how you seek to renew our acquaintance; recollect my daughter earns a pittance behind a counter—I take in work, and Paul now seeks the poorest means of earning an honest crust of bread.

LIVINGSTONE: And what would you say if I were not better off than yourselves—if I too were poor—if I—

PUFFY: You, poor, you who own a square mile of New York?

(*Enter Bloodgood.*)

LIVINGSTONE: Mr. Bloodgood!

BLOODGOOD: Ah, Livingstone—why do you not call to see us? You know our address—Madison square—my daughter Alida will be delighted.—By the way—I have some paper of yours at the bank, it comes due to-day—ten thousand dollars, I think—you bank at the Chemical?

LIVINGSTONE: Yes, I do—that is did,—bank there.

BLOODGOOD: Why don't you bank with me, a rich and careless fellow like you—

with a large account.

LIVINGSTONE: Yes—I—(*Aside.*) He is cutting the ground from under my feet.

PAUL: Mr. Bloodgood—pardon me, sir, but I was about to call on you to-day to solicit employment.

BLOODGOOD: I'm full, sir,—indeed I think of reducing salaries, everybody is doing so.

LIVINGSTONE: But you are making thousands a week?

BLOODGOOD: That is no reason that I should not take advantage of the times—(*Recognizing Puffy.*) Ah, Mr. Puffy, that note of yours.

PUFFY: Oh, Lord! (*Aside.*) It is the note Mrs. Fairweather gave me for her rent.

BLOODGOOD: My patience is worn out.

PUFFY: It's all right sir.

BLOODGOOD: Take care it is. (*Exit.*)

PUFFY: There goes the hardest cuss that ever went to law.

LIVINGSTONE: Paul—my dear friend—will you believe me—my feelings are the same towards you—nay more tender, more sincere than ever—but there are circumstances I cannot explain.

MRS. FAIRWEATHER: Mr. Livingstone, say no more—we ask no explanation.

LIVINGSTONE: But I ask something—let me visit you—let me return to the place that I once held in your hearts.

PUFFY: 219 Division street—Puffy, Baker. Dinner at half past one—come to-day, sir—do, sir.

PAUL: We cannot refuse you.

MRS. FAIRWEATHER: I will go to Lucy's store and let her know. Ah! Mr. Livingstone—she has never confessed that she loved you—but you will find her cheek paler than it used to be. (*Exit.*)

PAUL: And now to hunt for work—to go from office to office pleading for employment—to be met always with the same answer—"we are full"—or "we are discharging hands"—Livingstone, I begin to envy the common laborer who has no fears, no care, beyond his food and shelter—I am beginning to lose my pity for the poor.

LIVINGSTONE: The poor!—whom do you call the poor? Do you know them? do you see them? They are more frequently found under a black coat than under a red shirt. The poor man is the clerk with a family, forced to maintain a decent suit of clothes, paid for out of the hunger of his children. The poor man is the artist who is obliged to pledge the tools of his trade to buy medicines for his sick wife. The lawyer who, craving for employment, buttons up his thin paletot to hide his shirtless breast. These needy wretches are poorer than the poor, for they are obliged to conceal their poverty with the false mask of content—smoking a cigar to disguise their hunger—they drag from their pockets their last quarter, to cast it with studied carelessness, to the beggar, whose mattress at home is lined with gold. These are the most miserable of the Poor of New York.

(*A small crowd has assembled round Livingstone during this speech; they take him for an orator; one of them takes down what he says on tablets.*)

(*Enter Policeman.*)

PUFFY AND CROWD: Bravo—Bravo—Hurrah—get on the bench!

POLICEMAN: Come—I say—this won't do.

LIVINGSTONE: What have I done.

POLICEMAN: No stumping to the population allowed in the Park.

LIVINGSTONE: Stumping!!

REPORTER: Oblige me with your name, sir, for the Herald.

LIVINGSTONE: Oh! (*Rushes off, followed by Paul.*)

SCENE II

Exterior of Bloodgood's Bank, Nassau Street.

(*Enter Bloodgood.*)

BLOODGOOD: (*Looking at papers.*) Four per cent a month—ha! if this panic do but last, I shall double my fortune! Twenty years ago this very month—ay, this very day—I stood in yonder bank, a ruined man. Shall I never forget that night—when I and my accomplice carried out the body of the old sailor and laid it there. (*Points.*) I never pass the spot without a shudder. But his money—that founded my new fortune.

(*Enter Alida.*)

Alida, my dear child, what brings you to this part of the city?

ALIDA: I want two thousand dollars.

BLOODGOOD: My dearest child, I gave you five hundred last week.

ALIDA: Pooh! what's five hundred? You made ten thousand in Michigan Southern last week—I heard you tell Mr. Jacob Little so.

BLOODGOOD: But—

ALIDA: Come, don't stand fooling about it; go in and get the money—I must have it.

BLOODGOOD: Well, my darling, if you must. Will you step in?

ALIDA: Not I. I'm not going into your dirty bank. I've seen all your clerks— they're not worth looking at.

BLOODGOOD: I'll go and fetch it. (*Exit.*)

ALIDA: This is positively the last time I will submit to this extortion. (*Opens a letter and reads.*) "My adored Alida—I fly to your exquisite feet; I am the most wretched of men. Last night, at Hall's I lost two thousand dollars—it must be paid before twelve o'clock. Oh, my queen! My angel! Invent some excuse to get this money from your father, and meet me at Maillard's at half-past eleven. When shall we meet again alone, in that box at the opera, where I can press my lips to your superb eyes, and twine my hands in your magnificent hair? *Addio carissima!* The Duke of Calcavella." I wonder if he showed that to any of his friends before he sent it!

(*Re-enter Bloodgood, followed by Puffy.*)

BLOODGOOD: I tell you, sir, it must be paid. I have given you plenty of time.

PUFFY: You gave me the time necessary for you to obtain execution in the Marine Court.

BLOODGOOD: Alida, my love, there is a draft for the money. (*Gives her notes. She takes them.*) And now, will you do me a favor? Do not be seen about so much, in public, with that foreign Duke.

ALIDA: I never ask you for a draft but you always give me a pill to take with it.

BLOODGOOD: I don't like him.

ALIDA: I do—bye-bye. (*Exit.*)

BLOODGOOD: How grand she looks! That girl possesses my whole heart.

PUFFY: Reserve a little for me, sir. This here note, it was give to me by my 2d floor in payment for rent. It's as good as gold, sir—when they are able to pay it. I'd sooner have it—

BLOODGOOD: My Puffy, you are the worst kind of man; you are a weak honest fool. You are always failing—always the dupe of some new swindler.

PUFFY: Lord love you, sir! if you was to see the folks you call swindlers—the kindest, purest, 2d floor as ever drew God's breath. I told them that this note was all right—for if they know'd I was put about, along of it, I believe they'd sell the clothes off their backs to pay it.

BLOODGOOD: (*Aside.*) This fellow is a fool. But I see, if I levy execution the note will be paid. (*Aloud.*) Very good, Mr. Puffy. I will see about it.

PUFFY: You will! I knew it—there—when folks says you're a hard man—I says—no—no mor'n a rich man's got to be.

BLOODGOOD: Very good (*Aside.*) I'll put an execution on his house at once. (*Aloud.*) Good morning, Mr. Puffy. (*Exit.*)

PUFFY: Good morning, sir. So, I'm floated off that mud bank. Lord! if he had seized my goods and closed me up—I'd never a dared to look Mrs. Fairweather in the face agin. (*Exit.*)

SCENE III

The interior of Puffy's house. A poor but neat room—window at back. Mrs. Fairweather is arranging dinner.

(*Enter Lucy, with a box.*)

LUCY: My dear mother.

MRS. FAIRWEATHER: My darling Lucy. Ah, your eye is bright again. The thought of seeing Mark Livingstone has revived your smile.

LUCY: I have seen him. He and Paul called at Madame Victorine's.

MRS. FAIRWEATHER: Is your work over, Lucy, already?

LUCY: What we expected has arrived, mother. This dress is the last I shall receive from Madame Victorine—she is discharging her hands.

MRS. FAIRWEATHER: More misfortunes—and Paul has not been able to obtain employment.

(*A knock. Enter Mrs. Puffy.*)

MRS. PUFFY: May I come in? it's only Mrs. Puffy. I've been over the oven for two hours! Knowing you had company—I've got a pigeon pie—such a pie!—um—oo—mutton kidneys in it—and hard biled eggs—love ye!—then I've got a chicken, done up a way of my own! I'll get on a clean gown and serve it up myself.

MRS. FAIRWEATHER: But my dear Mrs. Puffy—really we did not mean to incur any expense—

MRS. PUFFY: Expense! why, wasn't them pigeons goin' to waste—they was shot by Dan—and we can't abide pigeons, neither Puffy nor I. Then the rooster was running round—always raisn' hereafter early in the mornin'—a noosance, it was—

(*Enter Dan.*)

DAN: Beg pardon ladies—I just stepped in—

LUCY: Good day, Dan.

DAN: Day, Miss!—(*Aside to Mrs. Puffy.*) Oh! mother, ain't she pootty this morning.

MRS. PUFFY: (*Smoothing her hair.*) What have you got there, Dan'el?

DAN: When I was paying the man for them birds—(*Mrs. Puffy kicks him.*)—Creation! mother—you're like the stocks—you can't move a'thout crushin' somebody—well, he'd got this here pair o' boots ornder his arm—why, ses I, if ever der was a foot created small enough to go into them thar, it is Miss Lucy's—so I brought them for you to look at.

LUCY: They are too dear for me, Dan, pray give them back.

DAN: Well, ye see—the man has kinder gone, Miss—he said he'd call again—some time next fall—

MRS. FAIRWEATHER: Dan—Mrs. Puffy—you are good, kind, dear souls—when the friends of our better days have deserted us—when the rich will scarcely deign to remember us—you, without any design, but with the goodness of God in your hearts—without any hope but that of hiding your kindness, you help me. Give me your hands—I owe you too much already—but you must bestow on us no more out of your poverty.

MRS. PUFFY: Lord, Mrs! just as if me and Puffy could bestow anything—and what's Dan fit for?

DAN: Yes—what's I'm fit for?

MRS. FAIRWEATHER: Well, I will accept your dinner to-day on one condition—that you will all dine with us.

MRS. PUFFY: Oh—my! Dine with up-town folks!

LUCY: Yes indeed, Dan, you must.

DAN: Lord, miss! I aint no account at dinin' with folks—I take my food on the fust pile of bricks, anyhow.

MRS. PUFFY: I'm accustomed to mine standin', behind the counter.

DAN: We never set down to it, square out—except on Sundays.

MRS. PUFFY: Then it don't seem natural—we never eat, each of us is employed a helping of the other.

DAN: I'll fix it! Father, and mother, and I, will all wait on you.

LUCY: (*Laughing.*) That's one way of dining together, certainly.

(*Enter Paul and Livingstone.*)

LIVINGSTONE: Here we are. Why, what a comfortable little cage this is!

DAN: Let me take your coat and hat, sir.

LIVINGSTONE: Thank you. (*Exit Dan and Mrs. Puffy.*) How like the old times, eh, Lucy? (*Sits by her.*)

MRS. FAIRWEATHER: (*Aside to Paul.*) Well, Paul, have you obtained employment?

PAUL: No, mother; but Livingstone is rich—he must have influence, and he will assist me.

MRS. FAIRWEATHER: Heaven help us! I fear that the worst is not come.

PAUL: Nonsense, mother—cheer up! Is there anything you have concealed from me?

MRS. FAIRWEATHER: No—nothing you need know. (*Aside.*) If he knew that for five weeks we have been subsisting on the charity of these poor people.

(*Enter Mrs. Puffy with a pie, followed by Dan with a roast chicken and Puffy, loaded with plates and various articles of dinner service.*)

MRS. PUFFY: Here it is.

LUCY: Stay—we must lay more covers; help me, Paul.

LIVINGSTONE: Let me assist you. (*They join another table to the first.*)

MRS. FAIRWEATHER: Mr. and Mrs. Puffy and Dan dine with us.

PAUL: Bravo!

LIVINGSTONE: Hail Columbia! (*Dan begins dancing about.*)

LUCY: Why, Dan—what's the matter?

DAN: Oh, nothing, miss.

LUCY: How red your face is!

DAN: Don't mind, miss.

MRS. PUFFY: Oh Lord! I forgot that dish; it has been in the oven for an hour.

DAN: It ain't at all hot. (*Paul touches it and jumps away.*) It's got to burn into the bone afore George Washington No. 4 gives in.

(*Lays down the plate—they all sit.*)

PUFFY: Now, this is agreeable—I have not felt so happy since I started my forty horse power oven.

LIVINGSTON: This pie is magnificent. (*Mrs. Puffy rises.*)

MRS. PUFFY: Oh, sir, you make me feel good.

DAN: (*Holding the table.*) Mother can't express her feelings without upsetting the table.

(*Enter two Sheriff's Officers.*)

PAUL: What persons are these?

PUFFY: What do you want?

FIRST SHERIFF'S OFFICER: I am the Deputy Sheriff—I come at the suit of Gideon Bloodgood, against Susan Fairweather and Jonas Puffy—amount of debt and costs, one hundred and fifty dollars.

PAUL: My mother!

PUFFY: He said he would see about it—Oh, Mrs. Fairweather—I hope you will forgive me—I couldn't help it.

DEPUTY SHERIFF: I do not want to distress you; Mr. Livingstone will perhaps pay the debt—or give me his check.

PAUL: Livingstone!

LIVINGSTONE: (*After a pause.*) I cannot help you. Yes, I will rather appear what I am a ruined man, than seem a contemptible one—I am penniless, broken—for weeks I have been so—but I never felt poverty till now.

Tableau.

END OF ACT II

ACT III

A Room in the house of Gideon Bloodgood; the furniture and ornaments are in a style of exaggerated richness, white satin and gold. Bloodgood is discovered writing at a table on one side, Alida seated reading a newspaper on the other.

BLOODGOOD: What are you reading?

ALIDA: The New York *Herald.*

BLOODGOOD: You seem interested in it?

ALIDA: Very. Shall I read aloud?

BLOODGOOD: Do. (*Goes on writing.*)

ALIDA: (*Reads.*) "Wall street is a perch, on which a row of human vultures sit, whetting their beaks, ready to fight over the carcass of a dying enterprise. Amongst these birds of prey, the most vulturous is perhaps Gid Bloodgood. This popular financier made his fortune in the lottery business. He then dabbled a little in the slave trade, as the Paraquita case proved,—last week by a speculation in flour he made fifty thousand dollars, this operation raised the price of bread four cents a loaf, and now there are a thousand people starving in the hovels of New York—we nominate Gid for Congress, expense to be paid by the admiring crowd—send round the hat." Father! (*Rises.*) Are you not rich?

BLOODGOOD: Why do you ask?

ALIDA: Because people say that riches are worshipped in New York, that wealth alone graduates society. This is false, for I am young, handsome and your heiress—yet I am refused admission into the best families here whose intimacy I have sought.

BLOODGOOD: Refused admission! Is not Fifth Avenue open to you?

ALIDA: Fifth Avenue! that jest is stale. Fifth Avenue is a shop where the richest fortunes are displayed like the dry goods in Stewart's windows, and like them, too, are changed daily. But why do we not visit those families at whose names all men and all journals bow with respect, the Livingstones, the Astors, Van Renssalaers. Father, these families receive men less rich than you—and honor many girls who don't dress as well as I do, nor keep a carriage.

BLOODGOOD: Is not the Duke of Calcavella at my feet?

ALIDA: The Duke de Calcavella is an adventurer to whom you lend money, who escorts me to my box at the opera that he may get in free.

BLOODGOOD: You minx, you know you love him.

ALIDA: I am not speaking of love—but of marriage.

BLOODGOOD: Marriage!

ALIDA: Yes, marriage! This society in New York which has shut its doors against me, it is from amongst these families that I have resolved to choose a husband.

BLOODGOOD: (*Rising.*) Alida, do you already yearn to leave me? For you alone I have hoarded my wealth—men have thought me miserly, when I have had but one treasure in the world and that was you, my only child. To the rest of my fellow creatures I have been cold and calculating, because in you alone was buried all the love my heart could feel—my fortune, take it, gratify your caprices—take it all, but leave me your affection.

ALIDA: You talk as if I were still a child.

BLOODGOOD: I would to God you were! Oh, Alida, if you knew how fearful a thing it is for a man like me to lose the only thing in the world that ties him to it!

ALIDA: Do you wish me to marry the Duke de Calcavella?

BLOODGOOD: A *roue*, a gambler! Heaven forbid!

ALIDA: Besides, they say he has a wife in Italy.

BLOODGOOD: I shall forbid him the house.

ALIDA: No, you won't.

BLOODGOOD: His reputation will compromise yours.

ALIDA: Judge my nature by your own—I may blush from anger—never from shame.

(*Enter Edwards.*)

EDWARDS: Mr. Mark Livingstone.

ALIDA: Livingstone! This is the first time that name has ever been announced in this house.

BLOODGOOD: He comes on business. Tell Mr. Livingstone I cannot see him. Beg him to call at my office to-morrow.

ALIDA: Show him up.

BLOODGOOD: Alida!

ALIDA: (*Sharply to Edwards.*) Do you hear me?

BLOODGOOD: This is tyranny—I—I—(*In a rage to Edwards.*) Well, blockhead, why do you stand staring there? Don't you hear the order? Show him up. (*Exit Edwards.*)

ALIDA: Livingstone!

(*Enter Mark Livingstone.*)

MARK: Mr. Bloodgood—Miss Bloodgood—(*Bows.*) I am most fortunate to find you at home.

ALIDA: I trust that Mrs. Livingstone your mother, and Miss Livingstone your sister, are well?

MARK: (*Coldly.*) I thank you. (*Gaily.*) Allow me to assure you that you were the belle of the opera last night.

ALIDA: Yet you did not flatter me with your presence in our box.

MARK: You noticed my absence! You render me the happiest and proudest member of my club.

ALIDA: By the way, papa, I thought you were going to be a member of the Union.

MARK: Ahem! (*An awkward silence.*) He was black-balled last week.

BLOODGOOD: I think, Mr. Livingstone you have some business with me.

ALIDA: Am I in the way?

MARK: Not at all—the fact is, Miss Bloodgood—my business can be explained in three words.

BLOODGOOD: Indeed!

MARK: I am ruined.

ALIDA: Ruined!

MARK: My father lived in those days when fancy stocks were unknown, and consequently was in a position to leave me with a handsome fortune. I spent it—extravagantly—foolishly. My mother, who loves me "not wisely but too well," heard that my name was pledged for a large amount,—Mr. Bloodgood held my paper—she sold out all her fortune without my knowledge, and rescued my credit from dishonor.

BLOODGOOD: Allow me to observe, I think she acted honorably, but foolishly.

MARK: (*Bows to Bloodgood.*) She shared my father's ideas on these matters; well (*Turns to Alida*) finding I was such good pay, your father lent me a further sum of money, with which I speculated in stocks to recover my mother's loss—I bulled the market—lost—borrowed more—the crisis came—I lost again—until I found myself ruined.

BLOODGOOD: (*Rising.*) Mr. Livingstone, I anticipate the object of your present visit—you desire some accommodation—I regret that it is out of my power to accord it. If you had applied to me a few days earlier I might have been able to—but—a—at the present moment it is quite impossible.

MARK: (*Aside.*) Impossible—the usual expression—I am familiar with it. (*Rising— aloud.*) I regret exceedingly that I did not fall on that more fortunate moment to which you allude—a thousand pardons for my untimely demand—

BLOODGOOD: I hope you believe I am sincere when I say—

MARK: Oh! I am sure of it. Accept my thanks—good morning, Miss Bloodgood.

BLOODGOOD: (*Ringing the bell.*) I trust you will not be put to serious inconvenience.

MARK: Oh, no. (*Aside.*) A revolver will relieve me of every difficulty. (*Aloud.*) Good day, Mr. Bloodgood. (*Exit.*)

BLOODGOOD: I like his impudence! To come to me for assistance! Let him seek it of his aristocratic friends—his club associates who blackballed me last week.

ALIDA: (*Who has been seated writing at table.*) Father, come here.

BLOODGOOD: What is it?

ALIDA: I am writing a letter which I wish you to sign.

BLOODGOOD: To whom?

ALIDA: To Mr. Livingstone.

BLOODGOOD: To Livingstone!

ALIDA: Read it.

BLOODGOOD: (*Reads.*) "My dear sir, give yourself no further anxiety about your debt to me; I will see that your notes are paid—and if the loan of ten thousand dollars will serve you, I beg to hold that amount at your service, to be repaid at your convenience. Yours truly." (*Throwing down letter.*) I will write nothing of the kind.

ALIDA: You are mistaken—you will write nothing else.

BLOODGOOD: With what object?

ALIDA: I want to make a purchase.

BLOODGOOD: Of what?

ALIDA: Of a husband—a husband who is a gentleman—and through whom I can gain that position you cannot with all your wealth obtain—you see—the thing is cheap—there's the pen. (*She rings a bell.*)

BLOODGOOD: Is your mind so set on this ambition?

ALIDA: If it cost half your fortune. (*Bloodgood signs.*)

(*Enter Edwards.*)

(*To servant.*) Deliver this letter immediately.

EDWARDS: (*Takes the letter and is going out, when he runs against Badger, who is cooly entering.*) I have told you already that my master is not to be seen.

BADGER: So you did—but you see how mistaken you were. There he is—I can see him distinctly.

BLOODGOOD: Badger! (*To Edwards.*) You may go, Edwards.

BADGER: (*To Edwards.*) James—get out.

BLOODGOOD: What can he want here?

BADGER: Respected Gideon, excuse my not calling more promptly, but since my return from California, this is my first appearance in fashionable society.

ALIDA: (*Proudly.*) Who is this fellow?

BADGER: Ah, Alida, how is the little tootles? You forget me.

ALIDA: How can I recollect every begging imposter who importunes my father.

BADGER: Charming! The same as ever—changed in form—but the heart, my dear Gideon, the same ever, is hard and dry as a biscuit.

ALIDA: Father, give this wretch a dollar and let him go.

BADGER: Hullo! Miss Bloodgood, when I hand round the hat it is time enough to put something in it. Gideon, ring and send that girl of yours to her nurse.

ALIDA: Is this fellow mad?

BLOODGOOD: Hush! my dear!

ALIDA: Speak out your business—I am familiar with all my father's affairs.

BADGER: All? I doubt it.

(*Enter Edwards, followed by Lucy.*)

EDWARDS: This way, Miss. (*To Alida.*) Here is your dress maker.

ALIDA: (*Eyeing Lucy.*) Ha! you are the young person I met this morning walking with Mr. Livingstone?

LUCY: Yes, Madam.

ALIDA: Hum! follow me, and let me see if you can attend on ladies as diligently as you do on gentlemen. (*Exeunt Alida and Lucy.*).

BLOODGOOD: (*Looking inquiringly at Badger.*) So you are here again. I thought you were dead.

BADGER: No; here I am—like a bad shilling, come back again. I've been all over the world since we parted twenty years ago. Your 3,000 dollars lasted me for some months in California. Believe me, had I known that instead of absconding, you remained in New York, I would have hastened back again ten years ago, to share your revived fortunes.

BLOODGOOD: I am at a loss to understand your allusions, sir—nor do I know the object of your return to this city. We have plenty of such persons as you in New York.

BADGER: The merchants of San Francisco did not think so, for they subscribed to send me home.

BLOODGOOD: What do you mean?

BADGER: I mean the Vigilance Committee.

BLOODGOOD: What do you intend to do here?

BADGER: Reduced in circumstance and without character, the only resource left to me is to start a bank.

BLOODGOOD: Well, Mr. Badger; I cannot see in what way these things can affect me!

BADGER: Can't you? Ahem! Do you ever read the Sunday papers?

BLOODGOOD: Never.

BADGER: I've got a romance ready for one of them—allow me to give you a sketch of it.

BLOODGOOD: Sir—

BADGER: The scene opens in a bank on Nassau street. Twenty years ago a very respectable old sea captain, one winter's night, makes a special deposit of one hundred thousand dollars—nobody present but the banker and one clerk. The old captain takes a receipt and goes on his way rejoicing—but, lo! and behold you!—in half an hour he returns—having ascertained a fact or two, he demands his money back, but while receiving it he is seized by a fit of apoplexy, and he dies on the spot. End of Chapter One.

BLOODGOOD: Indeed, Mr. Badger, your romance is quite original.

BADGER: Ain't it! never heard it before, did you?—no! Good! Chapter Two. (*Pointedly.*) The banker and his clerk carried the body out on the sidewalk, where it was discovered, and the next day the Coroner's Jury returned a verdict accordingly. The clerk receiving 3,000 dollars hush money left for parts unknown. The banker remained in New York, and on the profits of this plunder established a colossal fortune. End of Part No. 1—to be continued in our next.

BLOODGOOD: And what do you suppose such a romance will be worth?

BADGER: I've come to you to know.

BLOODGOOD: I am no judge of that.

BADGER: Ain't you?—well—in Part No. 2, I propose to relate that this history is true in every particular, and I shall advertise for the heirs of the dead man.

BLOODGOOD: Ha! you know his name then?

BADGER: Yes, but I see you don't. I wrote the acknowledgement which you signed—you had not even the curiosity then to read the name of your victim.

BLOODGOOD: Really, Mr. Badger, I am at a loss to understand you. Do you mean to insinuate that this romance applies in any way to me?

BADGER: It has a distant reference.

BLOODGOOD: Your memory is luxurious—perhaps it can furnish some better evidence of this wonderful story than the word of a convict ejected from California as a precaution of public safety.

BADGER: You are right—my word is not worth much.

BLOODGOOD: I fear not.

BADGER: But the receipt, signed by you, is worth a great deal.

BLOODGOOD: (*Starting.*) Ha! you lie!

BADGER: Let us proceed with my romance. When the banker and his clerk searched for the receipt, they could not find it—a circumstance which only astonished one of the villains—because the clerk had picked up the document and secured it in his pocket. I don't mean to insinuate that this applies in any way to you.

BLOODGOOD: Villain!

BADGER: Moral: As a general rule, never destroy receipts—it is no knowing when they may not prove useful.

BLOODGOOD: Were it so, this receipt is of no value in your hands—the heirs of the dead man can alone establish a claim.

BADGER: (*Rising.*) That's the point—calculate the chance of my finding them, and let me know what it is worth.

BLOODGOOD: What do you demand?

BADGER: Five thousand dollars.

BLOODGOOD: Five thousand devils!

BADGER: You refuse?

BLOODGOOD: I defy you—find the heir if you can.

(*Enter Edwards.*)

EDWARDS: Mr. Paul Fairweather!

(*Enter Paul. Badger starts, then falls laughing in a chair.*)

BLOODGOOD: Your business, sir, with me.

PAUL: Oh, pardon me, Mr. Bloodgood—but the officers have seized the furniture of our landlord—of your tenant—for a debt owed by my mother. I come to ask your mercy—utter ruin awaits two poor families.

BADGER: Oh, Supreme Justice! there is the creditor, and there is the debtor.

PAUL: My mother—my sister—I plead for them, not for myself.

BLOODGOOD: I have waited long enough.

BADGER: (*Rising.*) So have I. (*To Paul.*) Have you no friends or relations to help you?

PAUL: None, sir: My father is dead.

(*Bloodgood returns to his table.*)

BLOODGOOD: Enough of this. (*Rings the bell.*)

BADGER: Not quite; I feel interested in this young gentlemen—don't you?

BLOODGOOD: Not at all; therefore my servant will show you both out—so you may talk this matter over elsewhere.

BADGER: (*To Paul.*) Your name is familiar to me—was your father in trade?

PAUL: He was a sea captain.

BADGER: Ah! he died nobly in some storm, I suppose—the last to leave his ship?

PAUL: No, sir, he died miserably! Twenty years ago, his body was found on the side walk on Liberty street, where he fell dead by apoplexy.

BLOODGOOD: (*Rising.*) Ah!

(*Enter Edwards.*)

BADGER: James, show us out—we'll talk over this matter elsewhere.

BLOODGOOD: No—you—you can remain. Leave us, Edwards.

BADGER: Ah, I told you that the young man was quite interesting. Alphonse, get out.

(*Exit Edwards.*)

BLOODGOOD: My dear Mr. Badger, I think we have a little business to settle together?

BADGER: Yes, my dear Gideon. (*Aside to him.*) Stocks have gone up—I want fifty thousand dollars for that receipt.

BLOODGOOD: Fifty thousand!

BADGER: (*Aside.*) You see the effect of good news on the market—quite astonishing; ain't it.

BLOODGOOD: If you will step down to the dining-room, you will find lunch ready—refresh yourself, while I see what can be done for this young man.

BADGER: (*Aside.*) What are you up to? You want to fix him—to try some game to euchre me. Go it! I've got the receipt; you're on the hook—take out all the line you want. (*Calls.*) Ho! without there!

(*Enter Edwards.*)

Maximilian, vamos! Show me to the banquetting-hall. (*Exit, with Edwards.*)

BLOODGOOD: Your situation interests me; but surely, at your age—you can find employment.

PAUL: Alas, sir, in these times, it is impossible. I would work, yes, at any kind of labor—submit to anything, if I could save my mother and sister from want.

BLOODGOOD: Control your feelings; perhaps I can aid you.

PAUL: Oh, sir, I little expected to find in you a benefactor.

BLOODGOOD: My correspondents at Rio Janeiro require a book-keeper—are you prepared to accept this situation? But there is a condition attached to this employment that may not suit you—you must start by the vessel which sails to-morrow.

PAUL: To-morrow!

BLOODGOOD: I will hand you a thousand dollars in advance of salary, to provide for your mother and sister; they had better leave this city until they can follow you. You hesitate.

PAUL: Oh, sir, 'tis my gratitude that renders me silent.

BLOODGOOD: You accept? the terms are two thousand dollars a year.

PAUL: (*Seizing his hand.*) Mr. Bloodgood, the prayers of a family whom you have made happy, will prosper your life. God bless you, sir! I speak not for myself, but for those still more dear to me.

BLOODGOOD: Call again in an hour, when your papers of introduction and the money shall be ready.

PAUL: Farewell, sir. I can scarcely believe my good fortune. (*Exit.*)

BLOODGOOD: So, now to secure Badger. (*Sitting down and writing.*) He must, at any risk, be prevented from communicating with the mother and daughter until they can be sent into some obscure retreat. I doubt that he is in possession of this receipt, (*Rings a bell*) but I will take an assurance about that. (*Rings.*)

(*Enter Lucy.*)

LUCY: I will do my best, miss, to please you. Oh, let me hasten from this house!

(*Enter Mark Livingstone.*)

MARK: Lucy!

LUCY: Mark!

MARK: What brings you here?

LUCY: What brings the poor into the saloons of the rich?

(*Enter Alida, unseen by the others.*)

ALIDA: (*Aside.*) Mr. Livingstone here, and with this girl!

MARK: My dear Lucy, I have news, bright news, that will light up a smile in your eyes—I am once more rich. But before I relate my good fortune, let me hear from you the consent to share it.

LUCY: What do you mean?

MARK: I mean, dearest one, that I love you—I love you with all my reckless, foolish, worthless heart.

ALIDA: (*Advancing.*) Mr. Livingstone, my father is waiting for you in his study.

MARK: A thousand pardons, Miss Bloodgood; I was not aware—excuse me. (*Aside.*) I wonder if she overheard me. (*To Lucy.*) I will see you again this evening. (*Exit.*)

ALIDA: (*To Lucy, who is going.*) Stay; one word with you. Mr. Livingstone loves you? Do not deny it, I have overheard you.

LUCY: Well, Miss Bloodgood, I have no account to render you in this matter.

ALIDA: I beg your pardon—he is to be my husband.

LUCY: Your husband?

ALIDA: Be quiet and listen. Mr. Livingstone is ruined—my father has come to his aid; but one word from me, and the hand, extended to save him from destruction, will be withdrawn.

LUCY: But you will not speak that word?

ALIDA: That depends—

LUCY: On what? his acceptance of your hand? he does not love you.

ALIDA: That is not the question.

LUCY: You have overheard that he loves *me.*

ALIDA: That is no concern of mine.

LUCY: And you will coldly buy this man for a husband, knowing that you condemn him to eternal misery!

ALIDA: You are candid, but not complimentary. Let us hope that in time he will forget you, and learn to endure me.

LUCY: Oh, you do not love him. I see, it is his name you require to cover the shame which stains your father's, and which all his wealth cannot conceal. Thank Heaven! his love for me will preserve him from such a cowardly scheme.

ALIDA: I will make him rich. What would you make him?

LUCY: I would make him happy.

ALIDA: Will you give him up?

LUCY: Never!

ALIDA: Be it so.

(*Re-enter Mark.*)

MARK: Lucy, dear Lucy, do you see that lady?—she is my guardian angel. To her I owe my good fortune—Mr. Bloodgood has told me all, and see, this letter is in her own handwriting; now, let me confess, Miss Bloodgood, that had I not been thus rescued from ruin, I had no other resource but a Colt's revolver.

LUCY: Mark!

MARK: Yes, Lucy—I had resolved I could not endure the shame and despair which beset me on all sides. But let us not talk of such madness—let us only remember that I owe her my life.

ALIDA: (*Aside.*) And I intend to claim the debt.

MARK: More than my life—I owe to her all that happiness which you will bestow upon me.

LUCY: Me! me!—Mark!—No, it is impossible.

MARK: Impossible!

LUCY: I cannot be your wife.

MARK: What mean you, Lucy?

LUCY: (*With supreme effort.*) I—I do not love you.

MARK: You jest, Lucy—yet, no—there are tears in your eyes.

LUCY: (*Looking away.*) Did I ever tell you that I loved you?

MARK: No, it is true—but your manner, your looks, I thought—

LUCY: You are not angry with me, are you?

MARK: I love you too sincerely for that, and believe me I will never intrude again on your family, where my presence now can only produce pain and restraint; may I hope, however, that you will retain enough kindness towards me, as to persuade your mother to accept my friendship? It will soothe the anguish you have innocently inflicted, if your family will permit me to assist them. Have you the generosity to make this atonement? I know it will pain you all—but you owe it to me. (*Lucy falls, weeping, in a chair.*) Pardon me, Miss Bloodgood. Farewell, Lucy. (*To Alida.*) I take my leave. (*Exit.*)

ALIDA: He has gone—you may dry your eyes.

LUCY: Oh! I know what starvation is—I have met want face-to-face, and I have saved him from that terrible extremity.

ALIDA: He offered you money; I should prefer that my husband should not have pecuniary relations with you—at least, not at present—so, as you are in want—here is some assistance. (*Offers her purse to Lucy.*)

LUCY: (*Rising.*) You insult me, Miss Bloodgood.

ALIDA: How can an offer of money insult anybody?

LUCY: You thought I sold my heart—no—I gave it. Keep your gold, it would soil my poverty; you have made two fellow-beings unhappy for life—God forgive you! (*Exit.*)

(*Re-enter Bloodgood.*)

BLOODGOOD: What is the matter, Alida?

(*Re-enter Badger.*)

BADGER: Your cook is perfect, your wine choice. (*He pockets the napkins.*) Well, now suppose we do a little business.

BLOODGOOD: (*Rings bell.*) It is time we began to understand each other.

(*Enter Edwards.*)

Has that letter been delivered?

(Edwards bows, and at a sign from Bloodgood, exits.)

BADGER: Do you wish to enter into particulars in the presence of this charming creature?
BLOODGOOD: Her presence will not affect our business.

(Re-enter Edwards, and two Police Officers.)

BADGER: Just as you please. What proposition have you to make?
BLOODGOOD: I propose to give you into custody for an attempt to extort money by threats and intimidation.
FIRST POLICEMAN: You are our prisoner.
BADGER: Arrested!
BLOODGOOD: Let him be searched; on his person will be found a receipt signed by me which he purloined from my desk yonder.
BADGER: Well played, my dear Gideon, but, knowing the character of the society into which I was venturing, I left the dear document safe at home. Good morning, Gid—Miss Bloodgood, yours. General—Colonel—take care of me. (*Goes up with Policemen.*)

END OF ACT III

ACT IV

SCENE I

Union Square—Night. The snow falls.

(Puffy discovered, with a pan of roasting chestnuts. Paul crouches in a corner of the street.)

PUFFY: Lord! how cold it is. I can't sell my chestnuts. I thought if I posted myself just there, so as to catch the grand folks as they go to the opera, they might fancy to take in a pocket-full, to eat during the performance.

(Enter Dan, with two trunks on his shoulder, followed by a Gentleman.)

DAN: There is the hotel. I'll wait here while you see if you can get a room. *(Exit Gentleman, into hotel.)*
PUFFY: Dan, my boy, what cheer?
DAN: This is the first job I've had to-day.
PUFFY: I've not taken a cent.
DAN: Have you been home to dinner?
PUFFY: No; I took a chestnut. There wasn't more than enough for the old woman and you, so I dined out.
DAN: I wasn't hungry much, so I boried a bit o' 'bacca.
PUFFY: Then the old woman had all the dinner, that's some comfort—one of us had a good meal to-day.
DAN: I don't know, father—she's just ugly enough to go and put it by for our supper.

(Enter Mrs. Puffy, with a tin can.)

PUFFY: Here she is.
MRS. PUFFY: Ain't you a nice pair? For five mortal hours I've been carryin' this dinner up and down Broadway.
DAN: I told you so.

MRS. PUFFY: You thought to give old mother the slip, you undootiful villin—but I've found ye both. Come, here's your suppers—I've kept it warm under my cloak.

PUFFY: Lay the table on the gentleman's trunk.

DAN: (*Looking into the tin can.*) A splendid lump of bread, and a chunk of beef!

PUFFY: Small feed for three human beings.

DAN: Here goes.

PUFFY: Stay, Dan. (*Placing his hands over the bread.*) God bless us, and pity the Poor of New York. Now I'll share the food in three.

DAN: (*Pointing to Paul.*) Father, that cuss in the corner there looks kinder bad— suppose you have the food in four.

MRS. PUFFY: I don't want more. Give him mine—I ain't at all cold.

DAN: Mother, there's a tear on the end of your nose—let me break it off.

MRS. PUFFY: Get out.

DAN: (*Takes a piece of bread, and goes to Paul.*) Hello, stranger! He's asleep.

MRS. PUFFY: Then don't wake him. Leave the bread in his lap. (*Dan places the bread, softly, beside Paul, and rejoins the party—they eat.*)

(*Enter a Gentleman, followed by Badger.*)

BADGER: (*Very ragged, with some opera books in one hand, and boxes of matches in the other.*) Book of the opera, sir? take a book, sir—they will charge you double inside. Well, buy a box of lucifers—a hundred for three cents. (*Dodging in front of him, to prevent him passing.*) Genuine Pollak's—try one. (*Exit Gentleman—Badger changes his tone, and calls after him.*) If you're short of cash, I'll lend you a shilling. He wants all he has got to pay his omnibus. Jerusha! ain't it cold! Tum-iddy-tum-iddy-tum. (*Performs a short dance, while he hums a banjo melody.*) I could play the banjo on my stomach, while all my shivering anatomy would supply the bones.

(*Enter Mrs. Fairweather.*)

MRS. FAIRWEATHER: I cannot return to our miserable home without food for my children. Each morning, we separate in search of work, in search of food, only to meet again at night—their poor faces thin with hunger. (*She clasps her hands in anguish.*) Ah! what's here? yes, this remains—it is gold!

BADGER: (*Overhearing her last word.*) Gold! Book of the opera, ma'am?

MRS. FAIRWEATHER: Tell me, friend, where can I buy a loaf of bread at this hour?

BADGER: There's a saloon open in the 4th Avenue. (*Aside.*) Gold—she said gold.

MRS. FAIRWEATHER: Will they accept this pledge for some food? (*Shows a ring to Badger.*)

BADGER: (*Eagerly.*) Let me see it. (*Looks around.*)

MRS. FAIRWEATHER: It is my wedding ring.

(*Badger examines it by the light of the Druggist's window.*)

BADGER: (*Aside.*) I can easily make off with it. (*Rubs his nose with the ring while he considers.*)

MRS. FAIRWEATHER: My children are starving—I must part with it to buy them bread.

BADGER: (*Whistles—hesitates—and returns the ring.*) Go along, go buy your children food, start, and don't show that ring to anybody else. You deserve to lose it for showing it to such a blackguard as I am. (*Exit Mrs. Fairweather.*)

(*Enter Bloodgood.*)

BLOODGOOD: What's the time? The opera must be nearly over. (*Looks at his watch by the light of the Druggist's window.*)

BADGER: Book of the opera, sir—only authorized edition. (*Recognizing him.*) Bloodgood!

BLOODGOOD: Badger! (*They advance. Bloodgood puts his hand into the breast of his coat.*)

BADGER: Ah, my dear Gideon—(*Suddenly.*) Take your hand out of your breast—come! none of that—I've a knife up my sleeve that would rip you up like a dried codfish before you could cock that revolver you have there so handy.

BLOODGOOD: (*Withdrawing his hand.*) You are mistaken.

BADGER: Oh, no! I am not. I have not been ten years in California for nothing—you were just thinking that you could blow out my brains, and swear that I was trying to garrote you.

BLOODGOOD: What do you want?

BADGER: I want your life—but legally. A week ago, I came out of prison—you had removed the Fairweather family—I could not find a trace of them but I found the receipt where I had concealed it. Tomorrow I shall place it in the hands of the District Attorney with my confession of our murder of the Sea Captain.

BLOODGOOD: Murder—

BADGER: Only think what a fine wood cut for the Police Gazette we shall make, carrying out the dead body between us.

BLOODGOOD: Demon!

BADGER: There will be a correct plan of your back office in the Herald—headed—the Bloodgood Tragedy.

BLOODGOOD: Come to my house to-morrow, and bring that document with you.

BADGER: No, sir—eel once caught twice shy. You owe a call. Come to my house to-night—and alone.

BLOODGOOD: Where do you live?

BADGER: Nineteen and a half Cross Street, Five Points—fifth floor back—my name is on the door in chalk.

BLOODGOOD: In an hour I will be there.

BADGER: In an hour. Don't forget to present my compliments to your charming daughter—sweet creature! the image of her father—how I should like to write something in her album. (*Exit Bloodgood. Enter two Gentlemen from Hotel—they talk. Cries.*) Here's lucifers—three cents a hundred. (*Gentlemen shake hands and separate. Following one off.*) Here's this miscellaneous stock of lumber, just imported from Germany, to be sold out—an alarming sacrifice, in consequence of the present state of the money market. (*Exit importuning the gentleman, who tries to escape.*)

PUFFY: Come mother, we must get home—

MRS. PUFFY: Dan, have you seen nothing of poor Mrs. Fairweather and her children?

DAN: No, mother—I can't find out where they have gone to—I guess they've quit New York.

MRS. PUFFY: God help them—wherever they are!

PUFFY: Come, mother.

(Music—Puffy and Mrs. Puffy go out—Dan goes up and speaks with a gentleman.)

(Enter Lucy.)

LUCY: This is the place. The sisters of charity in Houston Street told me that I might find work at this address. *(Reads paper.)* 14th Street. Oh, Heaven! be merciful to me, this is my last hope. *(Exit.)*

(Paul rises and comes forward.)

PAUL: My limbs are powerless. How long have I slept there?—another long day has passed—I have crept round the hotels—the wharves—I have begged for work—but they laughed at my poor thin form—the remnant of better days hung in tatters about me—and I was thrust from the door, by stronger wretches than I. To-day I applied to get employment as a waiter in a hotel—but no, I looked too miserable. Oh, my mother! my poor mother! my dear sister! were it not for you, I would lie down here and die where I was born, in the streets of New York.

DAN: All right, sir—to the Brevoort House. Here, you lazy cuss, shoulder this trunk, and earn a quarter—

(Enter a Porter.)

PAUL: Yes—oh, gladly!—

PORTER: It's myself will do that same. *(Paul and the Porter seize the trunk.)* Lave yer hoult—you dandy chap wid the black coat.

PAUL: He called to me.

PORTER: It is the likes of you—that ud be takin' the bread out of the mouths of honest folks.

PAUL: God help me! I have not tasted bread for two days.

PORTER: The Lord save us! why didn't ye say so?—take the trunk and welkim. *(Paul trying to lift it. Exit Dan.)*

GENTLEMAN: Come along, quick! *(Exit Gentleman.)*

PAUL: *(Unable to lift it, staggers back.)* I—I—can't—I am too weak from hunger.

PORTER: Look at this, my jewel. *(Tossing the trunk on his shoulder.)* That's the way of—id—all right, yer honor! *(Exit Porter.)*

PAUL: *(Falling against the lamp-post in despair, on his knees.)* Oh, God!—you who have refused to me the force to earn my bread, give me the resignation to bear your will.

(Re-enter Lucy.)

LUCY: The lady was from home—they told me to call next week—oh, could I see some kindly face—I would beg, yes—I would ask alms.

(*Enter a Gentleman.*)

Sir—pardon me—would you—
GENTLEMAN: Eh?
LUCY: (*Stammering.*) I—I—I—
GENTLEMAN: What do you want?
LUCY: (*Faintly.*) The—the—Bowery—if—if—you please—
GENTLEMAN: Just turn to the right, and keep straight on. (*Exit.*)
LUCY: Oh coward! coward!—I have not the courage to beg.

(*Enter Mrs. Fairweather.*)

MRS. FAIRWEATHER: They refused to take my ring—they said I had stolen it—
they drove me from the house. To what have I come!—to beg in the
streets—yes, for them, for my children!
PAUL: (*Rising.*) Let me return to our home—perhaps mother or Lucy may have
found work.
MRS. FAIRWEATHER: Sir! sir!—In the name of your mother—help my poor
children.
LUCY: (*Covering her face with one hand, and holding out the other.*) For pity's
sake—give me the price of—
PAUL: Mother!!
LUCY: My Brother!   } (*Together*)
MRS. FAIRWEATHER: My Son!
PAUL: Oh, mother! my own Lucy! my heart is broken! (*They embrace.*) Have you
concealed from me the extent of your misery?
MRS. FAIRWEATHER: My son! my poor children! I cannot see you die of hunger
and cold!
PAUL: Take Lucy home, mother—and I will bring you food.
MRS. FAIRWEATHER: Paul, promise me that nothing will tempt you to a dishonor-
able act.
PAUL: Do not fear, mother; the wretched have always one resource—they can die!
Do not weep, Lucy—in an hour I will be with you. (*Exeunt Lucy and Mrs.
Fairweather.*) I will go and await the crowd as they leave the Academy of Mu-
sic—amongst them Heaven will inspire some Christian heart to aid me.

SCENE II

The vestibule of the Academy of Music.

(*Enter Alida and Livingstone. Music within.*)

ALIDA: How strange that my father has not returned.
MARK: Allow me to look for the carriage.
ALIDA: I will remain here. (*Exit Livingstone.*) At last I have won the husband I
desire. He is entangled in my father's debt; in one month hence I shall be Livingstone's wife. Our box is now crowded with the first people in New
York.—The dear Duke still makes love to me—to which Livingstone appears
indifferent—so much the better—once Mrs. Livingstone he may do as he likes
and so will I.

(Enter Paul.)

PAUL: Ah 'tis she—Alida Bloodgood.
ALIDA: I wonder they permit such vagabonds to hang about the opera.

(Re-enter Livingstone.)

MARK: The carriage is ready—*(Recognizing Paul.)* Paul!
PAUL: Livingstone!
MARK: Great heaven! In what condition do I find you.
PAUL: We are poor—we are starving.
ALIDA: Give the poor fellow a dollar, and send him away.
MARK: My dear Alida, you do not know—this is a school fellow—an old friend—
ALIDA: I know that you are keeping me in the cold—ah! I see the Duke of Cacavella on the steps yonder, smoking a cigar. He will see me home, don't let me take you from your old friend. *(Exit.)*
MARK: *(Aside.)* Cold—heartless girl! *(Aloud.)* Come, Paul, come quickly, bring me to where I shall find your mother—your sister—stay, let me first go home, and get money, I will meet you at your lodgings—where do you live?
PAUL: Number nineteen and a half Cross Street—Five Points—I will wait for you at the door.
MARK: In less than an hour I shall be there. *(Exeunt.)*

SCENE III

No. 19½ Cross Street—Five Points. Two adjoining attic rooms: that of Badger, that of the Fairweather family. Music. Lucy is seated and Mrs. Fairweather is kneeling.

LUCY: Surely an hour has passed and Paul has not returned.
MRS. FAIRWEATHER: Oh, merciful father! protect my poor children.

(Enter Badger in his attic with his box of matches. He scrapes several which do not light. Mrs. Fairweather rises and goes to window.)

BADGER: One hundred matches like that for one cent. *(Lighting one.)* Oh, lucky chance! here's one that condescends. *(Lights a candle in a bottle.)*
MRS. FAIRWEATHER: Day after day goes by—no hope—the future worse than the present—dark—dark. Oh! this load of wretchedness is too much to bear.
LUCY: The candle is going out.
MRS. FAIRWEATHER: So much the better, I shall not be able to see your tears. *(Lucy rests her face on her hands.)*
BADGER: *(Taking a bottle from his pocket.)* There's the concentrated essence of comfort—the poor man's plaster for the inside.
LUCY: *(Aside.)* Is there no way to end this misery? None but death.
BADGER: *(Taking from pocket a slice of bread and meat wrapped in a bit of newspaper.)* Here's my supper. *(Addressing an imaginary servant.)* James, lay the table—spread the table cloth.—"Yes sa"—*(Places the newspaper over the table.)* It's cold here, there's a draught in this room, somewhere.—James, champagne. Thank you, James. *(Drinks and eats.)*

MRS. FAIRWEATHER: (*Aside, coming down.*) If Paul had only Lucy to support, they might live—why should I prolong my life only to hasten theirs.

BADGER: The draught comes from—(*Examining the wall.*)—yes there are great chinks in the wall—I must see my landlord and solicit repairs. A new family moved into the next room, yesterday; I wonder who they are?

LUCY: The wretched always have one resource—they can die!

BADGER: (*At his table eating—he has taken the blanket from his bed and wrapped it about his shoulders.*) Now let us do a little business. James, turn up the gas. Yes sa!—(*He snuffs out the candle with his fingers.*) Thank you. Ahem! James, Bloodgood is coming for the receipt bequeathed to me by the old sailor. What price shall we set upon it, James?

LUCY: (*Aside.*) When I am gone, there will be one mouth less to feed—Paul will have but one care to provide for.

MRS. FAIRWEATHER: (*Aside.*) In this room, we had some charcoal—there is enough left to bestow on me an easy death. (*Mrs. Fairweather exits.*)

BADGER: I think $50,000 would be the figure—Oh, what a prospect opens before me—50,000 dollars—I should resume specie payments.

LUCY: (*Looks into room.*) What is mother doing? ah, she is lighting the pan of charcoal on which we prepare our food—ah!—the thought!—could I induce her to leave me alone. Hem.—The deadly fumes of that fuel will bestow on me an easy death.

MRS. FAIRWEATHER: (*Re-enters.*) It is there—now, now, while I have the courage of despair.

BADGER: 50,000 dollars! I'll have a pair of fast trotters, and dine at Delmonico's. James, more champagne. (*Takes a drink from bottle.*) Thank you—

LUCY & MRS. FAIRWEATHER: (*Together.*) Mother—Lucy.

LUCY: Dear mother—I have just thought of a friend—a—a—fellow work girl, from whom I may get assistance—

MRS. FAIRWEATHER: Go, then, my child—yes—go at once.

LUCY: I fear to go alone. Come with me, you can wait at the corner of the street until I come out.

MRS. FAIRWEATHER: (*Putting on her bonnet. Aside.*) When she is out of sight, I can return and accomplish my purpose.

LUCY: (*Casting a cloak over her head. Aside.*) I will come back by another way.

MRS. FAIRWEATHER: Come, Lucy.

LUCY: I am ready, mother. (*Aside.*) She does not think that we are about to part forever.

MRS. FAIRWEATHER: (*Aside.*) My poor child!

LUCY: Kiss me—mother, for my heart is cold. (*They embrace.*)

BADGER: (*Cogitating.*) 50,000 dollars! I'll have a box at Grace Church and a pew at the opera.

LUCY: Mother, I am ready. (*Exeunt.*)

BADGER: (*Finding his bottle empty.*) What's the news? Let us consult my table cloth. What journal have we here. (*Reads.*) "Chevalier Greely has got a new hat."—It's the *Herald*—What's here?—(*Reads*) "You lie-villainy—you lie, and you know it." No! it's the *Tribune*.

(*Enter Bloodgood.*)

BLOODGOOD: Ah, Mr. Badger.

BADGER: Please wipe your feet, before you come in—my carpet is new. I am glad to see you. Take a seat upon the sofa. (*Pointing to bed.*)

BLOODGOOD: Come, sir; to business. You have the receipt with you, I suppose?

BADGER: You know I've got it, or you would not have come.

BLOODGOOD: How much do you want for it?

BADGER: Stay a moment. Let us see. You have had for twenty years in your possession, the sum of $100,000, the profits of one robbery—well, at eight per cent, this sum would be doubled.

BLOODGOOD: Let me see the document, and then we can estimate its value.

BADGER: (*Drawing receipt from pocket.*) Here it is.

BLOODGOOD: (*Springing towards him.*) Let me have it.

BADGER: Hands off!

BLOODGOOD: (*Drawing pistol.*) That paper, give it me, or I'll blow your brains out!

BADGER: (*Edging slowly towards the bed.*) Ah! that's your calculation.

BLOODGOOD: Now you are in my power.

BADGER: It's an old dodge, but ineffective. Come, no violence—I'll give you the paper.

BLOODGOOD: A bullet is a good argument.

BADGER: (*Drawing from beneath his pillow, two enormous pistols.*) A brace of bullets are better still!

BLOODGOOD: Damnation!

BADGER: Derringer's self-cocking. Drop your hand, or I'll blow you into pi.—So, you took me for a fool:—that's where you made a mistake. I took you for a thorough rascal, that's where I did *not* make a mistake. Now, to business.

BLOODGOOD: (*Surlily.*) How much do you want?

BADGER: Fifty thousand dollars!

BLOODGOOD: Be it so.

BADGER: In gold, or Chemicals.

BLOODGOOD: Very well. To-morrow—

BADGER: No—to-night.

BLOODGOOD: To-night!

BADGER: Yes; I wish to purchase a brown stone house on the avenue early in the morning.

BLOODGOOD: Come with me to my house in Madison Square.

BADGER: No, thank you. I'll expect you here in an hour with the money.

BLOODGOOD: (*Aside.*) He has me in his power—I must yield. (*Aloud.*) I will return, then, in an hour.

BADGER: Let me light you out. Mind the bannister—don't break your precious neck, at least, not to-night. No, go in front, will you? I prefer it.

BLOODGOOD: What for?

BADGER: (*With pistol and candle.*) A fancy of mine—a want of confidence. A want of confidence, in fact, pervades the community. (*Exeunt.*)

(*Re-enter Lucy.*)

LUCY: I took a cross street, and ran rapidly home. Now I am alone; the fumes of the charcoal will soon fill this small room. They say it is an easy death—but let me not hesitate—let me sleep the long sleep where there are no more tears, no more suffering. (*Exit into closet.*)

(*Re-enter Badger.*)

BADGER: So! that is settled. I hope he will be cautious and escape the garroters. James, my chibouque. (*Takes his pipe.*)

(*Re-enter Mrs. Fairweather.*)

MRS. FAIRWEATHER: Poor Lucy! I dared not look back upon her as we parted forever. Despair hastened my steps. My poor children! I have given you all I had, and now I hope my wretched life will serve you in your terrible need. Come, courage; let me prevent the fresh air from entering. (*Takes bits of linen and stops window and door.*)

BADGER: (*Snuffing.*) I smell charcoal—burning charcoal—where can it come from?

MRS. FAIRWEATHER: Now let me stop the door.

BADGER: (*Smoking.*) It's very odd; I've a queer feeling in my head; let me lie down awhile. (*Lies on his bed.*)

(*Enter Lucy, with a brazier of charcoal, alight.*)

MRS. FAIRWEATHER: That's done. (*Going towards closet, and meeting Lucy.*) Now the hour has come.

LUCY: The moment has arrived. (*Sets down the brazier.*)

MRS. FAIRWEATHER: Lucy!

LUCY: Mother!

MRS. FAIRWEATHER: My child, what is this? For what purpose are you here?

LUCY: And you, mother, why have you fastened those apertures so closely? Like me, you wish to die!

MRS. FAIRWEATHER: No, no, you shall not die! my darling child—you are young—life is before you—hope—happiness.

LUCY: The future! what is it? The man I love will soon wed another. I have no future, and the present is a torture.

MRS. FAIRWEATHER: Hush, my child, hush!

LUCY: Is it not better to die thus, than by either grief or hunger?

MRS. FAIRWEATHER: (*Falling in a chair.*) Already my senses fail me. Lucy my child, live, live!

LUCY: (*Falls at her feet.*) No; let us die together—thus, mother—as often as I knelt to you as a child, let me pray for those we love.

MRS. FAIRWEATHER: Oh, merciful Judge in heaven, forgive us—forgive my child—and let—your anger fall—on me—alone—

LUCY: God bless my dear brother—and you my dear Mark, may—you be—hap— (*Murmurs the rest of the prayer.*)

BADGER: It's very cold! I feel quite sleepy. I must not go to sleep. (*Sings in a low voice.*) "Oh, down in ole Virginny."

PAUL: (*Without, knocking.*) Mother, open the door, why is the door locked? Mother, mother! Open, mother, open! (*Knocks violently. Mrs. Fairweather, arising, tries to reach the door, but cannot, and falls. Paul bursts open the door and enters with Livingstone; they start back—Livingstone breaks the window, and Paul runs to his mother.*) Too late! too late! They have committed suicide!

MARK: They live still. Quick, bear them outside into the air. (*Carries Lucy out while Paul assists his mother into the next room.*)

BADGER: (*Starting up.*) How hot it is here—I cannot breath. Have I drunk too much? Nonsense! I could drink a dozen such bottles. Let me try my legs a bit—where's the door? I can't see it—my head spins round—come, Badger, no nonsense now. God! I'm suffocating! Am I going to die, to die! like that old sea captain? (*Tears off his cravat.*) Justice of Heaven! I am strangling. Help! Help! Bloodgood will return and find me helpless, then he will rob me of the receipt, as I robbed the old sailor—I know him of old—he is capable of it, but he shall not have it! There in its nook, if I have the strength to reach it—it is safe—safe. (*Drags himself along the floor, lifts up a loose board, puts the receipt beneath it and falls exhausted.*) There!

PAUL: (*Entering the room.*) I heard smothered cries for help—they came from this floor. (*Exit.*)

(*Enter Bloodgood.*)

BLOODGOOD: Here I am, Badger. (*Starts back, suffocated.*) What a suffocating atmosphere! where is he? ha! is he intoxicated?

PAUL: (*Entering room.*) Perhaps the cry came from here, dead?

BLOODGOOD: Paul Fairweather!

PAUL: Gideon Bloodgood!

BADGER: (*Raising his head.*) What names were those? Both of them! Together, here! (*To Paul.*) Listen—while I yet have breath to speak—listen! Twenty years ago, that man robbed your father of $100,000!

PAUL: Robbed!

BLOODGOOD: Scoundrel!

BADGER: I've got the proofs.

PAUL: The proofs?

BADGER: I have 'em safe—you'll find 'em—th—ah—(*Falls backward insensible; Paul and Bloodgood stand aghast.*)

END OF ACT IV

ACT V

SCENE I

Brooklyn Heights, overlooking the city of New York and its harbors. The stage is occupied by a neat garden, on a natural terrace of the heights—a frame cottage stands, prettily built—a table with breakfast laid, at which Mrs. Fairweather and Paul are seated.

(Enter Mrs. Puffy, from the cottage, with a teapot.)

MRS. PUFFY: There's the tea. Bless me, how hot it is to-day! Who would think that we were in the month of February? *(Sits.)*
MRS. FAIRWEATHER: Your husband is late to breakfast.
PAUL: Here he comes.

(Enter Puffy, gaily.)

PUFFY: How is everybody? and above everybody, how is Miss Lucy this morning? *(Sits at table.)*
MRS. FAIRWEATHER: Poor child! her recovery is slow—the fever has abated, but she is still very weak.
PAUL: Her life is saved, for a whole month she hovered over the grave.
PUFFY: But how is it we never see Mr. Livingstone? our benefactor is like Santa Claus—he showers benefits and blessings on us all, yet never shows us his face.
MRS. FAIRWEATHER: He brought us back to this, our old home—he obtained employment for Paul in the Navy Yard.
PUFFY: He set me up again in my patent oven, and got me a government contract for Navy biscuit.
MRS. PUFFY: He is made of the finest flour that heaven ever put into human baking; he'll die of over-bigness of the heart.
MRS. FAIRWEATHER: That's a disease hereditary in your family.
PAUL: *(Rising.)* I will tell you why Livingstone avoids our gratitude. Because my sister Lucy refused his love—because he has sold his hand to Alida Bloodgood—and he has given us the purchase money.
PUFFY: And amongst those who have served us, don't let us forget poor Badger.

(Enter Badger, behind.)

BADGER: They are talking of me.

MRS. FAIRWEATHER: (*Rising.*) Forget him! forget the man who watched Lucy during her illness, with more than the tenderness of a brother! A woman never can forget anyone who has been kind to her children.

MRS. PUFFY: Them's my sentiments to a hair.

BADGER: You shan't have cause to change them.

PAUL: Badger!

BADGER: Congratulate me. I have been appointed to the police. The commissioners wanted a special service to lay on to Wall Street's savagery, it seems has concentrated there, and we want to catch a big offender.

MRS. PUFFY: They all go to Europe.

PUFFY: That accounts for the drain of specie.

(*Mr. and Mrs. Puffy take off the breakfast table.*)

MRS. FAIRWEATHER: I will tell Lucy that her nurse has come. (*Exit into cottage.*)

PAUL: Now, Badger, the news.

BADGER: Bad, sir. To-night Mr. Livingstone is to be married to Alida Bloodgood.

PAUL: What shall I do? I dare not accuse Bloodgood of this robbery, unless you can produce the proofs—and perhaps the wretch has discovered and destroyed them.

BADGER: I think not. When I recovered from the effects of the charcoal, the day after my suffocation, I started for my lodging—I found the house shut up, guarded by a servant of Bloodgood's—the banker had bought the place. But I had concealed the document too cunningly; he has not found it.

PAUL: But knowing this man to be a felon, whom we may be able at any hour to unmask, can we allow Livingstone to marry his daughter?

(*Enter Livingstone.*)

LIVINGSTONE: Paul, I have come to bid you farewell, and to see Lucy for the last time—

(*Enter Lucy.*)

LUCY: For the last time, why so—(*Paul and Badger run to assist her forward.*)

LIVINGSTONE: Lucy, dear Lucy.

BADGER: Now take care—sit down—

LUCY: Ah, my good kind nurse. (*She sits.*) You are always by my side.

BADGER: Always ready with a dose of nasty medicine, ain't I—well now I've got another dose ready—do you see this noble kind heart, Lucy; it looks through two honest blue eyes into your face—well tell me what you see there—

LUCY: Why do you ask me? (*Troubled.*)

BADGER: Don't turn your eyes away—the time has come when deception is a crime, Lucy—look in his face, and confess the infernal scheme by which Alida Bloodgood compelled you to renounce your love.

LIVINGSTONE: Alida!

LUCY: Has she betrayed me—

BADGER: No! you betrayed yourself—one night in the ravings of your fever, when I held your hands in the paroxysm of your frenzy, I heard the cries that came from your poor wounded heart; shall I repeat the scene.

LUCY: (*Hiding her face in her hands.*) No, no.

LIVINGSTONE: Paul, is this true? have I been deceived?

PAUL: You have—Lucy confessed to me this infamous bargain, extorted from her by Alida Bloodgood; and to save you from ruin she sacrificed her love—

LIVINGSTONE: Lucy! dear Lucy, look up. It was for your sake alone that I accepted this hated union—to save you and yours from poverty—but whisper one word, tell me that ruin of fortune is better than ruin of the heart. (*Lucy falls upon his neck.*)

BADGER: Hail Columbia! I know a grand party at Madison Square that will cave in to-night—hi!—I shall be there to congratulate that sweet girl.

(*Enter Dan.*)

DAN: Mother! mother! where's my hat, quick, there's a fire in New York. (*He runs into the house and re-enters with a telescope, looks off toward the city.*)

BADGER: Yes, and there is a fire here too, but one we don't want to put out—

PAUL: Now Mark, I can confess to you that documents exist—proofs of felony against Bloodgood, which may at any moment consign him to the State Prison and transfer to our family his ill-gotten wealth.

LIVINGSTONE: Proofs of felony?

DAN: The fire is in Chatham Street.

PAUL: Twenty years ago he robbed my father of 100,000 dollars.

BADGER: And I was his accomplice in the act; we shared the plunder between us—

DAN: No it isn't in Chatham Street—I see it plainly—it is in Cross Street, Five Points.

BADGER: (*Starting.*) Cross Street—where, where— (*Runs up.*)

LIVINGSTONE: But if these proofs—these documents exist, where are they?

DAN: It is the tenement house two doors from the corner.

BADGER: Damnation! it is our old lodging! you ask where are these proofs, these documents? they are yonder, in the burning house—fired by Bloodgood to destroy the papers he could not find—curses on him!

(*Enter Mrs. Puffy, with Dan's hat.*)

MRS. PUFFY: Here's your hat, Dan.

BADGER: Quick! Dan, my son—for our lives! Dan! the fortunes of Lucy and Paul and the old woman are all in that burning house.

(*Dan begins to thrust his trousers into his boots. Enter Mrs. Fairweather and Puffy.*)

DAN: To save it or perish in the flames. Count me in. (*They run out.*)

Tableau

SCENE II

Stage dark. The exterior of the tenement house, No. 19½ Cross Street, Five Points—the shutters of all the windows are closed. A light is seen through the round holes in the shutters of the upper windows—presently a flame rises—it is extinguished—then revives. The light seen to descend as the bearer of it passes down the staircase, the door opens cautiously—Bloodgood, disguised, appears—he looks round—closes the door again—locks it.

BLOODGOOD: In a few hours, this accursed house will be in ruins. The receipt is concealed there—and it will be consumed in the flames. (*The glow of fire is seen to spread from room to room.*) Now Badger—do your worst—I am safe! (*Exit.*)

(*The house is gradually enveloped in fire, a cry outside is heard "Fi-er!" "Fi-er!" It is taken up by other voices more distant. The tocsin sounds—other churches take up the alarm—bells of Engines are heard. Enter a crowd of persons. Enter Badger, without coat or hat—he tries the door—finds it fast; seizes a bar of iron and dashes in the ground floor window, the interior is seen in flames. Enter Dan.*)

DAN: (*Seeing Badger climbing into the window.*) Stop! Stop! (*Badger leaps in and disappears. Shouts from the mob; Dan leaps in—another shout, Dan leaps out again black and burned, staggers forward and seems overcome by the heat and smoke. The shutters of the garret fall and discover Badger in the upper floor. Another cry from the crowd, a loud crash is heard, Badger disappears as if falling with the inside of the building. The shutters of the windows fall away, and the inside of the house is seen, gutted by the fire; a cry of horror is uttered by the mob. Badger drags himself from the ruins, and falls across the sill of the lower window. Dan and two of the mob run to help him forward but recoil before the heat; at length they succeed in rescuing his body—which lies center stage. Livingstone, Paul, and Puffy, rush on. Dan kneels over Badger and extinguishes the fire which clings to parts of his clothes.*)

SCENE III

The Drawing-Room in Bloodgood's mansion, in Madison Square—illuminated. Music within.

(*Enter Bloodgood.*)

BLOODGOOD: The evidence of my crime is destroyed—no power on earth can reveal the past. (*Enter Alida, dressed as a bride.*) My dearest child, to-night you will leave this roof; but from this home in your father's heart, none can displace you.

ALIDA: Oh, dear papa, do take care of my flounces—you men pat one about as if a dress was put on only to be rumpled.

BLOODGOOD: The rooms below are full of company. Has Livingstone arrived?

ALIDA: I did not inquire. The duke is there, looking the picture of misery, while all my female friends pretend to congratulate me—but I know they are dying with envy and spite.

BLOODGOOD: And do these feelings constitute the happiest day of your life? Alida, have you no heart?

ALIDA: Yes, father, I have a heart—but it is like yours. It is an iron safe in which are kept the secrets of the past.

(*Enter Edwards.*)

EDWARDS: The clergyman is robed, sir, and ready to perform the ceremony.
BLOODGOOD: Let the bridesmaids attend Miss Bloodgood. (*The curtains are raised, and the Bridemaids enter. Bloodgood goes up and off, and immediately returns with the bridal party.*) Welcome, my kind friends. (*Alida speaks aside with the duke.*) Your presence fills me with pride and joy—but where is the bridegroom? Has no one seen my son-in-law?
EDWARDS: (*Announcing.*) Mr. Mark Livingstone.

(*Enter Livingstone.*)

BLOODGOOD: Ah! at last. What a strange costume for a bridegroom.
ALIDA: (*Turns, and views Livingstone.*) Had I not good reasons to be assured of your sincerity, Mr. Livingstone, your appearance would lead me to believe that you looked upon this marriage as a jest, or a masquerade.
LIVINGSTONE: As you say, Miss Bloodgood, it is a masquerade—but it is one where more than one mask must fall.
BLOODGOOD: (*Aside.*) What does he mean?
ALIDA: You speak in a tone of menace. May—
BLOODGOOD: Perhaps I had better see Mr. Livingstone alone—he may be under some misapprehension.
LIVINGSTONE: I am under none, sir—although I believe you may be; and what I have to say and do, demands no concealment. I come here to decline the hand of your daughter. (*Movement amongst the crowd.*)
BLOODGOOD: You must explain this public insult.
LIVINGSTONE: I am here to do so, but I do not owe this explanation to you; I owe it to myself, and those friends I see here, whose presence under your roof is a tribute to the name I bear. My friends, I found myself in this man's debt; he held in pledge all I possessed—all but my name; that name he wanted to shelter the infamy in which his own was covered, and I was vile enough to sell it.
BLOODGOOD: Go on, sir; go on.
LIVINGSTONE: With your leave, I will.
ALIDA: These matters you were fully acquainted with, I presume, when you sought my hand.
LIVINGSTONE: But I was not acquainted with the contents of these letters—written by you, to the Duke of Calcavella.
BLOODGOOD: Dare you insinuate that they contain evidence derogatory to the honor of my child?
LIVINGSTONE: No, sir; but I think Miss Bloodgood will agree with me, that the sentiments expressed in these letters entitle her to the hand of the duke rather than to mine. (*He hands letters to Alida.*)
ALIDA: Let him go, father.
LIVINGSTONE: Not yet. You forget that my friends here are assembled to witness a marriage, and all we require is a bride.
BLOODGOOD: Yes; a bride who can pay your debts.

(*Enter Paul, Lucy, and Mrs. Fairweather.*)

PAUL: No, sir; a bride who can place the hand of a pure and loving maiden in that of a good and honest man.

BLOODGOOD: How dare you intrude in this house?

PAUL: Because it is mine; because your whole fortune will scarcely serve to pay the debt you owe the widow and the children of Adam Fairweather!

BLOODGOOD: Is my house to be invaded by beggars like these! Edwards send for the police. Is there no law in New York for ruffians?

(Enter Badger, in the uniform of an officer of police.)

BADGER: Yes, plenty—and here's the police.

BLOODGOOD: Badger!

BADGER: What's left of him.

BLOODGOOD: *(Wildly.)* Is this a conspiracy to ruin me?

BADGER: That's it. We began it twenty years ago; we've been hatching it ever since; we let you build up a fortune; we tempted you to become an incendiary; we led you on from misdemeanor to felony—and that's what I want you for.

BLOODGOOD: What do you mean?

BADGER: My meaning is set forth very clearly in an affidavit, on which the Recorder, at this very late hour for business, issued this warrant for your arrest.

(Enter two Policemen. Alida falls in a chair.)

BLOODGOOD: Incendiary! Dare you charge a man of my standing in this city, with such a crime, without any cause?

BADGER: Cause! you wanted to burn up this receipt, which I was just in time to rescue from the flames!

BLOODGOOD: *(Drawing a knife.)* Fiend! you escaped the flames here—now go to those hereafter!

BADGER: Hollo! *(Disarms Bloodgood, and slips a pair of handcuffs on him.)* Gideon—my dear Gideon—don't lose your temper. *(Throws him back, manacled, on the sofa.)*

PAUL: Miss Bloodgood, let me lead you from this room.

ALIDA: *(Rises, and crosses to her father.)* Father.

BLOODGOOD: Alida, my child.

ALIDA: Is this true? *(A pause.)* It is—I read it in your quailing eye—on your paling lips. And it was for this that you raised me to the envied position of the rich man's heiress—for this you roused my pride—for this you decked me in jewels—to be the felon's daughter. Farewell.

BLOODGOOD: Alida—my child—my child—it was for you alone I sinned—do not leave me.

ALIDA: What should I do in this city? can I earn my bread? what am I fit for—with your tainted name and my own sad heart? *(Throws down her bride's coronet.)* I am fit for the same fate as yours—infamy. *(Exit.)*

BADGER: Duke, you had better see that lady out. *(Exit Duke.)* Gideon, my dear, allow me to introduce you to two friends of mine, who are anxious to make your acquaintance.

BLOODGOOD: Take me away; I have lost my child—my Alida; take me away; hide me from all the world.

PAUL: Stay! Mr. Bloodgood, in the midst of your crime there was one virtue; you loved your child; even now your heart deplores her ruin—not your own.

Badger, give me that receipt. (*Takes the receipt from Badger.*) Do you acknowledge this paper to be genuine?

BLOODGOOD: I do.

PAUL: (*Tears it.*) I have no charge against you. Let him be released. Restore to me my fortune, and take the rest; go, follow your child; save her from ruin, and live a better life.

BLOODGOOD: I cannot answer you as I would. (*Turns aside in tears and goes out with Policemen and Badger, who releases Bloodgood.*)

LIVINGSTONE: That was nobly done, Paul. Now my friends, since all is prepared for my marriage let the ceremony proceed.

MRS. FAIRWEATHER: But where is Mrs. Puffy?

BADGER: Here they are, outside, but they won't come in.

PAUL: Why not?

BADGER: They are afraid of walking on the carpets.

LIVINGSTONE: Bring them in.

BADGER: That's soon done. (*Exit.*)

MRS. FAIRWEATHER: Poor, good, kind people— the first to share our sorrow, the last to claim a part in our joy.

(*Enter Badger and Dan—Puffy and one Policeman—Mrs. Puffy and the other Policeman.*)

BADGER: They wouldn't come—I was obliged to take 'em in custody.

DAN: Oh! mother, where's this?

MRS. PUFFY: I'm walkin' on a feather bed.

PUFFY: He wouldn't let me wipe my shoes.

LIVINGSTONE: Come in—these carpets have never been trodden by more honest feet, these mirrors have never reflected kinder faces—come in—breathe the air here—you will purify it.

MRS. PUFFY: Oh, Dan, what grand folks—ain't they?

DAN: Canvass backs every one on 'em.

LIVINGSTONE: And now, Lucy, I claim your hand. (*Music inside.*) All is ready for the ceremony.

BADGER: You have seen the dark side of life—you can appreciate your fortune, for you have learned the value of wealth.

MRS. FAIRWEATHER: No, we have learned the value of poverty. (*Gives her hand to Puffy.*) It opens the heart.

PAUL: (*To the public.*) Is this true? have the sufferings we have depicted in this mimic scene, touched your hearts, and caused a tear of sympathy to fill your eyes? I so, extend to us your hands.

MRS. FAIRWEATHER: No, not to us—but when you leave this place, as you return to your homes, should you see some poor creatures, extend your hands to them, and the blessings that will follow you on your way will be the most grateful tribute you can pay to the Poor of New York.

END

UNCLE TOM'S CABIN

George Aiken
Harriet Beecher Stowe

THE CAST:

Uncle Tom
George Harris
George Shelby
St. Clare
Phineas Fletcher
Gumption Cute
Mr. Wilson
Deacon Perry
Shelby
Haley
Legree
Tom Loker
Marks
Sambo
Quimbo
Doctor
Waiter
Harry, a child
Eva
Eliza
Cassy
Marie
Ophelia
Chloe
Topsy

ACT I

SCENE I

Plain Chamber. Enter Eliza, meeting George.

ELIZA: Ah! George, is it you? Well, I am so glad you've come. (*George regards her mournfully.*) Why don't you smile, and ask after Harry?

GEORGE: (*Bitterly.*) I wish he'd never been born! I wish I'd never been born myself!

ELIZA: (*Sinking her head upon his breast and weeping.*) Oh George!

GEORGE: There now, Eliza, it's too bad for me to make you feel so. Oh! how I wish you had never seen me—you might have been happy!

ELIZA: George! George! how can you talk so? What dreadful thing has happened, or is going to happen? I'm sure we've been very happy till lately.

GEORGE: So we have, dear. But oh! I wish I'd never seen you, nor you me.

ELIZA: Oh, George! how can you?

GEORGE: Yes, Eliza, it's all misery! misery! The very life is burning out of me! I'm a poor, miserable, forlorn drudge! I shall only drag you down with me, that's all! What's the use of our trying to do anything—trying to know anything—trying to be anything? I wish I was dead!

ELIZA: Oh! now, dear George, that is really wicked. I know how you feel about losing your place in the factory, and you have a hard master; but pray be patient—

GEORGE: Patient! Haven't I been patient? Did I say a word when he came and took me away—for no earthly reason—from the place where everybody was kind to me? I'd paid him truly every cent of my earnings, and they all say I worked well.

ELIZA: Well, it *is* dreadful; but, after all, he is your master, you know.

GEORGE: My master! And who made him my master? That's what I think of. What right has he to me? I'm as much a man as he is. What right has he to make a dray-horse of me?—to take me from things I can do better than he can, and put me to work that any horse can do? He tries to do it; he says he'll bring me down and humble me, and he puts me to just the hardest, meanest and dirtiest work, on purpose.

ELIZA: Oh, George! George! you frighten me. Why, I never heard you talk so. I'm afraid you'll do something dreadful. I don't wonder at your feelings at all; but oh! do be careful—for my sake, for Harry's.

GEORGE: I have been careful, and I have been patient, but it's growing worse and worse—flesh and blood can't bear it any longer. Every chance he can get to insult and torment me he takes. He says that though I don't say anything, he sees that I've got the devil in me, and he means to bring it out; and one of these days it will come out, in a way that he won't like, or I'm mistaken.

ELIZA: Well, I always thought that I must obey my master and mistress, or I couldn't be a Christian.

GEORGE: There is some sense in it in your case. They have brought you up like a child—fed you, clothed you and taught you, so that you have a good education—that is some reason why they should claim you. But I have been kicked and cuffed and sworn at, and what do I owe? I've paid for all my keeping a hundred times over. I won't bear it!—no, I *won't!* Master will find out that I'm one whipping won't tame. My day will come yet, if he don't look out!

ELIZA: What are you going to do? Oh! George, don't do anything wicked; if you only trust in heaven and try to do right, it will deliver you.

GEORGE: Eliza, my heart's full of bitterness. I can't trust in heaven. Why does it let things be so?

ELIZA: Oh, George! we must all have faith. Mistress says that when all things go wrong to us, we must believe that heaven is doing the very best.

GEORGE: That's easy for people to say who are sitting on their sofas and riding in their carriages; but let them be where I am—I guess it would come some harder. I wish I could be good; but my heart burns and can't be reconciled. You couldn't, in my place, you can't now, if I tell you all I've got to say; you don't know the whole yet.

ELIZA: What do you mean?

GEORGE: Well, lately my master has been saying that he was a fool to let me marry off the place—that he hates Mr. Shelby and all his tribe—and he says he won't let me come here any more, and that I shall take a wife and settle down on his place.

ELIZA: But you were married to *me* by the minister, as much as if you had been a white man.

GEORGE: Don't you know I can't hold you for my wife if he chooses to part us? That is why I wish I'd never seen you—it would have been better for us both—it would have been better for our poor child if he had never been born.

ELIZA: Oh! but my master is so kind.

GEORGE: Yes, but who knows?—he may die, and then Harry may be sold to nobody knows who. What pleasure is it that he is handsome and smart and bright? I tell you, Eliza, that a sword will pierce through your soul for every good and pleasant thing your child is or has. It will make him worth too much for you to keep.

ELIZA: Heaven forbid!

GEORGE: So, Eliza, my girl, bear up now, and good by, for I'm going.

ELIZA: Going, George! Going where?

GEORGE: To Canada; and when I'm there I'll buy you—that's all the hope that's left us. You have a kind master, that won't refuse to sell you. I'll buy you and the boy—heaven helping me, I will!

ELIZA: Oh, dreadful! If you should be taken?

GEORGE: I won't be taken, Eliza—I'll *die* first! I'll be free, or I'll die.

ELIZA: You will not kill yourself?

GEORGE: No need of that; they will kill me, fast enough. I will never go down the river alive.

ELIZA: Oh, George! for my sake, do be careful. Don't lay hands on yourself, or anybody else. You are tempted too much, but don't. Go, if you must, but go carefully, prudently, and pray heaven to help you!

GEORGE: Well, then Eliza, hear my plan. I'm going home quite resigned, you understand, as if all was over. I've got some preparations made, and there are those that will help me; and in the course of a few days I shall be among the missing. Well, now, good by.

ELIZA: A moment—our boy.

GEORGE: (*Choked with emotion.*) True, I had forgotten him; one last look, and then farewell!

ELIZA: And heaven grant it be not forever! (*Exeunt.*)

SCENE II

A dining room. Table and chairs. Dessert, wine, etc., on table. Shelby and Haley discovered at table.

SHELBY: That is the way I should arrange the matter.

HALEY: I can't make trade that way—I positively can't, Mr. Shelby. (*Drinks.*)

SHELBY: Why, the fact is, Haley, Tom is an uncommon fellow! He is certainly worth that sum anywhere—steady, honest, capable, manages my whole farm like a clock!

HALEY: You mean honest, as niggers go. (*Fills glass.*)

SHELBY: No; I mean, really, Tom is a good, steady, sensible, pious fellow. He got religion at a camp-meeting, four years ago, and I believe he really *did* get it. I've trusted him since then, with everything I have—money, house, horses, and let him come and go round the country, and I always found him true and square in everything.

HALEY: Some folks don't believe there is pious niggers, Shelby, but *I do.* I had a fellow, now, in this yer last lot I took to Orleans—'twas as good as a meetin' now, really, to hear that critter pray; and he was quite gentle and quiet like. He fetched me a good sum, too, for I bought him cheap of a man that was 'bliged to sell out, so I realized six hundred on him. Yes, I consider religion a valeyable thing in a nigger, when it's the genuine article and no mistake.

SHELBY: Well, Tom's got the real article, if ever a fellow had. Why last fall I let him go to Cincinnati alone, to do business for me and bring home five hundred dollars. "Tom," says I to him, "I trust you, because I think you are a Christian—I know you wouldn't cheat." Tom comes back sure enough, I knew he would. Some low fellows, they say, said to him—"Tom, why don't you make tracks for Canada?" "Ah, master trusted me, and I couldn't," was his answer. They told me all about it. I am sorry to part with Tom, I must say. You ought to let him cover the whole balance of the debt and you would, Haley, if you had any conscience.

HALEY: Well, I've got just as much conscience as any man in business can afford to keep, just a little, you know, to swear by, as twere; and then I'm ready to do anything in reason to 'blige friends, but this yer, you see, is a leetle too hard on a fellow—a leetle too hard! (*Fills glass again.*)

SHELBY: Well, then, Haley, how will you trade?

HALEY: Well, haven't you a boy or a girl that you could throw in with Tom?

SHELBY: Hum! none that I could well spare; to tell the truth, it's only hard necessity makes me willing to sell at all. I don't like parting with any of my hands, that's a fact. (*Harry runs in.*) Hulloa! Jim Crow! (*Throws a bunch of raisins towards him.*) Pick that up now! (*Harry does so.*)

HALEY: Bravo, little 'un! (*Throws an orange, which Harry catches. He sings and dances around the stage.*) Hurrah! Bravo! What a young 'un! That chap's a case, I'll promise. Tell you what, Shelby, fling in that chap, and I'll settle the business. Come, now, if that ain't doing the thing up about the rightest!

(*Eliza enters. Starts on beholding Haley, and gazes fearfully at Harry, who runs and clings to her dress, showing the orange, etc.*)

SHELBY: Well, Eliza?

ELIZA: I was looking for Harry, please, sir.

SHELBY: Well, take him away, then.

(*Eliza grasps the child eagerly in her arms, and casting another glance of apprehension at Haley, exits hastily.*)

HALEY: By Jupiter! there's an article, now. You might make your fortune on that ar gal in Orleans any day. I've seen over a thousand in my day, paid down for gals not a bit handsomer.

SHELBY: I don't want to make my fortune on her. Another glass of wine. (*Fills the glasses.*)

HALEY: (*Drinks and smacks his lips.*) Capital wine—first chop. Come, how will you trade about the gal? What shall I say for her? What'll you take?

SHELBY: Mr. Haley, she is not to be sold. My wife wouldn't part with her for her weight in gold.

HALEY: Ay, ay! women always say such things, 'cause they hain't no sort of calculation. Just show 'em how many watches, feathers and trinkets one's weight in gold would buy, and that alters the case, I reckon.

SHELBY: I tell you, Haley, this must not be spoken of—I say no, and I mean no.

HALEY: Well, you'll let me have the boy tho'; you must own that I have come down pretty handsomely for him.

SHELBY: What on earth can you want with the child?

HALEY: Why, I've got a friend that's going into this yer branch of the business—wants to buy up handsome boys to raise for the market. Well, what do you say?

SHELBY: I'll think the matter over and talk with my wife.

HALEY: Oh, certainly, by all means; but I'm in a devil of a hurry and shall want to know as soon as possible, what I may depend on.

(*Rises and puts on his overcoat, which hangs on a chair. Takes hat and whip.*)

SHELBY: Well, call up this evening, between six and seven, and you shall have my answer.

HALEY: All right. Take care of yourself, old boy! (*Exit.*)

SHELBY: If anybody had ever told me that I should sell Tom to those rascally traders, I should never have believed it. Now it must come for aught I see, and Eliza's child too. So much for being in debt, heigho! The fellow sees his advantage and means to push it. (*Exit.*)

SCENE III

Snowy landscape. Uncle Tom's Cabin. Snow on roof. Practicable door and window. Dark stage. Music. Enter Eliza hastily, with Harry in her arms.

ELIZA: My poor boy! they have sold you, but your mother will save you yet!

(*Goes to Cabin and taps on window. Aunt Chloe appears at window with a large white night-cap on.*)

CHLOE: Good Lord! what's that? My sakes alive if it ain't Lizy! Get on your clothes, old man, quick! I'm gwine to open the door.

(*The door opens and Chloe enters followed by Uncle Tom in his shirt sleeves holding a tallow candle.*)

TOM: (*Holding the light towards Eliza.*) Lord bless you! I'm skeered to look at ye, Lizy! Are ye tuck sick, or what's come over ye?

ELIZA: I'm running away, Uncle Tom and Aunt Chloe, carrying off my child! Master sold him!

TOM & CHLOE: Sold him!

ELIZA: Yes, sold him! I crept into the closet by mistress' door tonight and heard master tell mistress that he had sold my Harry and you, Uncle Tom, both, to a trader, and that the man was to take possession to-morrow.

CHLOE: The good lord have pity on us! Oh! it don't seem as if it was true. What has he done that master should sell *him?*

ELIZA: He hasn't done anything—it isn't for that. Master don't want to sell, and mistress—she's always good. I heard her plead and beg for us, but he told her 'twas no use—that he was in this man's debt, and he had got the power over him, and that if he did not pay him off clear, it would end in his having to sell the place and all the people and move off.

CHLOE: Well, old man, why don't you run away, too? Will you wait to be toted down the river, where they kill niggers with hard work and starving? I'd a heap rather die than go there, any day! There's time for ye, be off with Lizy—you've got a pass to come and go any time. Come, bustle up, and I'll get your things together.

TOM: No, no—I ain't going. Let Eliza go—it's her right. I wouldn't be the one to say no—'tain't in natur' for her to stay; but you heard what she said? If I must be sold, or all the people on the place, and everything go to rack, why, let me be sold. I s'pose I can bar it as well as any one. Mas'r always found me on the spot—he always will. I never have broken trust, nor used my pass no ways contrary to my word, and I never will. It's better for me to go alone, than to break up the place and sell all. Mas'r ain't to blame, and he'll take care of you and the poor little 'uns! (*Overcome.*)

CHLOE: Now, old man, what is you gwine to cry for? Does you want to break this old woman's heart? (*Crying.*)

ELIZA: I saw my husband only this afternoon, and I little knew then what was to come. He told me he was going to run away. Do try, if you can, to get word to him. Tell him how I went and why I went, and tell him I'm going to try and find Canada. You must give my love to him, and tell him if I never see him again on earth, I trust we shall meet in heaven!

TOM: Dat is right, Lizy, trust in the Lord—he is our best friend—our only comforter.

ELIZA: You won't go with me, Uncle Tom?

TOM: No; time was when I would, but the Lord's given me a work among these yer poor souls, and I'll stay with 'em and bear my cross with 'em till the end. It's different with you—it's more'n you could stand, and you'd better go if you can.

ELIZA: Uncle Tom, I'll try it!

TOM: Amen! The lord help ye!

(*Exit Eliza and Harry.*)

CHLOE: What is you gwine to do, old man! What's to become of you?

TOM: (*Solemnly.*) Him that saved Daniel in the den of lions—that saved the children in the fiery furnace—Him that walked on the sea and bade the winds be still—He's alive yet! and I've faith to believe he can deliver me.

CHLOE: You is right, old man.

TOM: The Lord is good unto all that trust him, Chloe. (*Exeunt into cabin.*)

SCENE IV

Room in Tavern by the river side. A large window in flat, through which the river is seen, filled wth floating ice. Moon light. Table and chairs brought on. Enter. Phineas.

PHINEAS: Chaw me up into tobaccy ends! how in the name of all that's onpossible am I to get across that yer pesky river? It's a reg'lar blockade of ice! I promised Ruth to meet her to-night, and she'll be into my har if I don't come. (*Goes to window.*) Thar's a conglomerated prospect for a loveyer! What in creation's to be done? That thar river looks like a permiscuous ice-cream shop come to an awful state of friz. If I war on the adjacent bank, I wouldn't care a teetotal atom. Rile up, you old varmit, and shake the ice off your back!

(*Enter Eliza and Harry.*)

ELIZA: Courage, my boy—we have reached the river. Let it but roll between us and our pursuers, and we are safe! (*Goes to window.*) Gracious powers! the river is choked with cakes of ice!

PHINEAS: Holloa, gal!—what's the matter? You look kind of streaked.

ELIZA: Is there any ferry or boat that takes people over now?

PHINEAS: Well, I guess not; the boats have stopped running.

ELIZA: (*In dismay.*) Stopped running?

PHINEAS: Maybe you're wanting to get over—anybody sick? Ye seem mighty anxious.

ELIZA: I—I—I've got a child that's very dangerous. I never heard of it till last night, and I've walked quite a distance to-day, in hopes to get to the ferry.

PHINEAS: Well, now, that's onlucky; I'm re'lly consarned for ye. Thar's a man, a piece down here, that's going over with some truck this evening, if he duss to; he'll be in here to supper to-night, so you'd better set down and wait. That's a smart little chap. Say, young'un, have a chaw tobaccy? (*Takes out a large plug and a bowie-knife.*)

ELIZA: No, no! not any for him.

PHINEAS: Oh! he don't use it, eh? Hain't come to it yet? Well, I have. (*Cuts off a large piece, and returns the plug and knife to pocket.*) What's the matter with the young 'un? He looks kind of white in the gills!

ELIZA: Poor fellow! he is not used to walking, and I've hurried him on so.

PHINEAS: Tuckered, eh? Well, there's a little room there, with a fire in it. Take the baby in there, make yourself comfortable till that thar ferryman shows his countenance—I'll stand the damage.

ELIZA: How shall I thank you for such kindness to a stranger?

PHINEAS: Well, if you don't know how, why, don't try; that's the teetotal. Come, vamose! (*Exit, Eliza and Harry.*) Chaw me into sassage meat, if that ain't a perpendicular fine gal! she's a reg'lar A No. 1 sort of female! How'n thunder am I to get across this refrigerated stream of water? I can't wait for that ferryman. (*Enter Marks.*) Halloa! what sort of a critter's this? (*Advances.*) Say, stranger, will you have something to drink?

MARKS: You are excessively kind: I don't care if I do.

PHINEAS: Ah! he's a human. Holloa, thar! bring us a jug of whisky instantaneously, or expect to be teetotally chawed up! Squat yourself, stranger, and go in for enjoyment. (*They sit at table.*) Who are you, and what's your name?

MARKS: I am a lawyer, and my name is Marks.

PHINEAS: A land shark, eh? Well, I dont' think no worse on you for that. The law is a kind of necessary evil; and it breeds lawyers just as an old stump does fungus. Ah! here's the whisky. (*Enter Waiter, with jug and tumblers. Places them on table.*) Here, you—take that shin-plaster. (*Gives bill.*) I don't want any change—thar's a gal stopping in that room—the balance will pay for her—d'ye hear?—vamose! (*Exit Waiter. Fills glass.*) Take hold, neighbor Marks—don't shirk the critter. Here's hoping your path of true love may never have an ice-choked river to cross! (*They drink.*)

MARKS: Want to cross the river, eh?

PHINEAS: Well, I do, stranger. Fact is, I'm in love with the teetotalist pretty girl, over on the Ohio side, that ever wore a Quaker bonnet. Take another swig, neighbor. (*Fills glasses, and they drink.*)

MARKS: A Quaker, eh?

PHINEAS: Yes—kind of strange, ain't it? The way of it was this:—I used to own a grist of niggers—had 'em to work on my plantation, just below here. Well, stranger, do you know I fell in with that gal—of course I was considerably smashed—knocked into a pretty conglomerated heap—and I told her so. She said she wouldn't hear a word from me so long as I owned a nigger!

MARKS: You sold them, I suppose?

PHINEAS: You're teetotally wrong, neighbor. I gave them all their freedom, and told 'em to vamose!

MARKS: Ah! yes—very noble, I dare say, but rather expensive. This act won you your lady-love, eh?

PHINEAS: You're off the track again, neighbor. She felt kind of pleased about it, and smiled, and all that; but she said she could never be mine unless I turned Quaker! Thunder and earth! what do you think of that? You're a lawyer—come, now, what's your opinion? Don't you call it a knotty point?

MARKS: Most decidedly. Of course you refused.

PHINEAS: Teetotally; but she told me to think better of it, and come to-night and give her my final conclusion. Chaw me into mince meat, if I haven't made up my mind to do it!

MARKS: You astonish me!

PHINEAS: Well, you see, I can't get along without that gal;—she's sort of fixed my flint, and I'm sure to hang fire without her. I know I shall make a queer sort of Quaker, because you see, neighbor, I ain't precisely the kind of material to make a Quaker out of.

MARKS: No, not exactly.

PHINEAS: Well, I can't stop no longer. I must try to get across that candaverous river some way. It's getting late—take care of yourself, neighbor lawyer. I'm a teetotal victim to a pair of black eyes. Chaw me up to feed hogs, if I'm not in a ruinatious state! (*Exit.*)

MARKS: Queer genius, that, very! (*Enter Tom Loker.*) So you've come at last.

LOKER: Yes. (*Looks into jug.*) Empty! Waiter! more whisky!

(*Waiter enters, with jug, and removes the empty one. Enter Haley.*)

HALEY: By the land! if this yer ain't the nearest, now, to what I've heard people call Providence! Why, Loker, how are ye?

LOKER: The devil! What brought you here, Haley?

HALEY: (*Sitting at table.*) I say, Tom, this yer's the luckiest thing in the world. I'm in a devil of a hobble, and you must help me out!

LOKER: Ugh! aw! like enough. A body may be pretty sure of that when you're glad to see 'em, or can make something off of 'em. What's the blow now?

HALEY: You've got a friend here—partner, perhaps?

LOKER: Yes, I have. Here, Marks—here's that ar fellow that I was with in Natchez.

MARKS: (*Grasping Haley's hand.*) Shall be pleased with his acquaintance. Mr. Haley, I believe?

HALEY: The same, sir. The fact is, gentlemen, this morning I bought a young 'un of Shelby up above here. His mother got wind of it, and what does she do but cut her lucky with him; and I'm afraid by this time that she has crossed the river, for I tracked her to this very place.

MARKS: So, then, ye're fairly sewed up, ain't ye? He! he! he! it's neatly done, too.

HALEY: This young 'un business makes lots of trouble in the trade.

MARKS: Now, Mr. Haley, what is it? Do you want us to undertake to catch this gal?

HALEY: The gal's no matter of mine—she's Shelby's—it's only the boy. I was a fool for buying the monkey.

LOKER: You're generally a fool!

MARKS: Come now, Loker, none of your huffs; you see, Mr. Haley's a-puttin' us in a way of a good job. I reckon: just hold still—these yer arrangements are my forte. This yer gal, Mr. Haley—how is she? what is she?

(*Eliza appears, with Harry, listening.*)

HALEY: Well, white and handsome—well brought up. I'd have given Shelby eight hundred or a thousand, and then made well on her.

MARKS: White and handsome—well brought up! Look here now, Loker, a beautiful opening. We'll do a business here on our own account. We does the catchin'; the boy, of course, goes to Mr. Haley—we takes the gal to Orleans to speculate on. Ain't it beautiful? (*They confer together.*)

ELIZA: Powers of mercy, protect me! How shall I escape these human blood-hounds? Ah! the window—the river of ice! That dark stream lies between me and liberty! Surely the ice will bear my trifling weight. It is my only chance of escape—better sink beneath the cold waters, with my child locked in my arms, than have him torn from me and sold into bondage. He sleeps upon my breast—Heaven, I put my trust in thee! (*Gets out of window.*)

MARKS: Well, Tom Loker, what do you say?

LOKER: It'll do!

(*Strikes his hand violently on the table. Eliza screams. They all start to their feet. Eliza disappears. Music, chord.*)

HALEY: By the land, there she is now! (*They all rush to the window.*)

MARKS: She's making for the river!

LOKER: Let's after her!

(*Music. They all leap through the window. Change.*)

SCENE V

Snow. Landscape. Music. Enter Eliza, with Harry, hurriedly.

ELIZA: They press upon my footsteps—the river is my only hope. Heaven grant me strength to reach it, ere they overtake me! Courage, my child!—we will be free—or perish! (*Rushes off. Music continued.*)

(*Enter Loker, Haley and Marks.*)

HALEY: We'll catch her yet; the river will stop her!

MARKS: No, it won't, for look! she has jumped upon the ice! She's a brave gal, anyhow!

LOKER: She'll be drowned!

HALEY: Curse that young 'un! I shall lose him, after all.

LOKER: Come on, Marks, to the ferry!

HALEY: Aye, to the ferry!—a hundred dollars for a boat!

(*Music. They rush off.*)

SCENE VI

The entire depth of stage, representing the Ohio River filled with Floating Ice. Set bank on right and in front. Eliza appears, with Harry, on a cake of ice, and floats slowly across to left. Haley, Loker, and Marks, on bank right, observing. Phineas on opposite shore.

END OF ACT I

ACT II

SCENE I

A Handsome Parlor. Marie discovered reclining on a sofa.

MARIE: (*Looking at a note.*) What can possibly detain St. Clare? According to this note he should have been here a fortnight ago. (*Noise of carriage without.*) I do believe he has come at last.

(*Eva runs in.*)

EVA: Mamma! (*Throws her arms around Marie's neck, and kisses her.*)
MARIE: That will do—take care, child—don't you make my head ache! (*Kisses her languidly.*)

(*Enter St. Clare, Ophelia, and Tom, nicely dressed.*)

ST. CLARE: Well, my dear Marie, here we are at last. The wanderers have arrived, you see. Allow me to present my cousin, Miss Ophelia, who is about to undertake the office of our housekeeper.
MARIE: (*Rising to a sitting posture.*) I am delighted to see you. How do you like the appearance of our city?
EVA: (*Running to Ophelia.*) Oh! is it not beautiful? My own darling home!—is it not beautiful?
OPHELIA: Yes, it is a pretty place, though it looks rather old and heathenish to me.
ST. CLARE: Tom, my boy, this seems to suit you?
TOM: Yes, mas'r, it looks about the right thing.
ST. CLARE: See here, Marie, I've brought you a coachman, at last, to order. I tell you, he is a regular hearse for blackness and sobriety, and will drive you like a funeral, if you wish. Open your eyes, now, and look at him. Now, don't say I never think about you when I'm gone.
MARIE: I know he'll get drunk.
ST. CLARE: Oh! no he won't. He's warranted a pious and sober article.
MARIE: Well, I hope he may turn out well; it's more than I expect, though.
ST. CLARE: Have you no curiosity to learn how and where I picked up

Tom?

EVA: *Uncle* Tom, papa; that's his name.

ST CLARE: Right, my little sunbeam!

TOM: Please, mas'r, that ain't no 'casion to say nothing bout me.

ST. CLARE: You are too modest, my modern Hannibal. Do you know, Marie, that our little Eva took a fancy to Uncle Tom—whom we met on board the steamboat—and persuaded me to buy him.

MARIE: Ah! she is so odd.

ST. CLARE: As we approached the landing, a sudden rush of the passengers precipitated Eva into the water—

MARIE: Gracious heavens!

ST. CLARE: A man leaped into the river, and, as she rose to the surface of the water, grasped her in his arms, and held her up until she could be drawn on the boat again. Who was that man, Eva?

EVA: Uncle Tom! (*Runs to him. He lifts her in his arms. She kisses him.*)

TOM: The dear soul!

OPHELIA: (*Astonished.*) How shiftless!

ST CLARE: (*Overhearing her.*) What's the matter now, pray?

OPHELIA: Well, I want to be kind to everybody, and I wouldn't have anything hurt, but as to kissing—

ST. CLARE: Niggers! that you're not up to, hey?

OPHELIA: Yes, that's it—how can she?

ST. CLARE: Oh! bless you, it's nothing when you are used to it!

OPHELIA: I could never be so shiftless!

EVA: Come with me, Uncle Tom, and I will show you about the house. (*Crosses with Tom.*)

TOM: Can I go mas'r?

ST. CLARE: Yes, Tom; she is your little mistress—your only duty will be to attend to her! (*Tom bows and exits.*)

MARIE: Eva, my dear!

EVA: Well, mamma?

MARIE: Do not exert yourself too much!

EVA: No, mamma! (*Runs out.*)

OPHELIA: (*Lifting up her hands.*) How shiftless!

(*St. Clare sits next to Marie on sofa. Ophelia next to St. Clare.*)

ST. CLARE: Well, what do you think of Uncle Tom, Marie?

MARIE: He is a perfect behemoth!

ST. CLARE: Come, now, Marie, be gracious, and say something pretty to a fellow!

MARIE: You've been gone a fortnight beyond the time!

ST. CLARE: Well, you know I wrote you the reason.

MARIE: Such a short, cold letter!

ST. CLARE: Dear me! the mail was just going, and it had to be that or nothing.

MARIE: That's just the way; always something to make your journeys long and letters short!

ST. CLARE: Look at this. (*Takes an elegant velvet case from his pocket.*) Here's a present I got for you in New York—a Daguerreotype of Eva and myself.

MARIE: (*Looks at it with a dissatisfied air.*) What made you sit in such an awkward position?

ST. CLARE: Well, the position may be a matter of opinion, but what do you think of the likeness?

MARIE: (*Closing the case snappishly.*) If you don't think anything of my opinion in one case, I suppose you wouldn't in another.

OPHELIA: (*Senteniously, aside.*) How shiftless!

ST. CLARE: Hang the woman! Come, Marie, what do you think of the likeness? Don't be nonsensical now.

MARIE: It's very inconsiderate of you, St. Clare, to insist on my talking and looking at things. You know I've been lying all day with the sick headache, and there's been such a tumult made ever since you came, I'm half dead!

OPHELIA: You're subject to the sick headache, ma'am?

MARIE: Yes, I'm a perfect martyr to it!

OPHELIA: Juniper-berry tea is good for sick head-ache; at least, Molly, Deacon Abraham Perry's wife, used to say so; and she was a great nurse.

ST. CLARE: I'll have the first juniper-berries that get ripe in our garden by the lake brought in for that especial purpose. Come, cousin, let us take a stroll in the garden. Will you join us, Marie?

MARIE: I wonder how you can ask such a question, when you know how fragile I am. I shall retire to my chamber, and repose till dinner time.(*Exit.*)

OPHELIA: (*Looking after her.*) How shiftless!

ST. CLARE: Come, cousin! (*As he goes out.*) Look out for the babies! If I step upon anybody, let them mention it.

OPHELIA: Babies under foot! How shiftless! (*Exeunt.*)

SCENE II

A Garden. Tom discovered, seated on a bank, with Eva on his knee—his buttonholes are filled with flowers, and Eva is hanging a wreath around his neck. Music at opening of scene. Enter St. Clare and Ophelia, observing.

EVA: Oh, Tom! you look so funny.

TOM: (*Sees St. Clare and puts Eva down.*) I begs pardon, mas'r, but the young missis would do it. Look yer, I'm like the ox, mentioned in the good book, dressed for the sacrifice.

ST. CLARE: I say, what do you think, Pussy? Which do you like the best—to live as they do at your uncle's, up in Vermont, or to have a house-full of servants, as we do?

EVA: Oh! of course our way is the pleasantest.

ST. CLARE: (*Patting her head.*) Why so?

EVA: Because it makes so many more round you to love, you know.

OPHELIA: Now, that's just like Eva—just one of her odd speeches.

EVA: Is it an odd speech, papa?

ST. CLARE: Rather, as this world goes, Pussy. But where has my little Eva been?

EVA: Oh! I've been up in Tom's room, hearing him sing.

ST. CLARE: Hearing Tom sing, hey?

EVA: Oh, yes! he sings such beautiful things, about the new Jerusalem, and bright angels, and the land of Canaan.

ST. CLARE: I dare say; it's better than the opera, isn't it?

EVA: Yes; and he's going to teach them to me.

ST. CLARE: Singing lessons, hey? You are coming on.

EVA: Yes, he sings for me, and I read to him in my Bible, and he explains what it means. Come, Tom. (*She takes his hand and they exit.*)

ST. CLARE: (*Aside.*) Oh, Evangeline! Rightly named; hath not heaven made thee an evangel to me?

OPHELIA: How shiftless! How can you let her?

ST. CLARE: Why not?

OPHELIA: Why, I don't know; it seems so dreadful.

ST. CLARE: You would think no harm in a child's caressing a large dog even if he was black; but a creature that can think, reason and feel, and is immortal, you shudder at. Confess it, cousin. I know the feeling among some of you Northerners well enough. Not that there is a particle of virtue in our not having it, but custom with us does what Christianity ought to do: obliterates the feelings of personal prejudice. You loathe them as you would a snake or a toad, yet you are indignant at their wrongs. You would not have them abused but you don't want to have anything to do with them yourselves. Isn't that it?

OPHELIA: Well, cousin, there may be some truth in this.

ST. CLARE: What would the poor and lowly do without children? Your little child is your only true democrat. Tom, now, is a hero to Eva; his stories are wonders in her eyes; his songs and Methodist hymns are better than an opera, and the traps and little bits of trash in his pockets a mine of jewels, and he the most wonderful Tom that ever wore a black skin. This is one of the roses of Eden that the Lord has dropped down expressly for the poor and lowly, who get few enough of any other kind.

OPHELIA: It's strange, cousin; one might almost think you was a *professor*, to hear you talk.

ST. CLARE: A professor?

OPHELIA: Yes, a professor of religion.

ST. CLARE: Not at all; not a professor as you town folks have it, and, what is worse, I'm afraid, not a *practicer*, either.

OPHELIA: What makes you talk so, then?

ST. CLARE: Nothing is easier than talking. My forte lies in talking, and yours, cousin, lies in doing. And speaking of that puts me in mind that I have made a purchase for your department. There's the article now. Here, Topsy! (*Whistles.*)

(*Topsy runs on.*)

OPHELIA: Good gracious! what a heathenish, shiftless looking object! St. Clare, what in the world have you brought that thing here for?

ST. CLARE: For you to educate, to be sure, and train in the way she should go. I thought she was rather a funny specimen in the Jim Crow line. Here, Topsy, give us a song, and show us some of your dancing. (*Topsy sings a verse and dances a breakdown.*)

OPHELIA: (*Paralyzed.*) Well, of all things! If I ever saw the like!

ST. CLARE: (*Smothering a laugh.*) Topsy, this is your new mistress—I'm going to give you up to her. See now that you behave yourself.

TOPSY: Yes, mas'r.

ST. CLARE: You're going to be good, Topsy, you understand?

TOPSY: Oh, yes, mas'r.

OPHELIA: Now, St. Clare, what upon earth is this for? Your house is so full of these plagues now, that a body can't set down their foot without treading on 'em. I get up in the morning and find one asleep behind the door, and see one black head poking out from under the table—one lying on the door mat, and they are moping and mowing and grinning between all the railings, and tumbling over the kitchen floor! What on earth did you want to bring this one for?

ST. CLARE: For you to educate—didn't I tell you? You're always preaching about educating, I thought I would make you a present of a fresh caught specimen, and let you try your hand on her and bring her up in the way she should go.

OPHELIA: I don't want her, I am sure; I have more to do with 'em now than I want to.

ST. CLARE: That's you Christians, all over. You'll get up a society, and get some poor missionary to spend all his days among just such heathen; but let me see one of you that would take one into your house with you, and take the labor of their conversion upon yourselves.

OPHELIA: Well, I didn't think of it in that light. It might be a real missionary work. Well, I'll do what I can. (*Advances to Topsy.*) She's dreadful dirty and shiftless! How old are you, Topsy?

TOPSY: Dunno, missis.

OPHELIA: How shiftless! Don't know how old you are? Didn't anybody ever tell you? Who was your mother?

TOPSY: (*Grinning.*) Never had none.

OPHELIA: Never had any mother? What do you mean? Where was you born?

TOPSY: Never was born.

OPHELIA: You musn't answer me in that way. I'm not playing with you. Tell me where you was born, and who your father and mother were?

TOPSY: Never was born, tell you; never had no father, nor mother, nor nothin'. I war raised by a speculator, with lots of others. Old Aunt Sue used to take car on us.

ST. CLARE: She speaks the truth, cousin. Speculators buy them up cheap, when they are little, and get them raised for the market.

OPHELIA: How long have you lived with your master and mistress?

TOPSY: Dunno, missis.

OPHELIA: How shiftless! Is it a year, or more, or less?

TOPSY: Dunno, missis.

ST. CLARE: She does not know what a year is; she don't even know her own age.

OPHELIA: Have you ever heard anything about heaven, Topsy? (*Topsy looks bewildered and grins.*) Do you know who made you?

TOPSY: Nobody, as I knows on, he, he, he! I spect I growed. Don't think nobody never made me.

OPHELIA: The shiftless heathen! What can you do? What did you do for your master and mistress?

TOPSY: Fetch water—and wash dishes—and rub knives—and wait on folks—and dance breakdowns.

OPHELIA: I shall break down, I'm afraid, in trying to make anything of you, you shiftless mortal!

ST. CLARE: You find virgin soil there, cousin; put in your own ideas—you won't find many to pull up. (*Exit, laughing.*)

OPHELIA: (*Takes out her handkerchief. A pair of gloves falls. Topsy picks them up slyly and puts them in her sleeve.*) Follow me, you benighted innocent!

TOPSY: Yes, missis.

(*As Ophelia turns her back to her, she seizes the end of the ribbon she wears around her waist, and twitches it off. Ophelia turns and sees her as she is putting it in her other sleeve. Ophelia takes ribbon from her.*)

OPHELIA: What's this? You naughty, wicked girl, you've been stealing this?

TOPSY: Laws! why, that ar's missis' ribbon, a'nt it? How could it got caught in my sleeve?

OPHELIA: Topsy, you naughty girl, don't you tell me a lie—you stole that ribbon!

TOPSY: Missis, I declare for't, I didn't—never seed it till dis yer blessed minnit.

OPHELIA: Topsy, don't you know it's wicked to tell lies?

TOPSY: I never tells no lies, missis; it's just de truth I've been telling now and nothing else.

OPHELIA: Topsy, I shall have to whip you, if you tell lies so.

TOPSY: Laws missis, if you's to whip all day, couldn't say no other way. I never seed dat ar—it must a got caught in my sleeve. (*Blubbers.*)

OPHELIA: (*Seizes her by the shoulders.*) Don't you tell me that again, you barefaced fibber! (*Shakes her. The gloves fall on stage.*) There you, my gloves too—you outrageous young heathen! (*Picks them up.*) Will you tell me, now, you didn't steal the ribbon?

TOPSY: No, missis; stole de gloves, but didn't steal de ribbon. It was permiskus.

OPHELIA: Why, you young reprobate!

TOPSY: Yes—I's knows I's wicked!

OPHELIA: Then you know you ought to be punished. (*Boxes her ears.*) What do you think of that?

TOPSY: He, he, he! De Lord, missus; dat wouldn't kill a 'skeeter. (*Runs off laughing, Ophelia follows indignantly.*)

SCENE III

The Tavern by the River. Table and chairs. Jug and glasses on table. On flat is a printed placard, headed: "Four Hundred Dollars Reward—Runaway—George Harris!" Phineas is discovered, seated at table.

PHINEAS: So yer I am; and a pretty business I've undertook to do. Find the husband of the gal that crossed the river on the ice two or three days ago. Ruth said I must do it, and I'll be teetotally chawed up if I don't do it. I see they've offered a reward for him, dead or alive. How in creation am I to find the varmint? He isn't likely to go round looking natural, with a full description of his hide and figure staring him in the face. (*Enter Mr. Wilson.*) I say, stranger, how are ye?

(Rises and comes forward.)

WILSON: Well, I reckon.

PHINEAS: Any news? *(Takes out plug and knife.)*

WILSON: Not that I know of.

PHINEAS: *(Cutting a piece of tobacco and offering it.)* Chaw?

WILSON: No, thank ye—it don't agree with me.

PHINEAS: Don't, eh? *(Putting it in his own mouth.)* I never felt any the worse for it.

WILSON: *(Sees placard.)* What's that?

PHINEAS: Nigger advertised. *(Advances towards it and spits on it.)* There's my mind upon that.

WILSON: Why, now, stranger, what's that for?

PHINEAS: I'd do it all the same to the writer of that ar paper, if he was here. Any man that owns a boy like that, and can't find any better way of treating him, than branding him on the hand with the letter H, as that paper states, *deserves* to lose him. Such papers as this ar' a shame to old Kaintuck! that's my mind right out, if anybody wants to know.

WILSON: Well, now, that's a fact.

PHINEAS: I used to have a gang of boys, sir—that was before I fell in love— and I just told em:—"Boys," says I, "run now! Dig! put! jest when you want to. I never shall come to look after you!" That's the way I kept mine. Let 'em know they are free to run any time, and it jest stops their wanting to. It stands to reason it should. Treat 'em like men, and you'll have men's work.

WILSON: I think you are altogether right, friend, and this man described here is a fine fellow—no mistake about that. He worked for me some half dozen years in my bagging factory, and he was my best hand, sir. He is an ingenious fellow, too; he invented a machine for the cleaning of hemp—a really valuable affair; it's gone into use in several factories. His master holds the patent of it.

PHINEAS: I'll warrant ye; holds it, and makes money out of it, and then turns round and brands the boy in his right hand! If I had a fair chance, I'd mark him, I reckon, so that he'd carry it *one* while!

(Enter George Harris, disguised.)

GEORGE: *(Speaking as he enters.)* Jim, see to the trunks. *(Sees Wilson.)* Ah! Mr. Wilson here?

WILSON: Bless my soul, can it be?

GEORGE: *(Advances and grasps his hand.)* Mr. Wilson, I see you remember me Mr. Butler, of Oaklands. Shelby county.

WILSON: Ye—yes—yes—sir.

PHINEAS: Holloa! there's a screw loose here somewhere. That old gentlemen seems to be struck into a pretty considerable heap of astonishment. May I be teetotally chawed up! if I don't believe that's the identical man I'm arter. *(Crosses to George.)* How are ye, George Harris?

GEORGE: *(Starting back and thrusting his hands into his breast.)* You know me?

PHINEAS: Ha, ha, ha! I rather conclude I do; but don't get riled, I an't a bloodhound in disguise.

GEORGE: How did you discover me?

PHINEAS: By a teetotal smart guess. You're the very man I want to see. Do you know I was sent after you?

GEORGE: Ah! by my master?

PHINEAS: No; by your wife.

GEORGE: My wife! Where is she?

PHINEAS: She's stopping with a Quaker family over on the Ohio side.

GEORGE: Then she is safe?

PHINEAS: Teetotally!

GEORGE: Conduct me to her.

PHINEAS: Just wait a brace of shakes and I'll do it. I've got to go and get the boat ready. 'Twon't take me but a minute—make yourself comfortable till I get back. Chaw me up! but this is what I call doing things in short order. (*Exit.*)

WILSON: George!

GEORGE: Yes, George!

WILSON: I couldn't have thought it!

GEORGE: I am pretty well disguised, I fancy; you see I don't answer to the advertisment at all.

WILSON: George, this is a dangerous game you are playing; I could not have advised you to it.

GEORGE: I can do it on my own responsibility.

WILSON: Well, George, I suppose you're running away—leaving your lawful master, George, (I don't wonder at it) at the same time, I'm sorry, George, yes, decidedly. I think I must say that it's my duty to tell you so.

GEORGE: Why are you sorry, sir?

WILSON: Why to see you, as it were, setting yourself in opposition to the laws of your country.

GEORGE: *My* country! What country have *I*, but the grave? And I would to heaven that I was laid there!

WILSON: George, you've got a hard master, in fact he is—well, he conducts himself reprehensibly—I can't pretend to defend him. I'm sorry for you, now; it's a bad case—very bad; but we must all submit to the indications of providence. George, don't you see?

GEORGE: I wonder, Mr. Wilson, if the Indians should come and take you a prisoner away from your wife and children, and want to keep you all your life hoeing corn for them, if you'd think it your duty to abide in the condition in which you were called? I rather imagine that you'd think the first stray horse you could find an indication of providence, shouldn't you?

WILSON: Really, George, putting the case in that somewhat peculiar light— I don't know—under those circumstances—but what I might. But it seems to me you are running an awful risk. You can't hope to carry it out. If you're taken it will be worse with you than ever; they'll only abuse you, and half kill you, and sell you down river.

GEORGE: Mr. Wilson, I know all this. I *do* run a risk, but—(*Throws open coat and shows pistols and knife in his belt.*) There! I'm ready for them. Down South I never *will* go! no, if it comes to that, I can earn myself at least six feet of free soil—the first and last I shall ever own in Kentucky!

WILSON: Why, George, this state of mind is awful—it's getting really desperate. I'm concerned. Going to break the laws of your country?

GEORGE: My country again! Sir, I haven't any country any more than I have any father. I don't want anything of *your* country, except to be left alone—to go peaceably out of it; but if any man tries to stop me, let him take care, for I am desperate. I'll fight for my liberty, to the last breath I breathe!

You say your fathers did it, if it was right for them, it is right for me!

WILSON: (*Walking up and down and fanning his face with a large yellow silk handkerchief.*) Blast 'em all! Haven't I always said so—the infernal old cusses! Bless me! I hope I an't swearing now! Well, go ahead, George, go ahead. But be careful, my boy; don't shoot anybody, unless—well, you'd *better* not shoot—at least I wouldn't *hit* anybody, you know.

GEORGE: Only in self-defense.

WILSON: Well, well. (*Fumbling in his pocket.*) I suppose, perhaps, I an't following my judgment—hang it, I won't follow my judgment. So here, George. (*Takes out a pocket-book and offers George a roll of bills.*)

GEORGE: No, my kind, good sir, you've done a great deal for me, and this might get you into trouble. I have money enough, I hope, to take me as far as I need it.

WILSON: No; but you must, George. Money is a great help everywhere, can't have too much, if you get it honestly. Take it, *do* take it, *now* do, my boy!

GEORGE: (*Taking the money.*) On condition, sir, that I may repay it at some future time, I will.

WILSON: And now, George, how long are you going to travel in this way? Not long or far I hope? It's well carried on, but too bold.

GEORGE: Mr. Wilson, it is *so bold,* and this tavern is so near, that they will never think of it; they will look for me on ahead, and you yourself wouldn't know me.

WILSON: But the mark on your hand?

GEORGE: (*Draws off his glove and shows scar.*) That is a parting mark of Mr. Harris' regard. Looks interesting, doesn't it? (*Puts on glove again.*)

WILSON: I declare, my very blood runs cold when I think of it—your condition and your risks!

GEORGE: Mine has run cold a good many years; at present, it's about up to the boiling point.

WILSON: George, something has brought you out wonderfully. You hold up your head, and move and speak like another man.

GEORGE: (*Proudly.*) Because I'm a *freeman!* Yes, sir; I've said "master" for the last time to any man. *I'm free!*

WILSON: Take care! You are not sure; you may be taken.

GEORGE: All men are free and equal *in the grave,* if it comes to that, Mr. Wilson.

(*Enter Phineas.*)

PHINEAS: Them's my sentiment, to a teetotal atom, and I don't care who knows it! Neighbor, the boat is ready, and the sooner we make tracks the better. I've seen some mysterious strangers lurking about these diggings, so we'd better put.

GEORGE: Farewell, Mr. Wilson, and heaven reward you for the many kindnesses you have shown the poor fugitive!

WILSON: (*Grasping his hand.*) Your're a brave fellow, George. I wish in my heart you were safe through, though—that's what I do.

PHINEAS: And ain't I the man of all creation to put him through, stranger? Chaw me up if I don't take him to his dear little wife, in the smallest possible quantity of time. Come, neighbor, let's vamose.

GEORGE: Farewell, Mr. Wilson.

WILSON: My best wishes go with you, George. (*Exit.*)

PHINEAS: You're a trump, old Slow-and-Easy.

GEORGE: (*Looking off.*) Look! look!

PHINEAS: Consarn their picters, here they come! We can't get out of the house without their seeing us. We're teetotally treed!

GEORGE: Let us fight our way through them!

PHINEAS: No, that won't do; there are too many of them for a fair fight—we should be chawed up in no time. (*Looks round and sees trap door.*) Holloa! here's a cellar door. Just you step down here a few minutes, while I parley with them. (*Lifts trap.*)

GEORGE: I am resolved to perish sooner than surrender! (*Goes down trap.*)

PHINEAS: That's your sort! (*Closes trap and stands on it.*) Here they are!

(*Enter Haley, Marks, Loker and three Men.*)

HALEY: Say, stranger, you haven't seen a runaway darkey about these parts, eh?

PHINEAS: What kind of a darkey?

HALEY: A mulatto chap, almost as light-complexioned as a white man.

PHINEAS: Was he a pretty good-looking chap?

HALEY: Yes.

PHINEAS: Kind of tall?

HALEY: Yes.

PHINEAS: With brown hair?

HALEY: Yes.

PHINEAS: And dark eyes?

HALEY: Yes.

PHINEAS: Pretty well dressed?

HALEY: Yes.

PHINEAS: Scar on his right hand?

HALEY: Yes, yes.

PHINEAS: Well, I ain't seen him.

HALEY: Oh, bother! Come, boys, let's search the house. (*Exeunt.*)

PHINEAS: (*Raises trap.*) Now, then, neighbor George. (*George enters up trap.*) Now's the time to cut your lucky.

GEORGE: Follow me, Phineas. (*Exit.*)

PHINEAS: In a brace of shakes. (*Is closing trap as Haley, Marks, Loker, etc., re-enter.*)

HALEY: Ah! he's down in the cellar. Follow me, boys! (*Thrusts Phineas aside, and rushes down trap, followed by the others. Phineas closes trap and stands on it.*)

PHINEAS: Chaw me up! but I've got 'em all in a trap. (*Knocking below.*) Be quiet, you pesky varmints! (*Knocking.*) They're getting mighty oneasy. (*Knocking.*) Will you be quiet, you savagerous critters! (*The trap is forced open. Haley and Marks appear. Phineas seizes a chair and stands over trap—picture.*) Down with you or I'll smash you into apple-fritters! (*Tableau—closed in.*)

SCENE IV

A Plain chamber.

TOPSY: (*Without.*) You go 'long. No more nigger dan you be! (*Enters, shouts and laughter without—looks off.*) You seem to think yourself white folks. You ain't nerry one—black *nor* white. I'd like to be one or turrer. Law! you niggers, does you know you's all sinners? Well, you is—everybody is. White folks is sinners too—Miss Feely says so—but I 'spects niggers is the biggest ones. But Lor! ye ain't any on ye up to me. I's so awful wicked there can't nobody do nothin' with me. I used to keep old missis a-swarin' at me ha' de time. I 'spects I's de wickedest critter in de world. (*Song and dance introduced. Enter Eva.*)

EVA: Oh, Topsy! Topsy! you have been very wrong again.

TOPSY: Well, I 'spects I have.

EVA: What makes you do so?

TOPSY: I dunno; I 'spects it's cause I's so wicked.

EVA: Why did you spoil Jane's earrings?

TOPSY: 'Cause she's so proud. She called me a little black imp, and turned up her pretty nose at me 'cause she is whiter than I am. I was gwine by her room, and I seed her coral earrings lying on de table, so I threw dem on de floor, and put my foot on 'em, and scrunches 'em all to little bits— he! he! he! I's so wicked.

EVA: Don't you know that was very wrong?

TOPSY: I don't car'! I despises dem what sets up for fine ladies, when dey ain't nothing but cream-colored niggers! Dere's Miss Rosa—she gives me lots of 'pertinent remarks. T'other night she was gwine to a ball. She put on a beau'ful dress dat missis give her — wid her har curled, all nice and pretty. She hab to go down de back stairs—dem am dark—and I puts a pail of hot water on dem, and she put her foot into it, and den she go tumbling to de bottom of de stairs, and de water go all ober her, and spile her dress, and scald her dreadful bad! He! he! he! I's so wicked!

EVA: Oh! how could you!

TOPSY: Don't dey despise me cause I don't know nothing? Don't dey laugh at me 'cause I'm brack, and dey ain't?

EVA: But you shouldn't mind them.

TOPSY: Well, I don't mind dem; but when dey are passing under my winder, I trows dirty water on 'em, and dat spiles der complexions.

EVA: What does make you so bad, Topsy? Why won't you try and be good? Don't you love anybody, Topsy?

TOPSY: Can't recommember.

EVA: But you love your father and mother?

TOPSY: Never had none, ye know, I telled ye that, Miss Eva.

EVA: Oh! I know; but hadn't you any brother, or sister, or aunt, or—

TOPSY: No, none on 'em—never had nothing nor nobody. I's brack—no one loves me!

EVA: Oh! Topsy, I love you! (*Laying her hand on Topsy's shoulder.*) I love you because you haven't had any father, or mother, or friends. I love you, I want you to be good. I wish you would try to be good for my sake. (*Topsy looks astonished for a moment, and then bursts into tears.*) Only think of it, Topsy—*you* can be one of those spirits bright Uncle Tom sings about!

TOPSY: Oh! dear Miss Eva—dear Miss Eva! I will try—I will try. I never did care nothin' about it before.

EVA: If you try, you will succeed. Come with me. (*Crosses and takes Topsy's hand.*)

TOPSY: I will try; but den, I's so wicked! (*Exit Eva followed by Topsy, crying.*)

SCENE V

Chamber. Enter George, Eliza and Harry.

GEORGE: At length, Eliza, after many wanderings, we are united.

ELIZA: Thanks to these generous Quakers, who have so kindly sheltered us.

GEORGE: Not forgetting our friend Phineas.

ELIZA: I do indeed owe him much. 'Twas he I met upon the icy river's bank, after that fearful, but successful attempt, when I fled from the slave-trader with my child in my arms.

GEORGE: It seems almost incredible that you could have crossed the river on the ice.

ELIZA: Yes, I did. Heaven helping me, I crossed on the ice, for they were behind me—right behind—and there was no other way.

GEORGE: But the ice was all in broken-up blocks, swinging and heaving up and down in the water.

ELIZA: I know it was—I know it; I did not think I should get over, but I did not care—I could but die if I did not! I leaped on the ice, but how I got across I don't know; the first I remember, a man was helping me up the bank—that man was Phineas.

GEORGE: My brave girl! you deserve your freedom—you have richly earned it!

ELIZA: And when we get to Canada I can help you to work, and between us we can find something to live on.

GEORGE: Yes, Eliza, so long as we have each other, and our boy. Oh, Eliza, if these people only knew what a blessing it is for a man to feel that his wife and child belong to *him!* I've often wondered to see men that could call their wives and children *their own*, fretting and worrying about anything else. Why, I feel rich and strong, though we have nothing but our bare hands. If they will only let me alone now, I will be satisfied—thankful!

ELIZA: But we are not quite out of danger; we are not yet in Canada.

GEORGE: True, but it seems as if I smelt the free air, and it makes me strong!

(*Enter Phineas, dressed as a Quaker.*)

PHINEAS: (*With a snuffle.*) Verily, friends, how is it with thee?—hum!

GEORGE: Why, Phineas, what means this metamorphosis?

PHINEAS: I've become a Quaker, that's the meaning on't.

GEORGE: What—you?

PHINEAS: Teetotally! I was driven to it by a strong argument, composed of a pair of sparkling eyes, rosy cheeks, and pouting lips. Them lips would persuade a man to assassinate his grandmother! (*Assumes the Quaker tone again.*) Verily, George, I have discovered something of importance to the interests of thee and thy party, and it were well for thee to hear it.

GEORGE: Keep us not in suspense!

PHINEAS: Well, after I left you on the road, I stopped at a little, lone tavern, just below here. Well, I was tired with hard driving, and after my supper I stretched myself down on a pile of bags in the corner, and pulled a buffalo hide over me—and what does I do but get fast asleep.

GEORGE: With one ear open, Phineas?

PHINEAS: No, I slept ears and all for an hour or two, for I was pretty well tired; but when I came to myself a little, I found that there were some men in the room, sitting round a table, drinking and talking; and I thought, before I made much muster, I'd just see what they were up to, especially as I heard them say something about the Quakers. Then I listened with both ears and found they were talking about you. So I kept quiet, and heard them lay off all their plans. They've got a right notion of the track we are going to-night, and they'll be down after us, six or eight strong. So, now, what's to be done?

ELIZA: What *shall* we do, George?

GEORGE: I know what I shall do! (*Takes out pistols.*)

PHINEAS: Ay-ay, thou seest, Eliza, how it will work—pistols—phitz—poppers!

ELIZA: I see; but I pray it come not to that!

GEORGE: I don't want to involve any one with or for me. If you will lend me your vehicle, and direct me, I will drive alone to the next stand.

PHINEAS: Ah! well, friend, but thee'll need a driver for all that. Thee's quite welcome to do all the fighting thee knows; but I know a thing or two about the road that thee doesn't

GEORGE: But I don't want to involve you.

PHINEAS: Involve me! Why, chaw me—that is to say—when thee does involve me, please to let me know.

ELIZA: Phineas is a wise and skillful man. You will do well, George, to abide by his judgment. And, oh! George, be not hasty with these—young blood is hot! (*Laying her hand on pistols.*)

GEORGE: I will attack no man. All I ask of this country is to be left alone, and I will go out peaceably. But I'll fight to the last breath before they shall take from me my wife and son! Can you blame me?

PHINEAS: Mortal man cannot blame thee, neighbor George! Flesh and blood could not do otherwise. Woe unto the world because of offenses, but woe unto them through whom the offense cometh! That's gospel, teetotally!

GEORGE: Would not even you, sir, do the same, in my place?

PHINEAS: I pray that I be not tried; the flesh is weak—but I think my flesh would be pretty tolerably strong in such a case; I ain't sure, friend George, that I shouldn't hold a fellow for thee, if thee had any accounts to settle with him.

ELIZA: Heaven grant we be not tempted.

PHINEAS: But if we are tempted too much, why, consarn 'em! let them look out, that's all.

GEORGE: It's quite plain you was not born for a Quaker. The old nature has its way in you pretty strong yet.

PHINEAS: Well, I reckon you are pretty teetotally right.

GEORGE: Had we not better hasten our flight?

PHINEAS: Well, I rather conclude we had; we're full two hours ahead of them, if they start at the time they planned; so let's vamose. (*Exeunt.*)

SCENE VI

A Rocky Pass in the Hills. Large set rock and platform.

PHINEAS: (*Without.*) Out with you in a twinkling, every one, and up into these rocks with me! run *now*, if you *ever* did run! (*Music. Phineas enters, with Harry in his arms. George supporting Eliza.*) Come up here; this is one of our old hunting dens. Come up. (*They ascend the rock.*) Well, here we are. Let 'em get us if they can. Whoever comes here has to walk single file between those two rocks, in fair range of your pistols—d'ye see?

GEORGE: I do see. And now, as this affair is mine, let me take all the risk, and do all the fighting.

PHINEAS: Thee's quite welcome to do the fighting, George; but I may have the fun of looking on, I suppose. But see, these fellows are kind of debating down there, and looking up, like hens when they are going to fly up onto the roost. Hadn't thee better give 'em a word of advice, before they come up, just to tell 'em handsomely they'll be shot if they do.

(*Loker, Marks, and three Men enter.*)

MARKS: Well, Tom, your coons are fairly treed.

LOKER: Yes, I see 'em go up right here; and here's a path—I'm for going right up. They can't jump down in a hurry, and it won't take long to ferret 'em out.

MARKS: But, Tom, they might fire at us from behind the rocks. That would be ugly, you know.

LOKER: Ugh! always for saving your skin, Marks. No danger, niggers are too plaguy scared!

MARKS: I don't know why I shouldn't save my skin, it's the best I've got; and niggers do fight like the devil sometimes.

GEORGE: (*Rising on the rock.*) Gentlemen, who are you down there and what do you want?

LOKER: We want a party of runaway niggers. One George and Eliza Harris, and their son. We've got the officers here, and a warrant to take 'em too. D'ye hear? An't you George Harris, that belonged to Mr. Harris, of Shelby county, Kentucky?

GEORGE: I am George Harris. A Mr. Harris, of Kentucky, did call me his property. But now I'm a freeman, standing on heaven's free soil! My wife and child I claim as mine. We have arms to defend ourselves and we mean to do it. You can come up if you like, but the first one that comes within range of our bullets is a dead man!

MARKS: Oh, come—come, young man, this ar no kind of talk at all for you. You see we're officers of justice. We've got the law on our side, and the power and so forth; so you'd better give up peaceably, you see—for you'll certainly have to give up at last.

GEORGE: I know very well that you've got the law on your side, and the power; but you haven't got us. We are standing here as free as you are, and by the great power that made us, we'll fight for our liberty till we die! (*During this, Marks draws a pistol, and when he concludes fires at him. Eliza screams.*) It's nothing, Eliza; I am unhurt.

PHINEAS: (*Drawing George down.*) Thee'd better keep out of sight with thy speechifying; they're teetotal mean scamps.

LOKER: What did you do that for, Marks?

MARKS: You see, you get jist as much for him dead as alive in Kentucky.

GEORGE: Now, Phineas, the first man that advances I fire at; you take the second and so on. It won't do to waste two shots on one.

PHINEAS: But what if you don't hit?

GEORGE: I'll try my best.

PHINEAS: Creation! chaw me up if there a'nt stuff in you!

MARKS: I think I must have hit some on'em. I heard a squeal.

LOKER: I'm going right up for one. I never was afraid of niggers, and I an't a going to be now. Who goes after me?

(*Music. Loker dashes up the rock. George fires. He staggers for a moment, then springs to the top. Phineas seizes him. A struggle.*)

PHINEAS: Friend, thee is not wanted here! (*Throws Loker over the rock.*)

MARKS: (*Retreating.*) Lord help us—they're perfect devils!

(*Music. Marks and Party run off. George and Eliza kneel in an attitude of thanksgiving, with the Child between them. Phineas stands over them exulting. Tableau.*)

END OF ACT II

ACT III

SCENE I

Chamber. Enter St. Clare, followed by Tom.

ST. CLARE: (*Giving money and papers to Tom.*) There, Tom, are the bills, and the money to liquidate them.

TOM: Yes, mas'r.

ST. CLARE: Well, Tom, what are you waiting for? Isn't all right there?

TOM: I'm 'fraid not, mas'r.

ST. CLARE: Why, Tom, what's the matter? You look as solemn as a judge.

TOM: I feel very bad, mas'r. I allays have thought that mas'r would be good to everybody.

ST. CLARE: Well, Tom, haven't I been? Come, now, what do you want? There's something you haven't got, I suppose, and this is the preface.

TOM: Mas'r allays been good to me. I haven't nothing to complain of on that head; but there is one that mas'r isn't good to.

ST. CLARE: Why, Tom, what's got into you? Speak out—what do you mean?

TOM: Last night, between one and two, I thought so. I studied upon the matter then—mas'r isn't good to *himself.*

ST. CLARE: Ah! now I understand; you allude to the state in which I came home last night. Well, to tell the truth, I *was* slightly elevated—a little more champagne on board than I could comfortably carry. That's all, isn't it?

TOM: (*Deeply affected—clasping his hands and weeping.*) All! Oh! my dear young mas'r, I'm 'fraid it will be *loss of all—all,* body and soul. The good book says "it biteth like a serpent and stingeth like an adder," my dear mas'r.

ST. CLARE: You poor, silly fool! I'm not worth crying over.

TOM: Oh, mas'r! I implore you to think of it before it gets too late.

ST. CLARE: Well, I won't go to any more of their cursed nonsense, Tom— on my honor, I won't. I don't know why I haven't stopped long ago; I've always despised *it,* and myself for it. So now, Tom, wipe up your eyes and go about your errands.

TOM: Bless you, mas'r. I feel much better now. You have taken a load from poor Tom's heart. Bless you!

ST. CLARE: Come, come, no blessings; I'm not so wonderfully good, now.

There, I'll pledge my honor to you, Tom, you don't see me so again. (*Exit Tom.*) I'll keep my faith with him, too.

OPHELIA: (*Without.*) Come along, you shiftless mortal!

ST. CLARE: What new witchcraft has Topsy been brewing? That commotion is of her raising, I'll be bound.

(*Enter Ophelia, dragging in Topsy.*)

OPHELIA: Come here now; I will tell your master.

ST. CLARE: What's the matter now?

OPHELIA: The matter is that I cannot be plagued with this girl any longer. It's past all bearing; flesh and blood cannot endure it. Here I locked her up and gave her a hymn to study; and what does she do but spy out where I put my key, and has gone to my bureau, and got a bonnet-trimming and cut it all to pieces to make dolls' jackets! I never saw anything like it in my life!

ST. CLARE: What have you done to her?

OPHELIA: What have I done? What haven't I done? Your wife says I ought to have her whipped till she couldn't stand.

ST. CLARE: I don't doubt it. Tell me of the lovely rule of woman. I never saw above a dozen women that wouldn't half kill a horse or servant, either, if they had their own way with them—let alone a man.

OPHELIA: I am sure, St. Clare, I don't know what to do. I've taught and taught—I've talked till I'm tired; I've whipped her, I've punished her in every way I could think of, and still she's just what she was at first.

ST. CLARE: Come here, Tops, you monkey! (*Topsy crosses to St. Clare, grinning.*) What makes you behave so?

TOPSY: 'Spects it's my wicked heart—Miss Feely says so.

ST. CLARE: Don't you see how much Miss Ophelia has done for you? She says she has done everything she can think of.

TOPSY: Lord, yes, mas'r! old missis used to say so, too. She whipped me a heap harder, and used to pull my ha'r, and knock my head agin the door; but it didn't do me no good. I 'spects if they's to pull every spear of ha'r out o' my head, it wouldn't do no good neither—I's so wicked! Laws! I's nothin' but a nigger, no ways! (*Goes up.*)

OPHELIA: Well, I shall have to give her up; I can't have that trouble any longer.

ST. CLARE: I'd like to ask you one question.

OPHELIA: What is it?

ST. CLARE: Why, if your doctrine is not strong enough to save one heathen child, that you can have at home here, all to yourself, what's the use of sending one or two poor missionaries off with it among thousands of just such? I suppose this girl is a fair sample of what thousands of your heathen are.

OPHELIA: I'm sure I don't know; I never saw such a girl as this.

ST. CLARE: What makes you so bad, Tops? Why won't you try and be good? Don't you love any one, Topsy?

TOPSY: (*Comes down.*) Dunno nothing 'bout love; I loves candy and sich, that's all.

OPHELIA: But, Topsy, if you'd only try to be good, you might.

TOPSY: Couldn't never be nothing but a nigger, if I was ever so good. If I could be skinned and come white, I'd try then.

ST. CLARE: People can love you, if you are black, Topsy. Miss Ophelia would love you, if you were good. (*Topsy laughs.*) Don't you think so?

TOPSY: No, she can't b'ar me, 'cause I'm a nigger—she'd's soon have a toad touch her. There can't nobody love niggers, and niggers can't do nothin'! I don't car'! (*Whistles.*)

ST. CLARE: Silence, you incorrigible imp, and begone!

TOPSY: He! he! he! didn't get much out of dis chile! (*Exit.*)

OPHELIA: I've always had a prejudice against negroes, and it's a fact—I never could bear to have that child touch me, but I didn't think she knew it.

ST. CLARE: Trust any child to find that out, there's no keeping it from them. but I believe all the trying in the world to benefit a child, and all the substantial favors you can do them, will never excite one emotion of gratitude, while that feeling of repugnance remains in the heart. It's a queer kind of a fact, but so it is.

OPHELIA: I don't know how I can help it—they are disagreeable to me, this girl in particular. How can I help feeling so?

ST. CLARE: Eva does, it seems.

OPHELIA: Well, she's so loving. I wish I was like her. She might teach me a lesson.

ST. CLARE: It would not be the first time a little child had been used to instruct an old disciple, if it were so. Come, let us seek Eva, in her favorite bower by the lake.

OPHELIA: Why, the dew is falling, she mustn't be out there. She is unwell, I know.

ST. CLARE: Don't be croaking, cousin—I hate it.

OPHELIA: But she has that cough.

ST. CLARE: Oh, nonsense, of that cough—it is not anything. She has taken a little cold, perhaps.

OPHELIA: Well, that was just the way Eliza Jane was taken—and Ellen—

ST. CLARE: Oh, stop these hobgoblin, nurse legends. You old hands get so wise, that a child cannot cough or sneeze, but you see desperation and ruin at hand. Only take care of the child, keep her from the night air, and don't let her play too hard, and she'll do well enough. (*Exeunt.*)

SCENE II

The flat represents the lake. The rays of the setting sun tinge the waters with gold. A large tree. Beneath this a grassy bank, on which Eva and Tom are seated side by side. Eva has a Bible open on her lap. Music.

TOM: Read dat passage again, please, Miss Eva?

EVA: (*Reading.*) "And I saw a sea of glass, mingled with fire." (*Stopping suddenly and pointing to lake.*) Tom, there it is!

TOM: What, Miss Eva?

EVA: Don't you see there? There's a "sea of glass mingled with fire."

TOM: True enough, Miss Eva. (*Sings.*)

Oh, had I the wings of the morning,
I'd fly away to Canaan's shore;
Bright angels should convey me home,
To the New Jerusalem.

EVA: Where do you suppose New Jerusalem is, Uncle Tom?

TOM: Oh, up in the clouds, Miss Eva.

EVA: Then I think I see it. Look in those clouds, they look like great gates of pearl; and you can see beyond them—far, far off—it's all gold! Tom, sing about 'spirits bright.'

TOM: (*Sings.*)
I see a band of spirits bright,
That taste the glories there;
They are all robed in spotless white,
And conquering palms they bear.

EVA: Uncle Tom, I've seen *them.*

TOM: To be sure you have; you are one of them yourself. You are the brightest spirit I ever saw.

EVA: They come to me sometimes in my sleep—those spirits bright—
They are all robed in spotless white,
And conquering palms they bear.
Uncle Tom, I'm going there.

TOM: Where, Miss Eva?

EVA: ((*Pointing to the sky.*) I'm going *there,* to the spirits bright, Tom; I'm going before long.

TOM: It's jest no use tryin' to keep Miss Eva here; I've allays said so. She's got the Lord's mark in her forehead. She wasn't never like a child that's to live—there was always something deep in her eyes. (*Rises and comes forward. Eva also comes forward, leaving Bible on bank.*)

(*Enter St. Clare.*)

ST. CLARE: Ah! my little pussy, you look as blooming as a rose! You are better now-a-days, are you not?

EVA: Papa, I've had things I wanted to say to you a great while. I want to say them now, before I get weaker.

ST. CLARE: Nay, this is an idle fear, Eva; you know you grow stronger every day.

EVA: It's all no use, papa, to keep it to myself any longer. The time is coming that I am going to leave you, I am going, and never to come back.

ST. CLARE: Oh, now, my dear little Eva! you've got nervous and low spirited; you mustn't indulge such gloomy thoughts.

EVA: No, papa, don't deceive yourself, I am *not* any better; I know it perfectly well, and I am going before long. I am not nervous—I am not low spirited. If it were not for you, papa, and my friends, I should be perfectly happy. I want to go—I long to go!

ST. CLARE: Why, dear child, what has made your poor little heart so sad? You have everything to make you happy that could be given you.

EVA: I had rather be in heaven! There are a great many things here that makes me sad—that seem dreadful to me; I had rather be there; but I don't want to leave you—it almost breaks my heart!

ST. CLARE: What makes you sad, and what seems dreadful, Eva?

EVA: I feel sad for our poor people; they love me dearly, and they are all good and kind to me. I wish, papa, they were all *free!*

ST. CLARE: Why, Eva, child, don't you think they are well enough off now?

EVA: (*Not heeding the question.*) Papa, isn't there a way to have slaves made free? When I am dead, papa, then you will think of me and do it for my sake?

ST. CLARE: When you are dead, Eva? Oh, child, don't talk to me so. You are all I have on earth!

EVA: Papa, these poor creatures love their children as much as you do me. Tom loves his children. Oh, do something for them!

ST. CLARE: There, there, darling; only don't distress yourself, and don't talk of dying, and I will do anything you wish.

EVA: And promise me, dear father, that Tom shall have his freedom as soon as—(*Hesitating.*)—I am gone!

ST. CLARE: Yes, dear, I will do anything in the world—anything you could ask me to. There, Tom, take her to her chamber, this evening air is too chill for her. (*Music. Kisses her. Tom takes Eva in his arms, and exits. Gazing mournfully after Eva.*) Has there ever been a child like Eva? Yes, there has been; but their names are always on grave-stones, and their sweet smiles, their heavenly eyes, their singular words and ways, are among the buried treasures of yearning hearts. It is as if heaven had an especial band of angels, whose office it is to sojourn for a season here, and endear to them the wayward human heart, that they might bear it upward with them in their homeward flight. When you see that deep, spiritual light in the eye when the little soul reveals itself in words sweeter and wiser than the ordinary words of children, hope not to retain that child; for the seal of heaven is on it, and the light of immortality looks out from its eyes! (*Music. Exit.*)

SCENE III

A corridor. Proscenium doors on. Music. Enter Tom, he listens at door and then lies down. Enter Ophelia, with candle.

OPHELIA: Uncle Tom, what alive have you taken to sleeping anywhere and everywhere, like a dog, for? I thought you were one of the orderly sort, that liked to lie in bed in a Christian way.

TOM: (*Rises. Mysteriously.*) I do, Miss Feely, I do, but now—

OPHELIA: Well, what now?

TOM: We mustn't speak loud; Mas'r St. Clare won't hear on't; but Miss Feely, you know there must be somebody watchin' for the bridegroom.

OPHELIA: What do you mean, Tom?

TOM: You know it says in Scripture, "At midnight there was a great cry made, behold, the bridegroom cometh!" That's what I'm spectin' now, every night, Miss Feely, and I couldn't sleep out of hearing, noways.

OPHELIA: Why, Uncle Tom, what makes you think so?

TOM: Miss Eva, she talks to me. The Lord, he sends his messenger in the soul. I must be thar, Miss Feely; for when that ar blessed child goes into the kingdom, they'll open the door so wide, we'll all get a look in at the glory!

OPHELIA: Uncle Tom, did Miss Eva say she felt more unwell than usual tonight?

TOM: No; but she told me she was coming nearer—thar's them that tells it to the child, Miss Feely. It's the angels—it's the trumpet sound afore the break o' day!

OPHELIA: Heaven grant your fears be vain! Come in, Tom (*Exeunt.*)

SCENE IV

Eva's Chamber. Eva discovered on a couch. A table stands near the couch with a lamp on it. The light shines upon Eva's face, which is very pale. Scene half dark. Uncle Tom is kneeling near the foot of the couch, Ophelia stands at the head, St. Clare at back. Scene opens to plaintive music. After a strain enter Marie, hastily.

MARIE: St. Clare! Cousin! Oh! what is the matter now?

ST. CLARE: (*Hoarsely.*) Hush! she is dying!

MARIE: (*Sinking on her knees, beside Tom.*) Dying!

ST. CLARE: Oh! if she would only wake and speak once more. (*Bending over Eva.*) Eva, darling! (*Eva uncloses her eyes, smiles, raises her head and tries to speak.*) Do you know me, Eva?

EVA: (*Throwing her arms feebly about his neck.*) Dear papa. (*Her arms drop and she sinks back.*)

ST. CLARE: Oh heaven! this is dreadful! Oh! Tom, my boy, it is killing me!

TOM: Look at her, mas'r. (*Points to Eva.*)

ST. CLARE: (*A pause.*) She does not hear. Oh Eva! tell us what you see. What is it?

EVA: (*Feebly smiling.*) Oh! love! joy! peace! (*Dies*)

TOM: Oh! bless the Lord! it's over, dear mas'r, it's over.

ST. CLARE: (*Sinking on his knees.*) Farewell, beloved child! the bright eternal doors have closed after thee. We shall see thy sweet face no more. Oh! woe for them who watched thy entrance into heaven when they shall wake and find only the cold, gray sky of daily life and thou gone forever. (*Solemn music, slow curtain.*)

END OF ACT III

ACT IV

SCENE I

A street in New Orleans. Enter Gumption Cute, meeting Marks.

CUTE: How do ye dew?

MARKS: How are you?

CUTE: Well, now, squire, it's a fact that I am dead broke and busted up.

MARKS: You have been speculating, I suppose!

CUTE: That's just it and nothing shorter.

MARKS: You have had poor success, you say?

CUTE: Tarnation bad, now I tell you. You see I came to this part of the country to make my fortune.

MARKS: And you did not do it?

CUTE: Scarcely. The first thing I tried my hand at was keeping school. I opened an academy for the instruction of youth in the various branches of orthography, geography, and other graphies.

MARKS: Did you succeed in getting any pupils?

CUTE: Oh, lots on 'em! and a pretty set of dunces they were too. After the first quarter, I called on the repectable parents of the juveniles, and requested them to fork over. To which they politely answered—don't you wish you may get it?

MARKS: What did you do then?

CUTE: Well, I kind of pulled up stakes and left those diggins. Well then I went into Spiritual Rappings for a living. That paid pretty well for a short time, till I met with an accident.

MARKS: An accident?

CUTE: Yes; a tall Yahoo called on me one day, and wanted me to summon the spirit of his mother—which, of course, I did. He asked me about a dozen questions which I answered to his satisfaction. At last he wanted to know what she died of—I said, Cholera. You never did see a critter so riled as he was. 'Look yere, stranger,' said he, 'it's my opinion that you're a pesky humbug! for my mother was blown up in a *Steamboat!*' with that he left the premises. The next day the people furnished me with a conveyance, and I rode out of town.

MARKS: Rode out of town?

CUTE: Yes; on a rail!

MARKS: I suppose you gave up the spirits, after that?

CUTE: Well, I reckon I did; it had such an effect on my spirits.

MARKS: It's a wonder they didn't tar and feather you.

CUTE: There was some mention made of that, but when they said *feathers*, I felt as if I had wings and flew away.

MARKS: You cut and run?

CUTE: Yes; I didn't like their company and I cut it. Well, after that I let myself out as an overseer on a cotton plantation. I made a pretty good thing of that, though it was dreadful trying to my feelings to flog the darkies; but I got used to it after a while, and then I used to lather 'em like Jehu. Well, the proprietor got the fever and ague and shook himself out of town. The place and all the fixings were sold at auction and I found myself adrift once more.

MARKS: What are you doing at present?

CUTE: I'm in search of a rich relation of mine.

MARKS: A rich relation?

CUTE: Yes, a Miss Ophelia St. Clare. You see, a niece of hers married one of my second cousins—that's how I came to be a relation of hers. She came on here from Vermont to be housekeeper to a cousin of hers, of the same name.

MARKS: I know him well.

CUTE: The deuce you do!—well, that's lucky.

MARKS: Yes, he lives in this city.

CUTE: Say, you just point out the locality, and I'll give him a call.

MARKS: Stop a bit. Suppose you shouldn't be able to raise the wind in that quarter, what have you thought of doing?

CUTE: Well, nothing particular.

MARKS: How should you like to enter into a nice, profitable business—one that pays well?

CUTE: That's just about my measure—it would suit me to a hair. What is it?

MARKS: Nigger catching.

CUTE: Catching niggers! What on airth do you mean?

MARKS: Why, when there's a large reward offered for a runaway darkey, we goes after him, catches him, and gets the reward.

CUTE: Yes, that's all right so far—but s'pose there ain't no reward offered?

MARKS: Why, then we catches the darkey on our own account, sells him, and pockets the proceeds.

CUTE: By chowder, that ain't a bad speculation!

MARKS: What do you say? I want a partner. You see, I lost my partner last year, up in Ohio—he was a powerful fellow.

CUTE: Lost him! How did you lose him?

MARKS: Well, you see, Tom and I—his name was Tom Loker—Tom and I were after a mulatto chap, called George Harris, that run away from Kentucky. We traced him though the greater part of Ohio, and came up with him near the Pennsylvania line. He took refuge among some rocks, and showed fight.

CUTE: Oh! then runaway darkies show fight, do they?

MARKS: Sometimes. Well, Tom—like a headstrong fool as he was—rushed up the rocks, and a Quaker chap, who was helping this George Harris, threw him over the cliff.

CUTE: Was he killed?

MARKS: Well, I didn't stop to find out. Seeing that the darkies were stronger than I thought, I made tracks for a safe place.

CUTE: And what became of this George Harris?

MARKS: Oh! he and his wife and child got away safe into Canada. You see, they will get away sometimes though it isn't very often. Now what do you say? You are just the figure for a fighting partner. Is it a bargain?

CUTE: Well, I rather calculate our teams won't hitch, no how. By chowder, I hain't no idea of setting myself up as a target for darkies to fire at—that's a speculation that don't suit my constitution.

MARKS: You're afraid, then?

CUTE: No, I ain't, it's against my principles.

MARKS: Your principles—how so?

CUTE: Because my principles are to keep a sharp lookout for No. 1. I shouldn't feel wholesome if a darkie was to throw me over that cliff to look after Tom Loker. (*Exeunt arm-in-arm.*)

SCENE II

Gothic Chamber. Slow music. St. Clare discovered, seated on sofa. Tom at left.

ST. CLARE: Oh! Tom, my boy, the whole world is as empty as an egg shell.

TOM: I know it, mas'r, I know it. But oh! if mas'r could look up—up where our dear Miss Eva is—

ST. CLARE: Ah, Tom! I do look up; but the trouble is, I don't see anything when I do. I wish I could. It seems to be given to children and poor, honest fellows like you, to see what we cannot. How comes it?

TOM: Thou hast hid from the wise and prudent, and revealed unto babes; even so, Father, for so it seemed good in thy sight.

ST. CLARE: Tom, I don't believe—I've got the habit of doubting—I want to believe and I cannot.

TOM: Dear mas'r, pray to the good Lord: "Lord, I believe; help thou my unbelief."

ST. CLARE: Who knows anything about anything? Was all that beautiful love and faith only one of the ever-shifting phases of human feeling, having nothing real to rest on, passing away with the little breath? And is there no more Eva—nothing?

TOM: Oh! dear mas'r, there is. I know it; I'm sure of it. Do, do, dear mas'r, believe it!

ST. CLARE: How do you know there is, Tom? You never saw the Lord.

TOM: Felt Him in my soul, mas'r—feel Him now! Oh, mas'r! when I was sold away from my old woman and the children, I was jest a'most broken up—I felt as if there warn't nothing left—and then the Lord stood by me, and He says, "Fear not, Tom," and He brings light and joy into a poor fellow's soul—makes all peace; and I's so happy, and loves everybody, and feels willin' to be jest where the Lord wants to put me. I know it couldn't come from me, 'cause I's a poor, complaining creature—it comes from above, and I know He's willin' to do for mas'r.

ST. CLARE: (*Grasping Tom's hand.*) Tom, you love me!

TOM: I's willin' to lay down my life this blessed day for you.

ST. CLARE: (*Sadly.*) Poor, foolish fellow! I'm not worth the love of one good, honest heart like yours.

TOM: Oh, mas'r! there's more than me loves you—the blessed Saviour loves you.

ST. CLARE: How do you know that, Tom?

TOM: The love of the Saviour passeth knowledge.

ST. CLARE: (*Turns away.*) Singular! that the story of a man who lived and died eighteen hundred years ago can affect people so yet. But He was no man. (*Rises.*) No man ever had such long and living power. Oh! that I could believe what my mother taught me, and pray as I did when I was a boy! But, Tom, all this time I have forgotten why I sent for you. I'm going to make a freeman of you so have your trunk packed, and get ready to set out for Kentucky.

TOM: (*Joyfully.*) Bless the Lord!

ST. CLARE: (*Dryly.*) You haven't had such very bad times here, that you need be in such a rapture, Tom.

TOM: No, no, mas'r, 'tain't that; it's being a *freeman*—that's what I'm joyin' for.

ST. CLARE: Why, Tom, don't you think, for your own part, you've been better off than to be free?

TOM: No, *indeed*, Mas'r St. Clare—no, indeed!

ST. CLARE: Why, Tom, you couldn't possibly have earned, by your work, such clothes and such living as I have given you.

TOM: I know all that, Mas'r St. Clare—mas'r's been too good; but I'd rather have poor clothes, poor house, poor everything, and have 'em *mine*, than have the best, if they belong to somebody else. I had *so*, mas'r; I think it's natur', mas'r.

ST. CLARE: I suppose so, Tom; and you'll be going off and leaving me in a month or so—though why you shouldn't no mortal knows.

TOM: Not while mas'r is in trouble. I'll stay with mas'r as long as he wants me, so as I can be any use.

ST. CLARE: (*Sadly.*) Not while I'm in trouble, Tom? And when will my trouble be over?

TOM: When you are a believer.

ST. CLARE: And you really mean to stay by me till that day comes? (*Smiling and laying his hand on Tom's shoulder.*) Ah, Tom! I won't keep you till that day. Go home to your wife and children, and give my love to all.

TOM: I's faith to think that day will come—the Lord has a work for mas'r.

ST. CLARE: A work, hey? Well, now, Tom, give me your views on what sort of a work it is—let's hear.

TOM: Why, even a poor fellow like me has a work; and Mas'r St. Clare, that has larnin', and riches, and friends, how much he might do for the Lord.

ST. CLARE: Tom, you seem to think the Lord needs a great deal done for him.

TOM: We does for him when we does for his creatures.

ST. CLARE: Good theology, Tom. Thank you, my boy; I like to hear you talk. But go now, Tom, and leave me alone. (*Exit Tom.*) That faithful fellow's words have excited a train of thoughts that almost bear me, on the strong tide of faith and feeling, to the gates of that heaven I so vividly conceive. They seem to bring me nearer to Eva.

OPHELIA: (*Outside.*) What are you doing there, you limb of Satan? You've been stealing something, I'll be bound.

(*Ophelia drags in Topsy.*)

TOPSY: You go 'long, Miss Feely, 'tain't none o' your business.

ST. CLARE: Heyday! what is all this commotion?

OPHELIA: She's been stealing.

TOPSY: (*Sobbing.*) I hain't neither.

OPHELIA: What have you got in your bosom?

TOPSY: I've got my hand dar.

OPHELIA: But what have you got in your hand?

TOPSY: Nuffin'.

OPHELIA: That's a fib, Topsy.

TOPSY: Well, I 'spects it is.

OPHELIA: Give it to me, whatever it is.

TOPSY: It's mine—I hope I may die this bressed minute, if it don't belong to me.

OPHELIA: Topsy, I order you to give me that article; don't let me have to ask you again. (*Topsy reluctantly takes the foot of an old stocking from her bosom and hands it to Ophelia.*) Sakes alive! what is all this? (*Takes from it a lock of hair, and a small book, with a bit of crape twisted around it.*)

TOPSY: Dat's a lock of ha'r dat Miss Eva give me—she cut if from her own beau'ful head herself.

ST. CLARE: (*Takes book.*) Why did you wrap *this* (*Pointing to crape.*) around the book?

TOPSY: 'Cause—'cause—'cause 'twas Miss Eva's. Oh! don't take 'em away, please! (*Sits down on stage, and, putting her apron over her head, begins to sob vehemently.*)

OPHELIA: Come, come, don't cry; you shall have them.

TOPSY: (*Jumps up joyfully and takes them.*) I wants to keep 'em, 'cause dey makes me good; I ain't half so wicked as I used to was. (*Runs off.*)

ST. CLARE: I really think you can make something of that girl. Any mind that is capable of a *real sorrow* is capable of good. You must try and do something with her.

OPHELIA: The child has improved very much; I have great hopes of her.

ST. CLARE: I believe I'll go down the street, a few moments, and hear the news.

OPHELIA: Shall I call Tom to attend you?

ST. CLARE: No, I shall be back in an hour. (*Exit.*)

OPHELIA: He's got an excellent heart, but then he's so dreadful shiftless! (*Exit.*)

SCENE III

Front Chamber. Enter Topsy.

TOPSY: Dar's somethin' de matter wid me—I isn't a bit like myself. I haven't done anything wrong since poor Miss Eva went up in de skies and left us. When I's gwine to do anything wicked, I tinks of her, and somehow I can't do it. I's getting to be good, dat's a fact. I 'spects when I's dead I shall be turned into a little brack angel.

(*Enter Ophelia.*)

OPHELIA: Topsy, I've been looking for you; I've got something very particular to say to you.

TOPSY: Does you want me to say the catechism?

OPHELIA: No, not now.

TOPSY: (*Aside.*) Golly! dat's one comfort.

OPHELIA: Now, Topsy, I want you to try and understand what I am going to say to you.

TOPSY: Yes, missis, I'll open my ears drefful wide.

OPHELIA: Mr. St. Clare has given you to me, Topsy.

TOPSY: Den I b'longs to you, don't I? Golly! I thought I always belong to you.

OPHELIA: Not till to-day have I received any authority to call you my property.

TOPSY: I's your property, am I? Well, if you say so, I 'spects I am.

OPHELIA: Topsy, I can give you your liberty.

TOPSY: My liberty?

OPHELIA: Yes, Topsy.

TOPSY: Has you got 'um with you?

OPHELIA: I have, Topsy.

TOPSY: Is it clothes or wittles?

OPHELIA: How shiftless! Don't you know what your liberty is, Topsy?

TOPSY: How should I know when I never seed 'um?

OPHELIA: Topsy, I am going to leave this place; I am going many miles away—to my own home in Vermont.

TOPSY: Den what's to become of dis chile?

OPHELIA: If you wish to go, I will take you with me.

TOPSY: Miss Feely, I doesn't want to leave you no how, I loves you I does.

OPHELIA: Then you shall share my home for the rest of your days. Come, Topsy.

TOPSY: Stop, Miss Feely; does dey hab any oberseers in Varmount?

OPHELIA: No, Topsy.

TOPSY: Nor cotton plantations, nor sugar factories, nor darkies, nor whipping nor nothing?

OPHELIA: No, Topsy.

TOPSY: By Golly! de quicker you is gwine de better den.

(*Enter Tom, hastily.*)

TOM: Oh, Miss Feely! Miss Feely!

OPHELIA: Gracious me, Tom! what's the matter?

TOM: Oh, Mas'r St. Clare! Mas'r St. Clare!

OPHELIA: Well, Tom, well?

TOM: They've just brought him home and I do believe he's killed?

OPHELIA: Killed?

TOPSY: Oh dear! what's to become of de poor darkies now?

TOM: He's dreadful weak. It's just as much as he can do to speak. He wanted me to call you.

OPHELIA: My poor cousin! Who would have thought of it? Don't say a word to his wife, Tom; the danger may not be so great as you think; it would only distress her. Come with me; you may be able to afford some assistance. (*Exeunt.*)

SCENE IV

Handsome Chamber. St. Clare discovered seated on sofa. Ophelia, Tom and Topsy are clustered around him. Doctor back of sofa feeling his pulse. Scene opens to slow music.

ST. CLARE: (*Raising himself feebly.*) Tom—poor fellow!

TOM: Well, mas'r?

ST. CLARE: I have received my death wound.

TOM: Oh, no, no, mas'r!

ST. CLARE: I feel that I am dying—Tom, pray!

TOM: (*Sinking on his knees.*) I do, pray, mas'r! I do pray!

ST. CLARE: (*After a pause.*) Tom, one thing preys upon my mind—I have forgotten to sign your freedom papers. What will become of you when I am gone?

TOM: Don't think of that, mas'r.

ST. CLARE: I was wrong, Tom, very wrong, to neglect it. I may be the cause of much suffering to you hereafter. Marie, my wife—she—oh!—

OPHELIA: His mind is wandering.

ST. CLARE: (*Energetically.*) No! it is coming *home* at last! (*Sinks back.*) At last! at last! Eva, I come! (*Dies. Music—slow curtain.*)

END OF ACT IV

ACT V

SCENE I

An Auction Mart. Uncle Tom and Emmeline at back. Adolf, Skeggs, Marks, Mann, and various spectators discovered. Marks and Mann come forward.

MARKS: Hulloa, Alf! what brings you here?

MANN: Well, I was wanting a valet, and I heard that St. Clare's valet was going; I thought I'd just look at them.

MARKS: Catch me ever buying any of St. Clare's people. Spoiled niggers every one—impudent as the devil.

MANN: Never fear that; if I get 'em, I'll soon have their airs out of them— they'll soon find that they've another kind of master to deal with than St. Clare. 'Pon my word, I'll buy that fellow—I like the shape of him. (*Pointing to Adolf.*)

MARKS: You'll find it'll take all you've got to keep him—he's deucedly extravagant.

MANN: Yes, but my lord will find that he *can't* be extravagant with *me*. Just let him be sent to the calaboose a few times, and thoroughly dressed down, I'll tell you if it don't bring him to a sense of his ways. Oh! I'll reform him, up hill and down, you'll see. I'll buy him; that's flat.

(*Enter Legree, he goes up and looks at Adolf, whose boots are nicely blacked.*)

LEGREE: A nigger with his boots blacked—bah! (*Spits on them.*) Holloa, you! (*To Tom.*) Let's see your teeth. (*Seizes Tom by the jaw and opens his mouth.*) Strip up your sleeve and show your muscle. (*Tom does so.*) Where was you rais- ed?

TOM: In Kintuck, mas'r.

LEGREE: What have you done?

TOM: Had care of mas'r's farm.

LEGREE: That's a likely story. (*Turns to Emmeline.*) You're a nice-looking girl enough. How old are you? (*Grasps her arm.*)

EMMELINE: (*Shrieking.*) Ah! you hurt me.

SKEGGS: Stop that, you minx! No whimpering here. The sale is going to begin. (*Mounts the rostrum.*) Gentlemen, the next article I shall offer you to-day is Adolf, late valet to Mr. St. Clare. How much am I offered? (*Various bids are made. Adolf is knocked down to Mann for eight hundred dollars.*) Gentlemen, I now offer a prime article—the quadroon girl, Emmeline, only fifteen years of age, warranted in every respect. (*Business as before. Emmeline is sold to Legree for one thousand dollars.*) Now, I shall close to-day's sale by offering you the valuable article known as Uncle Tom, the most useful nigger ever raised. Gentlemen in want of an overseer, now is the time to bid.

(*Business as before. Tom is sold to Legree for twelve hundred dollars.*)

LEGREE: Now look here, you two belong to me. (*Tom and Emmeline sink on their knees.*)
TOM: Heaven help us, then!

(*Music. Legree stands over them exulting. Picture—closed in.*)

SCENE II

The Garden of Miss Ophelia's House in Vermont. Enter Ophelia and Deacon Perry.

DEACON: Miss Ophelia, allow me to offer you my congratulations upon your safe arrival in your native place. I hope it is your intention to pass the remainder of your days with us?
OPHELIA: Well, Deacon, I have come here with that express purpose.
DEACON: I presume you were not over-pleased with the South?
OPHELIA: Well, to tell you the truth, Deacon, I wasn't; I liked the country very well, but the people there are so dreadful shiftless.
DEACON: The result, I presume, of living in a warm climate.
OPHELIA: Well, Deacon, what is the news among you all here?
DEACON: Well, we live on in the same even jog-trot pace. Nothing of any consequence has happened—Oh! I forgot. (*Takes out handkerchief.*) I've lost my wife; my Molly has left me. (*Wipes his eyes.*)
OPHELIA: Poor soul! I pity you, Deacon.
DEACON: Thank you. You perceive I bear my loss with resignation.
OPHELIA: How you must miss her tongue!
DEACON: Molly certainly was fond of talking. She always would have the last word—heigho!
OPHELIA: What was her complaint, Deacon?
DEACON: A mild and soothing one, Miss Ophelia: she had a severe attack of the lockjaw.
OPHELIA: Dreadful!
DEACON: Wasn't it? When she found she couldn't use her tongue, she took it so much to heart that it struck to her stomach and killed her. Poor dear! Excuse my handkerchief; she's been dead only eighteen months.
OPHELIA: Why, Deacon, by this time you ought to be setting your cap for another wife.
DEACON: Do you think so, Miss Ophelia?
OPHELIA: I don't see why you shouldn't—you are still a good-looking man, Deacon.
DEACON: Ah! well, I think I do wear well—in fact, I may say remarkably

well. It has been observed to me before.

OPHELIA: And you are not much over fifty?

DEACON: Just turned of forty, I assure you.

OPHELIA: Hale and hearty?

DEACON: Health excellent—look at my eye! Strong as a lion—look at my arm!! A No. 1 constitution—look at my leg!!!

OPHELIA: Have you no thoughts of choosing another partner?

DEACON: Well, to tell you the truth, I have.

OPHELIA: Who is she?

DEACON: She is not far distant. (*Looks at Ophelia in an anguishing manner.*) I have her in my eye at this present moment.

OPHELIA: (*Aside.*) Really, I believe he's going to pop. Why, surely, Deacon, you don't mean to—

DEACON: Yes, Miss Ophelia, I do mean; and believe me, when I say— (*Looking off.*) The Lord be good to us, but I believe there is the devil coming!

(*Topsy runs on, with bouquet. She is now dressed very neatly.*)

TOPSY: Miss Feely, here is some flowers dat I hab been gathering for you. (*Gives bouquet.*)

OPHELIA: That's a good child.

DEACON: Miss Ophelia, who is this young person?

OPHELIA: She is my daughter.

DEACON: (*Aside.*) Her daughter! Then she must have married a colored man off South. I was not aware that you had been married, Miss Ophelia?

OPHELIA: Married! Sakes alive! what made you think I had been married?

DEACON: Good gracious, I'm getting confused. Didn't I understand you to say that this—somewhat tanned—young lady was your daughter?

OPHELIA: Only by adoption. She is my adopted daughter.

DEACON: O—oh! (*Aside.*) I breathe again.

TOPSY: By Golly! dat old man's eyes stick out of 'um head dre'ful. Guess he never seed anything like me afore.

OPHELIA: Deacon, won't you step into the house and refresh yourself after your walk?

DEACON: I accept your polite invitation. (*Offers his arm.*) Allow me.

OPHELIA: As gallant as ever, Deacon. I declare, you grow younger every day.

DEACON: You can never grow old, madam.

OPHELIA: Ah, you flatterer! (*Exeunt.*)

TOPSY: Dar dey go, like an old goose and gander. Guess dat ole gemblemun feels kind of confectionary—rather sweet on my old missis. By Golly! she's been dre'ful kind to me ever since I come away from de South; and I loves her, I does, 'cause she takes such car' on me and gives me dese fine clothes. I tries to be good too, and I's gettin 'long 'mazin' fast. I's not so wicked as I used to was. (*Looks out.*) Holloa! dar's some one comin' here. I wonder what he wants now. (*Retires, observing.*)

(*Enter Gumption Cute, very shabby, a small bundle, on a stick, over his shoulder.*)

CUTE: By chowder, here I am again. Phew, it's a pretty considerable tall piece of walking between here and New Orleans, not to mention the wear of shoe-leather. I guess I'm about done up. If this streak of bad luck lasts much longer, I'll borrow sixpence to buy a rope, and hang myself right straight up! When I went to call on Miss Ophelia, I swow if I didn't find out that she had left for Vermont; so I kind of concluded to make tracks in that direction myself and as I didn't have any money left, why I had to foot it, and here I am in old Varmount once more. They told me Miss Ophelia lived up here. I wonder if she will remember the relationship. (*Sees Topsy.*) By chowder, there's a darkey. Look here, Charcoal!

TOPSY: (*Comes forward.*) My name isn't Charcoal—it's Topsy.

CUTE: Oh! your name is Topsy, is it, you juvenile specimen of Day & Martin?

TOPSY: Tell you I don't know nothin' 'bout Day & Martin. I's Topsy and I belong to Miss Feely St. Clare.

CUTE: I'm much obleeged to you, you small extract of Japan, for your information. So Miss Ophelia lives up there in the white house, does she?

TOPSY: Well, she don't do nothin' else.

CUTE: Well, then, just locomote your pins.

TOPSY: What—what's dat?

CUTE: Walk your chalks!

TOPSY: By Golly! dere ain't no chalk 'bout me.

CUTE: Move your trotters.

TOPSY: How you does spoke! What you mean by trotters?

CUTE: Why, your feet, Stove Polish.

TOPSY: What does you want me to move my feet for?

CUTE: To tell your mistress, you ebony angel, that a gentleman wishes to see her.

TOPSY: Does you call yourself a gentleman! By Golly! you look more like a scar'crow.

CUTE: Now look here, you Charcoal, don't you be sassy. I'm a gentleman in distress; a done-up speculator; one that has seen better days—long time ago—and better clothes too, by chowder! My creditors are like my boots—they've no soles. I'm a victim to circumstances. I've been through much and survived it. I've taken walking exercise for the benefit of my health; but as I was trying to live on air at the same time, it was a losing speculation, 'cause it gave me such a dreadful appetite.

TOPSY: Golly! you look as if you could eat an ox, horns and all.

CUTE: Well, I calculate I could, if he was roasted—it's a speculation I should like to engage in. I have returned like the fellow that run away in Scripture; and if anybody's got a fatted calf they want to kill, all they got to do is to fetch him along. Do you know, Charcoal, that your mistress is a relation of mine?

TOPSY: Is she your uncle?

CUTE: No, no, not quite so near as that. My second cousin married her niece.

TOPSY: And does you want to see Miss Feely?

CUTE: I do. I have come to seek a home beneath her roof, and take care of all the spare change she don't want to use.

TOPSY: Den just you follow me, mas'r.

CUTE: Stop! By chowder, I've got a great idea. Say, you Day & Martin, how should you like to enter into a speculation?

TOPSY: Golly! I doesn't know what a spec—spec—cu—what-do-you-call-'um am.

CUTE: Well, now, I calculate I've hit upon about the right thing. Why should I degrade the manly dignity of the Cutes by becoming a beggar—expose myself to the chance of receiving the cold shoulder as a poor relation? By chowder, my blood biles as I think of it! Topsy, you can make my fortune, and your own, too. I've an idee in my head that is worth a million of dollars.

TOPSY: Golly! is your head worth dat? Guess you wouldn't bring dat out South for de whole of you.

CUTE: Don't you be too severe, now, Charcoal; I'm a man of genius. Did you ever hear of Barnum?

TOPSY: Barnum! Barnum! Does he live out South?

CUTE: No, he lives in New York. Do you know how he made his fortin?

TOPSY: What is him fortin, hey? Is it something he wears?

CUTE: Chowder, how green you are!

TOPSY: (Indignantly.) Sar, I hab you to know I's not green; I's brack.

CUTE: To be sure you are, Day & Martin. I calculate, when a person says another has a fortune, he means he's got plenty of money, Charcoal.

TOPSY: And did he make the money?

CUTE: Sartin sure, and no mistake.

TOPSY: Golly! now I thought money always growed.

CUTE: Oh, git out! You are too cute—you are cuterer than I am—and I'm Cute by name and cute by nature. Well, as I was saying, Barnum made his money by exhibiting a *woolly* horse; now wouldn't it be an all-fired speculation to show you as the woolly gal?

TOPSY: You want to make a sight of me?

CUTE: I'll give you half the receipts, by chowder!

TOPSY: Should I have to leave Miss Feely?

CUTE: To be sure you would.

TOPSY: Den you hab to get a woolly gal somewhere else, Mas'r Cute. (*Runs off.*)

CUTE: There's another speculation gone to smash, by chowder! (*Exit.*)

SCENE III

A Rude Chamber. Tom is discovered, in old clothes, seated on a stool. He holds in his hand a paper containing a curl of Eva's hair. The scene opens to the symphony of "Old Folds at Home."

TOM: I have come to de dark places; I's going through de vale of shadows. My heart sinks at times and feels just like a big lump of lead. Den it gits up in my throat and chokes me till de tears roll out of my eyes; den I take out dis curl of little Miss Eva's hair, and the sight of it brings calm to my mind and I feels strong again. (*Kisses the curl and puts it in his breast—takes out a silver dollar, which is suspended around his neck by a string.*) Dere's de bright silver dollar dat Mas'r George Shelby gave me the day I was sold away from old Kentuck, and I've kept it ever since. Mas'r George must have grown to be a man by this time. I wonder if I shall ever see him again.

(*Song. "Old Folks at Home." Enter Legree, Emmeline, Sambo and Quimbo.*)

LEGREE: Shut up, you black cuss! Did you think I wanted any of your infernal howling? (*Turns to Emmeline.*) We're home. (*Emmeline shrinks from him. He takes hold of her ear.*) You didn't ever wear earrings?

EMMELINE: (*Trembling.*) No, master.

LEGREE: Well, I'll give you a pair, if you're a good girl. You needn't be so frightened; I don't mean to make you work very hard. You'll have fine times with me and live like a lady; only be a good girl.

EMMELINE: My soul sickens as his eyes gaze upon me. His touch makes my very flesh creep.

LEGREE: (*Turns to Tom, and points to Sambo and Quimbo.*) Ye see what ye'd get if ye'd try to run off. These yer boys have been raised to track niggers and they'd just as soon chaw one on ye up as eat their suppers; so mind yourself. (*To Emmeline.*) Come, mistress, you go in here with me. (*Taking Emmeline's hand, and leading her off.*)

EMMELINE: (*Withdrawing her hand, and shrinking back.*) No, no! let me work in the fields; I don't want to be a lady.

LEGREE: Oh! you're going to be contrary, are you? I'll soon take all that out of you.

EMMELINE: Kill me, if you will.

LEGREE: Oh! you want to be killed, do you? Now come here, you Tom, you see I told you I didn't buy you jest for the common work; I mean to promote you and make a driver of you, and to-night ye may jest as well begin to get yer hand in. Now ye jest take this yer gal, and flog her; ye've seen enough on't to know how.

TOM: I beg mas'r's pardon—hopes mas'r won't set me at that. It's what I a'nt used to—never did, and can't do—no way possible.

LEGREE: Ye'll larn a pretty smart chance of things ye never did know before I've done with ye. (*Strikes Tom with whip, three blows. Music chord each blow.*) There! now will ye tell me ye can't do it?

TOM: Yes, mas'r! I'm willing to work night and day, and work while there's life and breath in me; but his yer thing I can't feel it right to do, and, mas'r, I *never* shall do it, *never!*

LEGREE: What! ye black beast! tell *me* ye don't think it right to do what I tell ye! What have any of you cussed cattle to do with thinking what's right? I'll put a stop to it. Why, what do ye think ye are? May be ye think yer a gentleman, master Tom, to be telling your master what's right and what a'nt! So you pretend it's wrong to flog the gal?

TOM: I think so, mas'r; 'twould be downright cruel, and it's what I never will do, mas'r. If you mean to kill me, kill me; but as to raising my hand agin any one here, I never shall—I'll die first!

LEGREE: Well, here's a pious dog at last, let down among us sinners—powerful holy critter he must be. Here, you rascal! you make believe to be so pious, didn't you never read out of your Bible, "Servants, obey your masters"? An't I your master? Didn't I pay twelve hundred dollars, cash, for all there is inside your cussed old black shell? An't you mine, body and soul?

TOM: No, no! My soul a'nt yours, mas'r; you haven't bought it—ye can't buy it; it's been bought and paid for by one that is able to keep it, and you can't harm it!

LEGREE: I can't? we'll see, we'll see! Here, Sambo! Quimbo! give this dog such a breaking in as he won't get over this month!

EMMELINE: Oh, no! you will not be so cruel—have some mercy! (*Clings to Tom.*)

LEGREE: Mercy? you won't find any in this shop! Away with the black cuss! Flog him within an inch of his life!

(*Music. Sambo and Quimbo seize Tom and drag him up stage. Legree seizes Emmeline, and throws her round. She falls on her knees, with her hands lifted in supplication. Legree raises his whip, as if to strike Tom. Picture closed in.*)

SCENE IV

Plain Chamber. Enter Ophelia, followed by Topsy.

OPHELIA: A person inquiring for me, did you say, Topsy?

TOPSY: Yes, missis.

OPHELIA: What kind of a looking man is he?

TOPSY: By golly! he's very queer looking man, anyway; and den he talks so dre'ful funny. What does you think?—yah! yah! he wanted to 'zibite me as de woolly gal! yah! yah!

OPHELIA: Oh! I understand. Some cute Yankee, who wants to purchase you, to make a show of—the heartless wretch!

TOPSY: Dat's just him, missis; dat's just his name. He tole me dat it was Cute—Mr. Cute Speculashum—dat's him.

OPHELIA: What did you say to him, Topsy?

TOPSY: Well, I didn't say much, it was brief and to the point—I tole him I wouldn't leave you, Miss Feely, no how.

OPHELIA: That's right, Topsy; you know you are very comfortable here— you wouldn't fare quite so well if you went away among strangers.

TOPSY: By golly! I know dat; you takes care on me, and makes me good. I don't steal any now, and I don't swar, and I don't dance breakdowns. Oh! I isn't so wicked as I used to was.

OPHELIA: That's right, Topsy; now show the gentleman, or whatever he is, up.

TOPSY: By golly! I guess he won't make much out of Miss Feely. (*Crosses and exits.*)

OPHELIA: I wonder who this person can be? Perhaps it is some old acquaintance, who has heard of my arrival, and who comes on a social visit.

(*Enter Cute.*)

CUTE: Aunt, how do ye do? Well, I swan, the sight of you is good for weak eyes. (*Offers his hand.*)

OPHELIA: (*Coldly drawing back.*) Really, sir, I can't say that I ever had the pleasure of seeing you before.

CUTE: Well, it's a fact that you never did. You see I never happened to be in your neighborhood afore now. Of course you've heard of me? I'm one of the Cutes—Gumption Cute, the first and only son of Josiah and Maria Cute, of Oniontown, on the Onion river in the north part of this ere State of Varmount.

OPHELIA: Can't say I ever heard the name before.

CUTE: Well then, I calculate your memory must be a little ricketty. I'm a relation of yours.

OPHELIA: A relation of mine! Why, I never heard of any Cutes in our family.

CUTE: Well, I shouldn't wonder if you never did. Don't you remember your niece, Mary?

OPHELIA: Of course I do. What a shiftless question!

CUTES: Well, you see my second cousin, Abijah Blake, married her. So you see that makes me a relation of yours.

OPHELIA: Rather a distant one, I should say.

CUTE: By chowder! I'm *near* enough, just at present.

OPHELIA: Well, you certainly are a sort of connection of mine.

CUTE: Yes, kind of sort of.

OPHELIA: And of course you are welcome to my house, as long as you wish to make it your home.

CUTE: By chowder! I'm booked for the next six months—this isn't a bad speculation.

OPHELIA: I hope you left all your folks well at home?

CUTE: Well, yes, they're pretty comfortably disposed of. Father and mother's dead, and Uncle Josh has gone to California. I am the only representative of the Cutes left.

OPHELIA: There doesn't seem to be a great deal of *you* left. I declare, you are positively in rags.

CUTE: Well, you see, the fact is, I've been speculating—trying to get bank-notes—specie-rags, as they say—but I calculate I've turned out rags of another sort.

OPHELIA: I'm sorry for your ill luck, but I am afraid you have been shiftless.

CUTE: By chowder! I've done all that a fellow could do. You see, somehow, everything I take hold of kind of bursts up.

OPHELIA: Well, well, perhaps you'll do better for the future; make yourself at home. I have got to see to some house-hold matters, so excuse me for a short time. (*Aside.*) Impudent and shiftless. (*Exit.*)

CUTE: By chowder! I rather guess that this speculation will hitch. She's a good-natured old critter; I reckon I'll be a son to her while she lives, and take care of her valuables arter she's a defunct departed. I wonder if they keep the vittles in this ere room? Guess not. I've got extensive accommodations for all sorts of eatables. I'm a regular vacuum, throughout—pockets and all. I'm chuck full of emptiness. (*Looks out.*) Holloa! who's this elderly individual coming up stairs? He looks like a compound essence of starch and dignity. I wonder if he isn't another relation of mine. I should like a rich old fellow now for an uncle.

(*Enter Deacon Perry.*)

DEACON: Ha! a stranger here!

CUTE: How d'ye do?

DEACON: You are a friend to Miss Ophelia, I presume?

CUTE: Well, I rather calculate that I am a leetle more than a friend.

DEACON: (*Aside.*) Bless me! what can he mean by those mysterious words? Can he be her—no I don't think he can. She said she wasn't—well, at all events, it's very suspicious.

CUTE: The old fellow seems kind of stuck up.

DEACON: You are a particular friend to Miss Ophelia, you say?

CUTE: Well, I calculate I am.

DEACON: Bound to her by any tender tie?

CUTE: It's something more than a tie—it's a regular double-twisted knot.

DEACON: Ah! just as I suspected. (*Aside.*) Might I inquire the nature of that tie?

CUTE: Well, it's the natural tie of relationship.

DEACON: A relation—what relation?

CUTE: Why, you see, my second cousin, Abijah Blake, married her niece, Mary.

DEACON: Oh! is that all?

CUTE: By chowder, ain't that enough?

DEACON: Then you are not her husband?

CUTE: To be sure I ain't. What put that ere idee into your cranium?

DEACON: (*Shaking him vigorously by the hand.*) My dear sir, I'm delighted to see you.

CUTE: Holloa! you ain't going slightly insane, are you?

DEACON: No, no fear of that; I'm only happy, that's all.

CUTE: I wonder if he's been taking a nipper?

DEACON: As you are a relation of Miss Ophelia's, I think it proper that I should make you my confidant; in fact, let you into a little scheme that I have lately conceived.

CUTE: Is it a speculation?

DEACON: Well, it is, just at present; but I trust before many hours to make it a surety.

CUTE: By chowder! I hope it won't serve you the way my speculations have served me. But fire away, old boy, and give us the prospectus.

DEACON: Well, then, my young friend, I have been thinking, ever since Miss Ophelia returned to Vermont, that she was just the person to fill the place of my lamented Molly.

CUTE: Say, you, you couldn't tell us who your lamented Molly was, could you?

DEACON: Why, the late Mrs. Perry, to be sure.

CUTE: Oh! then the lamented Molly was your wife?

DEACON: She was.

CUTE: And now you wish to marry Miss Ophelia?

DEACON: Exactly.

CUTE: (*Aside.*) Consarn this old porpoise! if I let him do that he'll Jew me out of my living. By chowder! I'll put a spoke in his wheel.

DEACON: Well, what do you say? will you intercede for me with your aunt?

CUTE: No! bust me up if I do!

DEACON: No?

CUTE: No, I tell you. I forbid the bans. Now, ain't you a purty individual, to talk about getting married, you old superannuated Methuselah specimen of humanity! Why, you've got one foot in eternity already, and t'other ain't fit to stand on. Go home and go to bed! have your head shaved, and send for a lawyer to make your will, leave your property to your heirs—if you hain't got any, why leave it to me—I'll take care of it, and charge nothing for the trouble.

DEACON: Really, sir, this language to one of my standing, is highly indecorous—it's more, sir, than I feel willing to endure, sir. I shall expect an explanation, sir.

CUTE: Now, you see, old gouty toes, you're losing your temper.

DEACON: Sir, I'm a deacon; I never lost my temper in all my life, sir.

CUTE: Now, you see, you're getting excited; you had better go; we can't have a disturbance here!

DEACON: No, sir! I shall not go, sir! I shall not go until I have seen Miss Ophelia. I wish to know if she will countenance this insult.

CUTE: Now keep cool, old stick-in-the-mud! Draw it mild, old timber-toes!

DEACON: Damn it all, sir, what—

CUTE: Oh! only think, now, what would people say to hear a deacon swearing like a trooper?

DEACON: Sir—I—you—this is too much, sir.

CUTE: Well, now, I calculate that's just about my opinion, so we'll have no more of it. Get out of this! start your boots, or by chowder! I'll pitch you from one end of the stairs to the other.

(*Enter Ophelia*)

OPHELIA: Hoity toity! What's the meaning of all these loud words?

CUTE: (*Together.*) Well, you see, Aunt—

DEACON: Miss Ophelia, I beg—

CUTE: Now, look here, you just hush your yap! How can I fix up matters if you keep jabbering?

OPHELIA: Silence! for shame, Mr. Cute. Is that the way you speak to the deacon?

CUTE: Darn the deacon!

OPHELIA: Deacon Perry, what is all this?

DEACON: Madam, a few words will explain everything. Hearing from this person that he was your nephew, I ventured to tell him that I cherished hopes of making you my wife, whereupon he flew into a violent passion, and ordered me out of the house.

OPHELIA: Does this house belong to you or me, Mr. Cute?

CUTE: Well, to you, I reckon.

OPHELIA: Then how dare you give orders in it?

CUTE: Well, I calculated that you wouldn't care about marrying old half a century there.

OPHELIA: That's enough; I will marry him; and as for you, (*Points.*) get out.

CUTE: Get out?

OPHELIA: Yes; the sooner the better.

CUTE: Darned if I don't serve him out first though.

(*Music. Cute makes a dash at Deacon, who gets behind Ophelia. Topsy enters, with a broom and beats Cute around stage. Ophelia faints in Deacon's arms. Cute falls, and Topsy butts him kneeling over him. Quick drop.*)

ACT VI

SCENE I

Dark landscape. An old, roofless shed. Tom is discovered in shed, lying on some old cotton bagging. Cassy kneels by his side, holding a cup to his lips.

CASSY: Drink all ye want. I knew how it would be. It isn't the first time I've been out in the night, carrying water to such as you.

TOM: (*Returning cup.*) Thank you, missis.

CASSY: Don't call me missis. I'm a miserable slave like yourself—a lower one than you can ever be! It's no use, my poor fellow, this you've been trying to do. You were a brave fellow. You had the right on your side; but it's all in vain for you to struggle. You are in the Devil's hands; he is the strongest, and you must give up.

TOM: Oh! how can I give up?

CASSY: You see *you* don't know anything about it; I do. Here you are, on a lone plantation, ten miles from any other, in the swamps; not a white person here who could testify, if you were burned alive. There's no law here that can do you, or any of us, the least good; and this man! there's no earthly thing that he is not bad enough to do. I could make one's hair rise, and their teeth chatter, if I should only tell what I've seen and been knowing to here; and it's no use resisting! Did I *want* to live with him? Wasn't I a woman delicately bred? and he!—Father in Heaven! what was he and is he? And yet I've lived with him these five years, and cursed every moment of my life, night and day.

TOM: Oh heaven! have you quite forgot us poor critters?

CASSY: And what are these miserable low dogs you work with, that you should suffer on their account? Every one of them would turn against you the first time they get a chance. They are all of them as low and cruel to each other as they can be; there's no use in your suffering to keep from hurting them?

TOM: What made 'em cruel? If I give out I shall get used to it and grow, little by little, just like 'em. No, no, Missis, I've lost everything, wife, and children, and home, and a kind master, and he would have set me free if he'd only lived a day longer—I've lost everything in *this* world, and now I can't lose heaven, too: no I can't get to be wicked besides all.

CASSY: But it can't be that He will lay sin to our account; he won't charge it to us when we are forced to it; he'll charge it to them that drove us to it. Can I do anything more for you? Shall I give you some more water?

TOM: Oh missis! I wish you'd go to Him who can give you living waters!

CASSY: Go to him! Where is he? Who is he?

TOM: Our Heavenly Father!

CASSY: I used to see the picture of him, over the altar, when I was a girl but *he isn't here!* there's nothing here but sin, and long, long despair! There, there, don't talk any more, my poor fellow. Try to sleep, if you can. I must hasten back, lest my absence be noted. Think of me when I am gone, Uncle Tom, and pray, pray for me.

(*Music. Exit Cassy. Tom sinks back to sleep.*)

SCENE II

Street in New Orleans. Enter George Shelby.

GEORGE: At length my mission of mercy is nearly finished, I have reached my journey's end. I have now but to find the house of Mr. St. Clare, re-purchase old Uncle Tom, and convey him back to his wife and children, in old Kentucky. Some one approaches; he may, perhaps, be able to give me the information I require. I will accost him. (*Enter Marks.*) Pray, sir, can you tell me where Mr. St. Clare dwells?

MARKS: Where I don't hink you'll be in a hurry to seek him.

GEORGE: And where is that?

MARKS: In the grave!

GEORGE: Stay, sir! you may be able to give me some information concerning Mr. St. Clare.

MARKS: I beg pardon, sir, I am a lawyer; I can't afford to *give* anything

GEORGE: But you would have no objections to selling it?

MARKS: Not the slightest.

GEORGE: What do you value it at?

MARKS: Well, say five dollars, that's reasonable.

GEORGE: There they are. (*Gives money.*) Now answer me to the best of your ability. Has the death of St. Clare caused his slaves to be sold?

MARKS: It has.

GEORGE: How were they sold?

MARKS: At auction—they went dirt cheap.

GEORGE: How were they bought—all in one lot?

MARKS: No, they went to different bidders.

GEORGE: Was you present at the sale?

MARKS: I was.

GEORGE: Do you remember seeing a negro among them called Tom?

MARKS: What, Uncle Tom?

GEORGE: The same—who bought him?

MARKS: A Mr. Legree.

GEORGE: Where is his plantation?

MARKS: Up in Louisiana, on the Red River; but a man never could find it, unless he had been there before.

GEORGE: Who could I get to direct me there?

MARKS: Well, stranger, I don't know of any one just at present 'cept myself, could find it for you; it's such an out-of-the-way sort of hole; and if you are a mind to come down handsomely, why, I'll do it.

GEORGE: The reward shall be ample.

MARKS: Enough said, stranger; let's take the steamboat at once. (*Exeunt.*)

SCENE III

A Rough Chamber. Enter Legree. Sits.

LEGREE: Plague on that Sambo, to kick up this yer row between Tom and the new hands. (*Cassy steals on and stands behind him.*) The fellow won't be fit to work for a week now, right in the press of the season.

CASSY: Yes, just like you.

LEGREE: Hah! you she-devil! you've come back, have you? (*Rises*)

CASSY: Yes, I have; come to have my own way, too.

LEGREE: You lie, you jade! I'll be up to my word. Either behave yourself or stay down in the quarters and fare and work with the rest.

CASSY: I'd rather, ten thousand times, live in the dirtiest hole at the quarters, than be under your hoof!

LEGREE: But you are under my hoof, for all that, that's one comfort; so sit down here and listen to reason. (*Grasps her wrist.*)

CASSY: Simon Legree, take care! (*Legree lets go his hold.*) You're afraid of me, Simon, and you've reason to be; for I've got the Devil in me!

LEGREE: I believe to my soul you have. After all, Cassy, why can't you be friends with me, as you used to?

CASSY: (*Bitterly.*) Used to!

LEGREE: I wish, Cassy, you'd behave yourself decently.

CASSY: *You* talk about behaving decently! and what have you been doing? You haven't even sense enough to keep from spoiling one of your best hands, right in the most pressing season, just for your devilish temper.

LEGREE: I was a fool, it's fact, to let any such brangle come up. Now when Tom set up his will he had to be broke in.

CASSY: You'll never break *him* in.

LEGREE: Won't I? I'd like to know if I won't? He'd be the first nigger that ever come it round me! I'll break every bone in his body but he shall give up. (*Enter Sambo, with a paper in his hand, stands bowing.*) What's that, you dog?

SAMBO: It's a witch thing, mas'r.

LEGREE: A what?

SAMBO: Something that niggers gits from witches. Keep 'em from feeling when they's flogged. He had it tied round his neck with a black string.

(*Legree takes the paper and opens it. A silver dollar drops on the stage, and a long curl of light hair twines around his finger.*)

LEGREE: Damnation. (*Stamping and writhing, as if the hair burned him.*) Where did this come from? Take it off! burn it up! burn it up! (*Throws the curl away.*) What did you bring it to me for?

SAMBO: (*Trembling.*) I beg pardon, mas'r; I thought you would like to see um.

LEGREE: Don't you bring me any more of your devilish things. (*Shakes his fist at Sambo who runs off. Legree kicks the dollar after him.*) Blast it! where did he get that? If it didn't look just like—whoo! I thought I'd forgot that. Curse me if I think there's any such thing as forgetting anything, any how.

CASSY: What is the matter with you, Legree? What is there in a simple curl of fair hair to appall a man like you—you who are familiar with every form of cruelty.

LEGREE: Cassy, to-night the past has been recalled to me—the past that I have so long and vainly striven to forget.

CASSY: Has aught on this earth power to move a soul like thine?

LEGREE: Yes, for hard and reprobate as I now seem, there has been a time when I have been rocked on the bosom of a mother, cradled with prayers and pious hymns, my now seared brow bedewed with the waters of holy baptism.

CASSY: (*Aside.*) What sweet memories of childhood can thus soften down that heart of iron?

LEGREE: In early childhood a fair-haired woman has led me, at the sound of Sabbath bells, to worship and to pray. Born of a hard-tempered sire, on whom that gentle woman had wasted a world of unvalued love, I followed in the steps of my fgather. Boisterous, unruly and tyrannical, I despised all her counsel, and would have none of her reproof, and, at an early age, broke from her to seek my fortunes on the sea. I never came home but once after that; and then my mother, with the yearning of a heart that must love something, and had nothing else to love, clung to me, and sought with passionate prayers and entreaties to win me from a life of sin.

CASSY: That was your day of grace, Legree; then good angels called you, and mercy held you by the hand.

LEGREE: My heart inly relented; there was a conflict, but sin got the victory, and I set all the force of my rough nature against the conviction of my conscience. I drank and swore, was wilder and more brutal than ever. And one night, when my mother, in the last agony of her despair, knelt at my feet, I spurned her from me, threw her senseless on the floor, and with brutal curses fled to my ship.

CASSY: Then the fiend took thee for his own.

LEGREE: The next I heard of my mother was one night while I was carousing among drunken companions. A letter was put in my hands. I opened it, and a lock of long, curling hair fell from it, and twined about my fingers, even as that lock twined but now. The letter told me that my mother was dead, and that dying she blest and forgave me! (*Buries his face in his hands.*)

CASSY: Why did you not even then renounce your evil ways?

LEGREE: There is a dread, unhallowed necromancy of evil, that turns things sweetest and holiest to phantoms of horror and afright. That pale, loving mother,—her dying prayers, her forgiving love,—wrought in my demoniac heart of sin only as a damning sentence, bringing with it a fearful looking for of judgment and fiery indignation.

CASSY: And yet you would not strive to avert the doom that threatened you.

LEGREE: I burned the lock of hair and I burned the letter; and when I saw them hissing and crackling in the flame, inly shuddered as I thought of everlasting fires! I tried to drink and revel, and swear away the memory; but often in the deep night, whose solemn stillness arraigns the soul in forced communion with itself, I have seen that pale mother rising by my bed-side, and felt the soft twining of that hair around my fingers, 'till the cold sweat would roll down my face, and I would spring from my bed in horror—horror! (*Falls in chair—After a pause.*) What the devil ails me? Large drops of sweat stand on my forehead, and my heart beats heavy and thick with fear. I thought I saw something white rising and glimmering in the gloom before me, and it seemed to bear my mother's face! I know one thing; I'll let that fellow Tom alone, after this. What did I want with his cussed paper? I believe I am bewitched sure enough! I've been shivering and sweating ever since! Where did he get that hair? It couldn't have been that! I *burn'd* that up, I know I did! It would be a joke if hair could rise from the dead! I'll have Sambo and Quimbo up here to sing and dance one of their dances, and keep off these horrid notions. Here, Sambo! Quimbo! (*Exit.*)

CASSY: Yes, Legree, that golden tress was charmed; each hair had in it a spell of terror and remorse for thee, and was used by a mightier power to bind thy cruel hands from inflicting uttermost evil on the helpless! (*Exit.*)

SCENE IV

Street. Enter Marks meeting Cute, who enters dressed in an old faded uniform.

MARKS: By the land, stranger, but it strikes me that I've seen you somewhere before.

CUTE: By chowder! do you know now, that's just what I was a going to say?

MARKS: Isn't your name Cute?

CUTE: You're right, I calculate. Yours is Marks, I reckon.

MARKS: Just so.

CUTE: Well, I swow, I'm glad to see you. (*They shake hands.*) How's your wholesome?

MARKS: Hearty as ever. Well, who would have thought of ever seeing you again. Why, I thought you was in Vermont?

CUTE: Well, so I was. You see I went there after that rich relation of mine— but the speculation didn't turn out well.

MARKS: How so?

CUTE: Why, you see, she took a shine to an old fellow—Deacon Abraham Perry—and married him.

MARKS: Oh, that rather put your nose out of joint in that quarter.

CUTE: Busted me right up, I tell you. The Deacon did the hand-some thing though, he said if I would leave the neighborhood and go out South again, he'd stand the damage. I calculate I didn't give him much time to change his mind, and so, you see, here I am again.

MARKS: What are you doing in that soldier rig?

CUTE: Oh, this is my sign.

MARKS: Your sign?

CUTE: Yes; you see, I'm engaged just at present in an all-fired good speculation, I'm a Fillibusterow.

MARKS: A what?

CUTE: A Fillubusterow! Don't you know what that is? It's Spanish for Cuban Volunteer; and means a chap that goes the whole perker for glory and all that ere sort of thing.

MARKS: Oh! you've joined the order of the Lone Star!

CUTE: You've hit it. You see I bought this uniform at a second hand clothing store, I puts it on and goes to a benevolent individual and I says to him,—appealing to his feelings,—I'm one of the fellows that went to Cuba and got massacred by the bloody Spaniards. I'm in a destitute condition—give me a trifle to pay my passage back, so I can whop the tyrannical cusses and avenge my brave fellow soger what got slewed there.

MARKS: How pathetic!

CUTE: I tell you it works up the feelings of benevolent individuals dreadfully. It draws tears from their eyes and money from their pockets. By chowder! one old chap gave me a hundred dollars to help on the cause.

MARKS: I admire a genius like yours.

CUTE: But I say, what are you up to?

MARKS: I am the traveling companion of a young gentleman by the name of Shelby, who is going to the plantation of a Mr. Legree of the Red River, to buy an old darkey who used to belong to his father.

CUTE: Legree—Legree? Well, now, I calculate I've heard that ere name afore.

MARKS: Do you remember that man who drew a bowie knife on you in New Orleans?

CUTE: By chowder! I remember the circumstance just as well as if it was yesterday; but I can't say that I recollect much about the man, for you see I was in something of a hurry about that time and didn't stop to take a good look at him.

MARKS: Well, that man was this same Mr. Legree.

CUTE: Do you know, now, I should like to pay that critter off!

MARKS: Then I'll give you an opportunity.

CUTE: Chowder! how will you do that?

MARKS: Do you remember the gentleman that interfered between you and Legree?

CUTE: Yes—well?

MARKS: He received the blow that was intended for you, and died from the effects of it. So, you see, Legree is a murderer, and we are only witnesses of the deed. His life is in our hands.

CUTE: Let's have him right up and make him dance on nothing to the tune of Yandee Doodle!

MARKS: Stop a bit. Don't you see a chance for a profitable speculation?

CUTE: A speculation! Fire away, don't be bashful, I'm the man for a speculation.

MARKS: I have made a deposition to the Governor of the state on all the particulars of that affair at Orleans.

CUTE: What did you do that for?

MARKS: To get a warrant for his arrest.

CUTE: Oh! and have you got it?

MARKS: Yes; here it is. (*Takes out paper.*)

CUTE: Well, now, I don't see how you are going to make anything by that bit of paper?

MARKS: But I do. I shall say to Legree, I have got a warrant against you for murder; my friend, Mr. Cute, and myself are the only witnesses who can appear against you. Give us a thousand dollars, and we will tear the warrant and be silent.

CUTE: Then Mr. Legree forks over a thousand dollars, and your friend Cute pockets five hundred of it, is that the calculation?

MARKS: If you will join me in the undertaking.

CUTE: I'll do it, by chowder!

MARKS: Your hand to bind the bargain.

CUTE: I'll stick by you thro' thick and thin.

MARKS: Enough said.

CUTE: Then shake. (*They shake hands.*)

MARKS: But I say, Cute, he may be contrary and show fight.

CUTE: Never mind, we've got the law on our side, and we're bound to stir him up. If he don't come down handsomely we'll present him with a neck-tie made of hemp!

MARKS: I declare you're getting spunky.

CUTE: Well, I reckon, I am. Let's go and have something to drink. Tell you what, Marks, if we don't get *him*, we'll have his hide, by chowder! (*Exeunt, arm in arm.*)

SCENE V

Rough Chamber. Enter Legree, followed by Sambo.

LEGREE: Go and send Cassy to me.

SAMBO: Yes, mas'r. (*Exit.*)

LEGREE: Curse the woman! she's got a temper worse than the devil; I shall do her an injury one of these days, if she isn't careful. (*Re-enter Sambo, frightened.*) What's the matter with you, you black scoundrel?

SAMBO: S'help me, mas'r, she isn't dere.

LEGREE: I suppose she's about the house somewhere?

SAMBO: No, she isn't, mas'r; I's been all over de house and I can't find nothing of her nor Emmeline.

LEGREE: Bolted, by the Lord! Call out the dogs! saddle my horse. Stop! are you sure they really have gone?

SAMBO: Yes, mas'r; I's been in every room 'cept the haunted garret and dey wouldn't go dere.

LEGREE: I have it! Now, Sambo, you jest go and walk that Tom up here, right away! (*Exit Sambo.*) The old cuss is at the bottom of this yer whole matter; and I'll have it out of his infernal black hide, or I'll know the reason why! I *hate* him—I *hate* him! And isn't he *mine?* Can't I do what I like with him? Who's to hinder, I wonder? (*Tom is dragged on by Sambo and Quimbo, Legree grimly confronting Tom.*) Well, Tom, do you know I've made up my mind to *kill* you?

TOM: It's very likely, Mas'r.

LEGREE: *I—have—done—just—that—thing,* Tom, unless you'll tell me what do you know about these yer gals? (*Tom is silent.*) D'ye hear? Speak!

TOM: I han't got anything to tell, mas'r.

LEGREE: Do you dare to tell me, you old black rascal, you don't know? Speak! Do you know anything?

TOM: I know, mas'r; but I can't tell anything. *I can die!*

LEGREE: Hark ye, Tom! ye think, 'cause I have let you off before, I don't mean what I say; but, this time, I have made *up my mind,* and counted the cost. You've always stood it out agin me; now, I'll *conquer ye or kill ye!* one or t'other. I'll count every drop of blood there is in you, and take 'em, one by one, 'till ye give up!

TOM: Mas'r, if you was sick, or in trouble, or dying, and I could save you, I'd *give* you my heart's blood; and, if taking every drop of blood in this poor old body would save your precious soul, I'd give 'em freely. Do the worst you can, my troubles will be over soon; but if you don't repent yours won't never end.

(*Legree strikes Tom down with the butt of his whip.*)

LEGREE: How do you like that?

SAMBO: He's most gone, mas'r!

TOM: (*Rises feebly on his hands.*) There an't no more you can do. I forgive you with all my soul. (*Sinks back, and is carried off by Sambo and Quimbo.*)

LEGREE: I believe he's done for finally. Well, his mouth is shut up at last—that's one comfort. (*Enter George Shelby, Marks and Cute.*) Strangers! Well what do you want?

GEORGE: I understand that you bought in New Orleans a negro named Tom?

LEGREE: Yes, I did buy such a fellow, and a devil of a bargain I had of it, too! I believe he's trying to die, but I don't know as he'll make it out.

GEORGE: Where is he? Let me see him?

SAMBO: Dere he is. (*Points to Tom.*)

LEGREE: How dare you speak? (*Drives Sambo and Quimbo off. George exits.*)

CUTE: Now's the time to nab him.

MARKS: How are you, Mr. Legree?

LEGREE: What the devil brought you here?

MARKS: This little bit of paper. I arrest you for the murder of Mr. St. Clare. What do you say to that?

LEGREE: This is my answer! (*Makes a blow at Marks, who dodges, and Cute receives the blow—he cries out and runs off, Marks fires at Legree, and follows Cute.*) I am hit!—the game's up! (*Falls dead. Quimbo and Sambo return and carry him off laughing.*)

(*George Shelby enters, supporting Tom. Music. They advance to front and Tom falls.*)

GEORGE: Oh! dear Uncle Tom! do wake—do speak once more! look up! Here's Master George—your own little Master George. Don't you know me?

TOM: (*Opening his eyes and speaking in a feeble tone.*) Mas'r George! Bless de Lord! it's all I wanted! They hav'n't forgot me! It warms my soul; it does my old heart good! Now I shall die content!

GEORGE: You shan't die! you mustn't die, nor think of it. I have come to buy you, and take you home.

TOM: Oh, Mas'r George, you're too late. The Lord has bought me, and is going to take me home.

GEORGE: Oh! don't die. It will kill me—it will break my heart to think what you have suffered, poor, poor fellow!

TOM: Don't call me, poor fellow! I *have* been poor fellow; but that's all past and gone now. I'm right in the door, going into glory! Oh, Mas'r George! *Heaven has come!* I've got the victory, the Lord has given it to me! Glory be to His name! (*Dies.*)

(Solemn music. George covers Uncle Tom with his cloak, and kneels over him. Clouds work on and conceal them, and then work off.)

SCENE VII

Gorgeous clouds, tinted with sunlight. Eva, robed in white, is discovered on the back of a milk-white dove, with expanded wings, as if just soaring upward. Her hands are extended in benediction over St. Clare and Uncle Tom who are kneeling and gazing up to her. Expressive music. Slow curtain.

END

UNDER THE GASLIGHT

Augustin Daly

THE CAST:

Ray Trafford, one of the New York "Bloods."

Snorkey, a returned veteran, established as a soldier messenger, but open to anything else

Byke, one of the men whom the law is always reaching for and never touches

Ed. Demilt, one of the rising Wall Street generation

Windel, his friend, "sound on the street"

Justice Bowling, of the Tombs Police Court

Counsellor Splinter, an attorney of the Tombs Court

Bermudas, one of the under crust, a sidewalk merchant prince, with a "banjo swarry"

Peanuts, a rival operator in papers and matches

Sam, a colored citizen, ready for suffrage when it is ready for him

Rafferdi, nee Rafferty, an Italian organist from Cork

The Sergeant of the River Patrol

Policeman 999

Martin

Peter Rich, the boy who was committed

The Signalman at Shrewsbury Bend

Members of the Tuesday Sociable, Court Officers, Dock Boys, etc.

Laura Courtland, the belle of society

Pearl Courtland, pretty, but no heart

Peachblossom, a girl who was never "brought up," with the doleful ditty of "the Knight, the Dame, and the Murderous Rival"

Old Judas, the right hand of Byke

Mrs. Van Dam, one of the voices of society

Sue Earlie, one of the echoes of the voice

Lizzie Liston, another echo

ACT I

SCENE I

Parlor at the Courtlands; deep window at back showing snowy exterior; street lamp lighted; time, night; the place elegantly furnished; chandelier. Ray Trafford is discovered lounging on tete-a-tete. Pearl is at door taking leave of Demilt, Windel, Mrs. Van Dam, and Sue Earlie, who are all dressed and muffled to go out.

MRS. VAN DAM: Good night! Of course we'll see you on Tuesday.

PEARL: To be sure you will.

DEMILT: Never spent a jollier hour. Good night, Ray.

RAY: (*On sofa.*) Good night.

MRS. VAN DAM: You won't forget the Sociable on Tuesday, Ray?

RAY: O, I won't forget.

ALL: (*At door.*) Good night—good night! (*Exit.*)

PEARL: Good night. (*Coming forward.*) O, dear! now they're gone, and the holiday's gone with them. (*Goes to window.*) There they go. (*Laughter without.*) Ray, do come and look at the Van Dam's new sleigh. How they have come out.

RAY: Yes, it's the gayest thing in the Park!

PEARL: (*Still at window.*) I wonder where they got the money, I thought you said Van Dam had failed!

RAY: Well, yes. He failed to pay, but he continues to spend.

PEARL: (*As if to those outside.*) Good night! (*Response from without as sleigh bells jingle—"Good night."*) I wish I was in there with you. It's delightful for a sleigh ride, if it wasn't New Year's. O! there's Demilt over! (*Laughter outside—cracking of whips—Ray saunters up to window. Sleigh bells jingle, sleigh music heard to die away. Ray and Pearl wave their handkerchiefs. Ray comes down and sits.*)

PEARL: (*Closing lace curtains.*) Isn't it a frightful thing to be shut up here on such a beautiful night, and New Year's of all others. Pshaw, we've had nothing but mopes all day. O, dear! I hate mourning, though it does become me, and I hate everything but fun, larks and dancing. (*Comes down.*)

RAY: Where in the world is Laura?

PEARL: O! do forget her for a second, can't you? She'll be here presently. You're not in the house a minute but it's, "Where's Laura?" "Why don't Laura come?"

RAY: (*Taking her hand.*) Well, if anybody in the world could make me forget her, it would be you. But if you had a lover, wouldn't you like him to be as constant as that?

PEARL: That's quite another thing.

RAY: But this doesn't answer my question—Where is she?

PEARL: I sent for her as soon as I saw you coming. She has hardly been down here a moment all this evening. O, dear! Now don't you think I'm a victim, to be cooped up in this way instead of receiving calls as we used to?

RAY: You forget that your mother died only last summer. (*Rising.*)

PEARL: No, I don't forget. Pshaw! You're just like Laura. She's only my cousin, and yet she keeps always saying—"Poor aunt Mary! let us not forget how she would have sorrowed for us."

RAY: (*Going towards back.*) Well, don't you know she would, too.

PEARL: I don't know anything about it. I was always at boarding school, and she only saw me once a year. Laura was always at home, and it's very different. But don't let's talk about it. To die—ugh! I don't want to die till I don't want to live—and that'll not be for a million of years. Come, tell me—where have you been to-day? How many calls did you make? (*Sitting in tete-a-tete.*)

RAY: About sixty.

PEARL: That's all? You're lazy. Demilt and Windel made a hundred and thirty, and they say that's nothing. Won't you have a cup of coffee?

RAY: No.

PEARL: Ain't you hungry?

RAY: No—you torment.

PEARL: O, dear! I suppose it's because you're going to be married shortly to Laura. If there's one time that a man's stupid to his friends, it's when he's going to be married shortly. Tell me whom you saw. (*Ray has sauntered off and is looking over cards on table.*) Where are you? Oh, you needn't be so impatient to see her. Do be agreeable; sit here and tell me something funny, or I shall drop down and fall asleep.

RAY: (*Over her shoulder.*) You witch! Why didn't I fall in love with you?

PEARL: (*Laughing.*) I don't know; why didn't you?

RAY: You never keep me waiting. (*Listening.*) Ah, that's her step! No.

PEARL: Do sit down.

RAY: (*Sitting.*) This calling's a great bore; but as you and Laura insisted I should go through it, I did. First I—(*Jumping up.*) I knew it was she. (*Goes to door, meets Laura, who enters.*) How you did keep me waiting. (*Kisses both her hands.*)

LAURA: And you, sir, we have been looking for you since eight o'clock.

RAY: O, I was fulfilling your orders. I've been engaged in the business of calling, from ten o'clock in the morning, till now—(*Looks at watch—*) ten at night.

LAURA: Well, you can make this your last one, for you have leave to spend a nice long hour chatting here before you go. Won't you have some supper. (*Goes to bell.*)

RAY: I don't care if I do. I'm rather famished.

PEARL: Well, I declare! Did Laura bring your appetite with her? (*Laura rings.*)

RAY: I don't know how it is, but she brings me a relish for everything in life, I believe. Laura, I think if I were to lose you I'd mope to death and starve to death.

LAURA: Well, that's as much as to say I'm a sort of Life Pill. (*Martin enters door.*) Supper. (*Martin exits.*)

RAY: You may joke about it,—but it's so. You take the lounge. (*Laura and Pearl sit on tete-a-tete.*)

PEARL: You don't want me to go away, do you? (*Putting her head on Laura's shoulder.*)

LAURA: Certainly not. What an idea!

PEARL: I'm sure you'll have time enough to be alone when you are married. And I do so want to talk and be talked to.

LAURA: Well, Ray shall talk to you.

PEARL: He was just going to tell me about his calls to-day.

LAURA: That's exactly what we want to hear about. Did you call on every one we told you to?

RAY: Every one. There was Miss—

PEARL: Did you go to Henrietta Liston's first?

RAY: Yes, and wasn't she dressed! Speaking of dress, are you doing to have your new pink for the Sociable, Tuesday?

LAURA: Yes, Pearl, and I will do credit to the occasion, as it is our first for a year.

RAY: (*Taking Laura's hand.*) And *our* last.

PEARL: Our last!

RAY: Laura's and mine. For when we are married, you know we shall be tabooed—where maids and bachelors only are permitted.

PEARL: O bless me! (*Rising.*) How do you do Mrs. Trafford.

LAURA: (*Rising sadly.*) I wish you hadn't said that Pearl. You know the old proverb: "Call a maid by a married name."

RAY: Nonsense! (*Putting his arm about Laura's waist.*) It's only a few days to wait, and we'll live long enough, you know. For nothing but death shall separate us. (*Martin appears at door.*)

PEARL: O, here's supper.

MARTIN: Beg pardon, Miss.

LAURA: What's the matter?

MARTIN: There's a person below, Miss, who says he's been sent with a bouquet for you, Miss, and must deliver it in person.

LAURA: For me? Whose servant is it?

MARTIN: I don't know, Miss, he looks like one of those soldier Messengers—red cap and all that.

LAURA: Show him up here. (*Exit Martin.*)

PEARL: How romantic. So late at night. It's a rival in disguise, Ray.

(*Martin re-enters showing in Snorkey, with an air of disdain. Snorkey has a large bouquet in his hand, and his hat is under the stump of his right arm, which is cut off.*)

LAURA: You wished to see me?

SNORKEY: Are you Miss Laura Courtland?

LAURA: Yes.

SNORKEY: Then I was told to give you this.

LAURA: By whom?

SNORKEY: Now, that's what I don't know myself! You see I was down by the steps of the Fifth Avenue Hotel, taking a light supper off a small toothpick, when a big chap dressed in black came by, and says he: "Hallo, come with me if you want to earn a quarter." That (*confidentially to all*) being my very frame of mind, I went up one street and down another, till we came here. "Just you take this up there," says he, "and ask for Miss Laura Courtland, and give it to her and no one else."

LAURA: It is some folly of our late visitors.

SNORKEY: I'm one of the Soldier Messengers, Miss. We take to it very well, considering we had so little running in Uncle Sam's service.

RAY: Stop a moment, my man. Were you not one of the Twenty-second's recruits?

SNORKEY: Yes, Captain; I remember you joined us in New York, and left us at Washington. Real fighting wasn't funny, you thought, and I began to think so too at Fredericksburg.

RAY: Poor devil.

SNORKEY: There was a South Carolina gentleman took such a fancy to me at Fredericksburg! Wouldn't have no denial, cut off my arm to remember me by; he was very fond of me. I wasn't any use to Uncle Sam then, so I came home, put a red band round my blue cap, and with my empty sleeve, as a character from my last place, set up for light porter and general messenger. All orders executed with neatness and dispatch.

PEARL: And Uncle Sam has forgotten you.

SNORKEY: Ah! Miss, don't blame Uncle Sam for that, he's got such a big family to look after, I can't find fault if he don't happen to remember all us poor stumps of fellows.

RAY: So it seems.

LAURA: (*Pearl takes bouquet.*) Poor fellow! (*To servant.*) Martin, be sure and give him a glass of wine before he goes.

SNORKEY: I'm much obliged, Miss—but I don't think it would be good for me on an empty stomach—after fasting all day.

LAURA: Well, Martin shall find you some supper, too.

SNORKEY: Is this Martin? What a nice young man. Mayn't he have a drop of something, too? He must have caught cold letting me in, he has got such a dreadful stiffness in the back of his neck. (*Martin exits.*)

RAY: (*Giving penciled address.*) Call on me at this place tomorrow and you shan't regret it.

SNORKEY: All right, Cap'n! I havn't forgot the Army Regulations about punctuality and promotion. Ladies, if ever either of you should want a Light Porter, think of Joe Snorkey—wages no objection. (*Exit.*)

PEARL: (*Who has been examining the bouquet.*) O! Laura, only look—here's a billet-doux!

RAY: Nonsense! Crazy head! Who would dare (*Takes bouquet*)—a letter! (*Takes a paper from bouquet.*)

LAURA: A letter?

PEARL: I am crazy—am I?

RAY: (*Reads superscription.*) "For Miss Laura Courtland. Confidential."

LAURA: (*Laughs.*) Ha! Ha! from some goose who has made one call too many today. Read it, Ray—(*Offering letter.*)

RAY: "Dear Laura . . ." (*Refusing the letter, and going to Pearl.*)

LAURA: (*Looks at it a moment, when the whole expression of face changes. Then reads slowly and deliberately.*) "I respectfully beg you to grant me the favor of an interview to-night. I have waited until your company retired. I am waiting across the street, now."

PEARL: (*Runs to window.*) A tall man in black is just walking away.

LAURA: "If you will have the door opened as soon as you get this I will step over; if you don't, I will ring; under all circumstances I will get in. There is no need to sign my name; you will remember me as the strange man whom you once saw talking with your mother in the parlor, and who frightened you so much." What can be the meaning of this?—Pearl—no—(*Goes to bell on table and rings.*)

RAY: Laura, you—

LAURA: Ask me nothing. I will tell you by and by. (*Enter Martin.*)

MARTIN: Miss—

LAURA: Admit no one till you bring me the name.

MARTIN: I was about to tell you, Miss, that a strange man has forced himself in at the door and asks to see you, but will give no name.

RAY: Kick the rascal out!

PEARL: Oh! don't let him come here.

MARTIN: He's a very strange-looking person, Miss.

RAY: I'll find out what this means! (*Is going to door when Byke appears at it smiling and bowing.*)

BYKE: I'll spare you the trouble, if you'll hear me a minute.

RAY: (*Violently.*) Who are you, fellow?

BYKE: Don't, I beg you. Don't speak so crossly; I might answer back—then you'd kick me out—and you'd never forgive yourself for it as long as I lived.

RAY: Your business? Come! Speak quickly and begone.

BYKE: Business! On this happy day! I came for pleasure—to see Miss Courtland, my little pupil—grown so—only think, sir! I knew her when she was only a little child. I taught her music—she was so musical—and so beautiful—I adored her, and her mother told me I needn't come again—But I did—and her mother was glad to see me. Wasn't she, little pupil?—(*To Laura, who is pale with terror, leaning on Pearl.*)—and begged me to stay—but I said no—I'd call occasionally—to see my dear little pupil, and to receive any trifling contribution her mother might give me. Won't you shake hands, little pupil? (*Advances suddenly, when Ray grasps him by the collar—Byke glares at him a moment. Then, quickly as before.*) Don't please, don't! The stuff is old, and I've no other.

RAY: The fellow's drunk! Leave the house.

BYKE: What! after sending that touching bouquet?

LAURA: It was you, then? I knew it.

BYKE: You see she knows me. Ah! mempry how it blooms again where the plough of time has passed.

LAURA: Leave this house at once.

BYKE: Not until I have spoken to you.

RAY: (*Seizing him.*) You miserable rascal.

BYKE: Don't, pray don't! I weigh a hundred and ninety-eight pounds, and if you attempt to throw me about you'll strain yourself.

LAURA: (*Crossing.*) Go. To-morrow in the morning I will see you.

BYKE: Thanks! I thank you, Miss, for your forebearance. (*To Ray.*) I am also obliged to you, sir, for not throwing me out at the window. I am indeed. I wish you good night, and many happy returns of the day. (*Bows and turns to go. Then familiarly to servant.*) Many calls to-day, John? (*Exit.*)

RAY: (*Runs to Laura, who is pale.*)

LAURA: (*Pointing after Byke.*) See that he goes. (*Exit Ray.*)

LAURA: (*Taking both of Pearl's hands in her own.*) Pearl, he must know every thing.

PEARL: O, dear! this is dreadful! I do hate scenes.

LAURA: He must know everything, I tell you; and you must relate all. He will ques tion—he will ponder—leave him nothing to ask.

PEARL: If you wish it, but—

LAURA: I desire it; speak of me as you will—but tell him the truth. (*Ray enters hastily.*) Stay with her. Don't follow me. (*Exit.*)

RAY: Pearl, what does this mean.

PEARL: O, it's only a little cloud that I want to clear up for you.

RAY: Cloud—how? where?

PEARL: Don't I tell you I am going to tell you. Sit down here by me. (*She sinks into tete-a-tete.*)

RAY: (*Promenading.*) He said he knew her. And she gave him an interview for to-morrow. That drunken wretch—

PEARL: Do sit down. I can never speak while you are walking about so. (*Gets up, brings him to a chair and makes him sit.*) Sit by me, won't you? For I've got something strange to tell you.

RAY: *You* serious! I'd as soon expect to see the lightning tamed. Well, I listen.

PEARL: I have something to say to you, Ray, which you must settle with your own heart. You love Laura, do you not?

RAY: Pearl, I do more, I adore her. I adore the very air that she breathes. I will never be happy without her. I can swear *that.*

PEARL: Laura is twenty now. How do you think she looked when I first saw her?

RAY: Were you at home when she first came into this earthly sphere?

PEARL: Yes.

RAY: Well then, I suppose she looked very small and very pink.

PEARL: She was covered with rags, barefooted, unkempt, crying and six years old.

RAY: (*Shocked.*) Explain.

PEARL: One night father and mother were going to the Opera. When they were crossing Broadway, the usual crowd of children accosted them for alms. As mother felt in her pocket for some change, her fingers touched a cold and trembling hand which had clutched her purse.

RAY: A pickpocket! Well.

PEARL: This hand my mother grasped in her own, and so tightly that a small, feeble voice uttered an exclamation of pain. Mother looked down, and there beside her was a little ragged girl.

RAY: The thief.

PEARL: Yes, but a thief hardly six years old, with a face like an angel's. "Stop!" said my mother. "What are you doing?" "Trying to steal," said the child. "Don't you know that it's wicked to do so?" asked my father. "No," said the girl, "but it's dreadful to be hungry." "Who told you to steal?" asked my mother. "She—there!" said the child, pointing to a squalid woman in a doorway oppo- site, who fled suddenly down the street. "That is Old Judas," said the girl.

RAY: Old Judas. What a name! But how does this story interest us?

PEARL: That child was Laura. My father was about to let her go unharmed—but my mother said, "No, it is not enough. We have a duty to perform, even to her," and acting on a sudden impulse, took her to our home. On being questioned there, the child seemed to have no recollection, save of misery and blows. My mother persuaded father, and the girl was sent to a country clergyman's for instruction, and there she remained for several years.

RAY: Pearl, you are joking with me.

PEARL: In beauty, and accomplishments, and dignity, Laura (as mother named her) exceeded every girl of her age. In gratitude she was all that father could have wished. She was introduced as you know, into society as my cousin, and no one dreams of her origin.

RAY: (*Starting up.*) Laura, an outcast—a thief!

PEARL: (*Rising.*) No, that is what she might have been.

RAY: And this man—to-night?

PEARL: All I know about him is, that four years ago this man came with a cruel looking woman, to see mother. There was a fearful scene between them, for Laura and I sat trembling on the stairs, and overheard some awful words. At last they went away, the man putting money into his pocket as he left.

RAY: But who were they?

PEARL: Laura never told me, and mother would not. But, of course, they must have been Laura's father and mother. (*Ray sinks on chair as if overcome.*)

PEARL: Mother made me promise never to tell anybody this, and you would have known nothing had not Laura made me speak. You see, she would not conceal anything from you. (*Going to him.*) Ray, why don't you speak—shall I go after Laura? Shall I tell her to come to you? Why don't you answer? (*Going.*) I'll go and tell her you want to see her. (*Pausing as she goes.*) I'm going to send her to you, Ray. (*Goes off still looking back at him.*)

RAY: (*Starting up.*) What a frightful story. Laura Courtland a thief! A drunken wretch who knows her history, and a squalid beggar woman who can claim her at any moment as their child. And I was about to marry her. Yes, and I love her. But what would my mother think? My friends? Society? No—no—no—I cannot think of it. I will write her—I will tell her—pshaw! she knows of course that I cannot wed her now. (*Goes to table.*) Here is paper. (*Sits.*) What am I about to do? What will be said of me? But I owe a duty to myself—to society—I must perform it. (*Writes.*) "Laura, I have heard all from your sister." What have I said—(*Crosses out last word*)—"from Pearl. You know that I love you, but my mother will demand of me a wife who will not blush to own her kindred, and who is not the daughter of obscurity and crime." It is just; it is I who have been deceived. (*Folds letter and addresses it.*) I will leave it for her. (*Puts on light overcoat, which hangs on chair at back.*) I must go before she returns. Her step—too late! (*Crams the letter into pocket of overcoat. Laura enters.*)

LAURA: (*Gently.*) Ray.

RAY: Miss—Miss Courtland. (*Laura looks at him a moment, smiles and then crosses without further noticing him, and sits down on tete-a-tete.*) What have I said? What ought I to have said? (*He takes a step towards her—she rises, without looking at him goes to window—looks out, then looks over books on table.*)

RAY: Laura—I—

LAURA: Pshaw, where is my book?

RAY: What book do you want, Laura?

LAURA: Sir.

RAY: (*Repulsed.*) Oh!—(*Pause*)—I've been a fool. How lovely she looks. (*He follows her mechanically to table.*) Can I find it for you? (Laura *picks up a book and reseats herself.*)

LAURA: Don't trouble yourself I beg.

RAY: (*Coming forward and leaning over her seat.*) Laura.

LAURA: (*Without lifting her head.*) Well.

RAY: (*Toying with her hair.*) Look at me.

LAURA: (*Turns round and looks full at him.*)

RAY: No, no, not that way; as you used to. You act as if I were a stranger.

LAURA: They are only strangers who call me Miss Courtland. (*Resumes reading.*)

RAY: Forgive me, I beg you to forgive me. (*Coming round and sitting beside her.*) I was mad — it was so sudden — this miserable story—but I don't care what they say. O! do listen to me. I thought you hated reading.

LAURA: I often wish that I were ugly, wretched and repulsive, like the heroine in this story. (*Seats herself.*)

RAY: (*Behind her.*) Why?

LAURA: Because, then I could tell who really loved me.

RAY: And don't you know?

LAURA: No; I do not.

RAY: Well, I know.

LAURA: Do tell me then, please.

RAY: He has told you so himself a hundred times.

LAURA: You.

RAY: I.

LAURA: (*Laughing heartily at him, then seriously.*) How happy must those women be, who are poor, and friendless, and plain, when some true heart comes and says: I wish to marry you.

RAY: Laura, you act very strangely to-night.

LAURA: Will you put this book away?

RAY: (*Throws it on table.*) There Laura. (*Seats himself beside her.*)

LAURA: (*Rising.*) There's Pearl calling me.

RAY: (*Rising and taking her hand.*) Laura, why don't you let me speak to you.

LAURA: About what?

RAY: About my love.

LAURA: For whom? Not me. This is only marriage and giving in marriage. I hate the very word.

RAY: You did not think so once.

LAURA: I wish I had. I am frightened now; I begin to understand myself better.

RAY: And I am frightened because I understand you less.

LAURA: Do not try to; good night. (*Stops by door as she is going out.*) Good night Mr. Trafford. (*Exit laughing.*)

RAY: I've been an ass. No, I wrong that noble animal. The ass recognized the angel, and I, like Balaam, was blind. But I see now. After all what have I to fear? (*Takes letter from pocket.*) No one knows of this, (*puts it in his pocket again.*) Let things go on, we'll be married, go straight to Europe, and live there ten years. That's the way we'll fix it. (*Exit. Scene closes in.*)

SCENE II

1st Grooves—The Gentlemen's coat-room at Delmonico's—opening for hat and coat. Chairs. Pier-glass on flat.

(*Enter Windel and Demilt muffled, and with umbrellas. They proceed to disrobe*

DEMILT: Phew! wet as the deuce, and cold, too. There'll be nobody here.
WINDEL: It's an awful night. The rooms are almost empty.
DEMILT: Sam! Where the dickens is that darkey? (*Enter Sam fetching in a chair, and boot-black, box and brush.*)
SAM: Here, sah.
DEMILT: (*Sitting in a chair.*) Hurry up with my boots. Who's here?
SAM: Berry few gemman, sah; only lebben overcoats and ten overshoes. Bless de Lord—dem overshoes is spilin the polishin business.
DEMILT: Look out and don't give me any knocks.
WINDEL: (*Handing in his coat at window and getting check for it.*) I wonder if the Courtland girls have come yet.
DEMILT: What did Laura Courtland ever see in Trafford to fall in love with? The Van Dam party is my fancy.
WINDEL: (*Brushing his hair at glass.*) She's ten years older than you, and has a husband.
DEMILT: Yes, a fine old banker, on whom she can draw for everything but attention and affection. She has to get that by her own business tact.

(*Other parties enter, exchange good-nights, and deposit their coats; some go out at once, some arrange themselves at glass.*)

DEMILT: That'll do, Sam, take my coat. (*Enter Ray.*)
WINDEL: Hallo! Trafford, this is a night, ain't it? Have the Courtlands come?
RAY: Not with me. Here, Sam, take my coat. (*His coat is pulled off by Sam, and four letters drop out.*) Stupid!
DEMILT: Save the pieces. Mind the love letters.
RAY: (*Picking them up.*) Look out well next time. There's that cursed letter I was going to send to Laura. Confound it, I must destroy it when I go home. (*Puts letters back in overcoat pocket. Ray gets his boots touched up.*)
DEMILT: I say, Trafford, what'll you take, and let a fellow read those? Windel, I guess if the girls could get into the cloak room, it would be better than the dead-letter office. What a time they'd have! Are you ready?
WINDEL: What's the use of hurrying? There's no life in the party till Laura Court land comes. By Jove, Trafford! you're in luck. She's the prettiest girl in New York.
RAY: And the best. (*March music is heard.*)
DEMILT: There's the march music; let's go. (*Gets a final brush as they all go off.*)
RAY: Come along. (*Exeunt.*)
SAM: (*Picking up a letter dropped from Ray's pocket.*) Dere's anoder of dem billy dooses; wonder if it am Mist' Trafford's. Eh, golly! musn't mix dem gentlemen's letters,—musn't mix 'em nohow,—or an oberruling providence wouldn't be able to stop fighting in dis city for de nex month. (*Exit, carrying a chair.*)

(*Scene draws off to dance music. Wait till change of music before change of Scene.*)

SCENE III

The Blue Room at Delmonico's. Waltz-music as the Scene opens. Waltzers in motion. Pearl is dancing with Mrs. Van Dam.

(Enter Trafford, Demilt, and Windel.)

PEARL: There's Ray. I've had enough; I want to speak with him. *(Bursts away from Mrs. Van Dam, runs up to Trafford. Demilt goes up to Mrs. Van Dam.)*
PEARL: *(To Ray.)* You lazy fellow, where have you been?
DEMILT: You're not tired, are you?
MRS. VAN DAM: I feel as fresh as a daisy.
DEMILT: Have a waltz with me. *(Waltz music, piano, as they dance. Windel goes to Sue Earlie.)*
RAY: *(Coming down with Pearl.)* Where's Laura?
PEARL: She wasn't ready, and I was dying to come. Been fixed since eight o'clock; so I came with Sue Earlie. So you made it up with Laura.
RAY: Yes. Don't say anything more about the horrid subject. We've made it all up. But what on earth keeps her to-night? It's eleven already. *(Looking at watch.)* Confound it, I tremble every moment she's out of my sight. I fear that terrible man and his secret.
MRS. VAN DAM: *(Coming up with Demilt.)* Trafford, you look very uneasy. What's the matter?
RAY: O, nothing. I think I ought to go for Laura. I will, too. *(Servant passes at back.)* Here! go up stairs for my overcoat. *(Gives the man a card, and he goes out.)*
MRS. VAN DAM: Nonsense! She'll be here in good time. You shan't leave us. Hold him, Pearl. We want a nine-pin quadrille, we haven't half enough gentlemen. Come, be jolly about it. You lovers are always afraid some one will carry your girls away.
RAY: *(Uneasy.)* I? I'm not afraid.
PEARL: Come, come! I never saw such a restless fellow.
(Servant enters with coat.)
SERVANT: Here's your coat, sir.
MRS. VAN DAM: Give it to me. I'm determined you shan't go. *(Takes coat carelessly.)* I'll make you a promise—if Laura isn't here in fifteen minutes you shall have your coat, and may go for her.
RAY: Well, I suppose I'll have to wait.
MRS. VAN DAM: There; take him off, Pearl. *(Ray goes up with Pearl. To Servant.)* Here take this back. *(Flings coat to Servant. As she does so, letters drop from it.)* Well, there's a mess. *(Sue Earlie and another lady run forward and pick up the letters.)* Love letters, of course!—*(Smelling them.)* Perfumed to suffocation.
SUE EARLIE: Here's one for Laura. It's unsealed and not delivered.
MRS. VAN DAM: *(Tremolo waltz music.)* A fair prize! Let's see it. *(Music. Takes and opens it. Puts on eye-glasses and reads.)* "Laura"—Well, come! That's cool for a lover. "I have heard all from"—something scratched out—ah!—"Your sister, Pearl—Your obscure origin—terrible family connexions—the secret of the tie which binds you to a drunken wretch—My mother, Society—will demand of me a wife who will not blush to own her kindred,—or start at the name

of outcast and thief! Signed, Ray Trafford."

(*All stand speechless and look at each other. All this time the rest have been dancing.*)

SUE EARLIE: What can it mean?

MRS. VAN DAM: It means that the rumors of ten years ago are proven. It was then suspected that the girl whom Mrs. Courtland brought every year from some unnamed place in the country, and introduced to everybody as her niece, was an impostor, which that foolish woman, in a freak of generosity, was thrusting upon society. The rumors died out for want of proof—and before Laura's beauty and dignity—but now they are confirmed. She is some beggar's child.

SUE EARLIE: What do you think we ought to do? (*Trafford surrenders Pearl to Demilt and comes down.*)

MRS. VAN DAM: Tell it—tell it everywhere, of course. The best blood of New York is insulted by the girl's presence. (*Trafford coming down.*)

RAY: What have you three girls got your heads together for? Some conspiracy, I know.

MRS. VAN DAM: (*To ladies.*) Go girls—tell it everywhere.

RAY: (*As the ladies distribute themselves about the groups.*) What is it all about? Your face is a portrait of mystery.

MRS. VAN DAM: (*Showing letter.*) Look at this, and tell me what it means.

RAY: (*Quickly.*) Where did you get this?

MRS. VAN DAM: It is you who must answer—and Society that will question. So Laura is not a Courtland?

RAY: (*Overcome.*) You know, then,—

MRS. VAN DAM: Everything; and will you marry this creature! You cannot. Society will not permit your sacrifice.

RAY: This is not your business. Give me that letter.

MRS. VAN DAM: Certainly; take it. But let me say one word—its contents are known. In an hour every tongue will question you about this secret,—every eye will inquire.

RAY: I implore you! Do not breathe a word for her sake. (*She turns scornfully away.*)

MRS. VAN DAM: The secret's not mine.

RAY: Who knows it?

MRS. VAN DAM: Look! (*Points to others who are grouped about whispering and motioning towards Ray. Pearl enters here and speaks to lady and gents.*)

RAY: (*Wildly.*) What will they do?

MRS. VAN DAM: Expose her! Expel her from society in which she is an intruder!

RAY: You dare not. (*Pearl comes forward.*)

PEARL: O, Ray! What is the meaning of this?

RAY: (*Bitterly.*) It means that society is a terrible avenger of insult. Have you ever heard of the Siberian wolves? When one of the pack falls through weakness, the others devour him. It is not an elegant comparison—but there is something wolfish in society. Laura has mocked it with a pretence, and society, which is made up of pretenses, will bitterly resent the mockery.

MRS. VAN DAM: Very good! This handsome thief has stolen your breeding as well as your brains, I see.

RAY: If you speak a word against her, I will say that what you utter is a lie!

MRS. VAN DAM: As you please, we will be silent. But you will find that the world speaks most forcibly when it utters no sound.

PEARL: O, go and prevent her coming here.

RAY: That I can do. (*Going up hastily sees Laura entering.*) Too late. (*He retreats.*)

MRS. VAN DAM: Come girls! Let us look after our things. They are no longer safe when such an accomplished thief enters.

(*Music low as Laura enters, continues while all except Pearl and Ray pass out, eyeing her superciliously.*)

PEARL: Ray, Ray, why do you not come to her?

MRS. VAN DAM: (*Surrounded by others.*) Are you not coming with us Trafford?

PEARL: (*To Laura.*) Let us go home.

LAURA: No; stay with *him*. (*Pointing to Ray, who has held off.*) He shall not suffer the disgrace long! (*About to faint, Ray runs forward—she proudly waves him away.*) It is Heaven's own blow!

Picture—Quick Curtain

END OF ACT I

ACT II

SCENE I

Interior of a basement. Street and railings seen through window at back. Stove with long pipe in fire-place. Table between two windows at back, with flowers, etc. Humble furniture. Table and three chairs. Closet (2nd Grooves). Peach-blossom is discovered polishing stove, a slip-shod girl a la Fanchon.

SONG—PEACHBLOSSOM:

A lordly knight and a lovely dame, were walking in the meadow,
But a jealous rival creeping came a-watching in the shadow;
They heeded not, but he whet his knife and dogg'd them in the shadow.
The knight was brave, and the dame was true, the rival fared but badly;
For the knight he drew and ran him through, and left him groaning sadly,
The knight and dame soon wedded were, with bells a-chiming gladly.

PEACHBLOSSOM: (*Talking while working.*) The stove won't shine. It's the fault of the polish I know. That boy that comes here, just fills the bottles with mud, and calls it stove polish. Only let me catch him. Ah! Ah! (*threatening gesture with brush.*) I declare I'd give it up if I didn't want to make everything look smart, before Miss Nina comes in. Miss Nina is the only friend I ever had, since I ran away from Mother Judas. I wonder where old Judas is now? I know she's drunk; she always was; perhaps that's why she never tried to find out what became of me. If she did she could not take me away. Miss Nina begged me off a policeman. I belong to her. I wonder why she ain't got any other friends? She's awful mysterious. Tells me never to let any strangers see her. She's afraid of somebody, I know. It looks just as if she was hiding. I thought only bad girls, such as I, had to hide. If I was good and pretty like her, I wouldn't hide from the President. (*Still polishing. Judas appears at window with basket of ornaments.*)
JUDAS: Hum! Is your ma in my dear?
PEACHBLOSSOM: (*Starting.*) Oh! (*Aside.*) Old Judas! She's found me out at last. No she h'aint, or she'd have got me by the hair before she spoke. That's *her* way.
JUDAS: (*Coming in at door. Peachblossom keeps her back towards her.*) Any old clothes to change for chany, my dear? Where's your ma's old skirts and shawls, my pet. Get 'em quick before mother comes in, and I'll give you a

beautiful chany mug or a tea-pot for them. Come here, my ducky—see the pretty—(*recognizes Peachblossom.*) Eh! why you jail-bird what are you doing here? Are you sneakin' it? Answer me, or I'll knock your head agin the wall. (*Catches her by the hair.*)

PEACHBLOSSOM: You just leave me be.. I'm honest I am! I'm good.

JUDAS: You're good? Where's my shoe? I'll take the goodness out of you.

PEACHBLOSSOM: Oh, oh! please don't beat me. I ain't good. I'm only trying to be.

JUDAS: You're only trying to be, eh? Trying to be good, and here's me as was a-weeping every night, thinking as you was sent up for six months. Who're you living with—you ain't a-keeping house, are you?

PEACHBLOSSOM: I'm living with Miss Nina.

JUDAS: Nina, what's she, concert-saloon girl?

PEACHBLOSSOM: No, she's a lady.

JUDAS: A lady—and have such baggage as you about. Where's my shoe, I'll make you speak the truth.

PEACHBLOSSOM: I don't know what she is. She met me when the police was taking me up for loafin' down Hudson Street, and she begged me off.

JUDAS: Has she any money?   .

PEACHBLOSSOM: No, she's poor.

JUDAS: Any nice clothes?

PEACHBLOSSOM: O, she's got good clothes.

JUDAS: Where are they?

PEACHBLOSSOM: Locked up, and she's got the key.

JUDAS: You're lying, I see it in your eye. You're always shamefaced when you are telling the truth, and now you're as bold as brass. Where's my shoe? (*Making a dash at her.*)

PEACHBLOSSOM: (*Shouting.*) There's Miss Nina (*As if curtseying to some one behind Judas.*) Good morning, miss.

JUDAS: (*Changing her tone.*) Ah! my pretty dear! What a good lady to take you in and give you a home. (*Turns and discovers the deception—in a rage.*) You hussy, (*Peachblossom retreats.*) wait till I get you in my clutches again, my lady; and it won't be long. Miss Nina takes care of you, does she. Who will take care of her? Let her look to it. (*Laura enters plainly dressed, at back.*) Beg pardon, Miss, I just called to see if you had any old clothes you'd like to exchange.

LAURA: No, I don't want anything, my good woman.

JUDAS: (*Eyeing her sharply and going to door.*) That's her—I'd know her anywheres! (*Malicious glance, and exit.*)

LAURA: You've been very good this morning, Blossom. The room is as nice as I could wish.

PEACHBLOSSOM: Please 'm, I tried because you are so good to me (*Laura taking off her shawl and things.*) Shall I sweep out the airy? (*Laura does not answer.*) I guess I'd better—then she'll be alone, as she loves to be. (*Takes broom and exit.*)

LAURA: (*Solus. Opening a package and taking out photographs.*) No pay yet for coloring, 'till I have practiced a week longer. Then I shall have all the work I can do. They say at the photographer's I color well, and the best pictures will be given me. The best! Already I have had beneath my brush so many faces that I know, friends of the old days. The silent eyes seem to wonder at me for bringing them to this strange and lowly home. (*Picking up letters from table.*) Letters; ah! answers to my advertisement for employment. No, only a circular "To the lady of this house." What's that! (*Starting.*) only Blossom sweeping. Every time there is a noise I dread the entrance of some one that knows me. But they could never find me in New York, I left them all too secretly and suddenly. None of them can expect I would have descended to this. But it is natural, everything will find its level. I sprang from poverty, and I return to it. Poor Pearl. How she must have wondered the next morning—Laura gone? But three months have passed, and they have forgotten me. Ray will cheer her. (*Wrangling outside, Peachblosssom bursts in dragging Bermudas, with his professional tape, pins, blacking and baskets.*)

PEACHBLOSSOM: Here he is m'm.

BERMUDAS: Leave go, I tell yer, or I'll make yer.

LAURA: What is the matter?

PEACHBLOSSOM: He's the boy that sold me that stove polish what isn't stove polish.

BERMUDAS: What is it then—s-a-a-y?

PEACHBLOSSOM: It's mud! it's mud at ten pence a bottle.

BERMUDAS: Ah! Where could I get mud? Ain't the streets clean? Mud's dearer than stove polish now.

PEACHBLOSSOM: And your matches is wet, and your pins won't stick, and your shoe-strings is rotten, there now!

BERMUDAS: Well, how am I to live; it ain't my fault, it's the taxes. Ain't I got to pay my income tax, and how am I to pay it if I gives you your money's worth? Do you think I'm Stewart—Sa-a-y?

LAURA: Do let the boy alone, Blossom. Send him away. (*Enter Peanuts at door flat.*)

PEANUTS: Extra! Hollo, Bermudas! how's your sister? Papers, Miss. Extra! Revolution in Mexico!

LAURA: Dear, dear, this is the way I'm worried from morning till night.

BERMUDAS: Here, just you get out! This is my beat.

PEANUTS: Vell, I ain't blacking or hairpins now, I'm papers—How'm I hurting you?

BERMUDAS: Vell, I'm papers at four o'clock, and this is my beat. Take care of me, I'm in training for a fight. I'm a bruiser, I am.

PEANUTS: Hold yer jaw. (*They fight.*)

PEACHBLOSSOM: (*Beats them with broom.*) Get out with you. Both of you (*Grand escapade and exit of boys.*)

LAURA: Don't let's be troubled in this way again. Have you got the things for dinner?

PEACHBLOSSOM: Lor, no, miss! It's twelve o'clock and I forgot! (*Peachblossom gets shawl, bit bonnet from hooks on the wall, basket from closet, while Laura opens her pocket-book for money.*)

LAURA: What did we have for dinner yesterday, Blossom?

PEACHBLOSSOM: Beefsteak, 'm. Let's have some leg o'mutton to-day. We've never had that.

LAURA: But I don't know how to cook it. Do you?

PEACHBLOSSOM: No, but I'd just slap it on, and it's sure to come out right.

LAURA: Slap it on what?

PEACHBLOSSOM: The gridiron.

LAURA: (*Giving money.*) No, we'd better not try a leg of mutton to-day. Get some lamp chops, we know how to manage them.

PEACHBLOSSOM: (*As she is going.*) Taters, as usual, 'mum?

LAURA: Yes; and stop Blossom—while you're buying the chops, just ask the butcher—off hand—you know—how he would cook a leg of mutton, if he were going to eat it himself—as if you wanted to know for yourself.

PEACHBLOSSOM: Yes'm—but I'm sure it's just as good broiled as fried. (*Exit.*)

LAURA: Now to be cook. (*Laughing.*) "The Tuesday Sociable" ought to see me now. Artist in the morning, cook at noon, artist in the afternoon. (*Snorkey raps at the door and enters.*)

SNORKEY: (*With letter.*) Beg pardon, is there anybody here as answers to the name of A. B. C.?

LAURA: (*Aside.*) My advertisement for work.—Yes, give it to me.

SNORKEY: (*Seeing her face.*) If I'd been taking something this morning, I'd say that I'd seen that face in a different sort of place from this.

LAURA: Is there anything to pay? Why do you wait?

SNORKEY: Nothing, Miss. It's all right. (*Going—and aside.*) But it ain't all right, Snorkey, old boy! (*Goes out after looking at her, stops at window, and gazes in.*)

LAURA: (*Without noticing him, opening letter.*) Yes, an answer to my advertisement. (*Reads.*) To A. B. C.: "Your advertisement promises that you are a good linguist, and can teach children of any age. I have two daughters for whom I wish to engage your services while on a tour of Europe. Call at seven o'clock, this evening, at No. 207 W. 34th Street. Annersley." Hope at last—a home, and in another land soon. I was sure the clouds would not always be black above me! (*Kisses letter. Snorkey re-entering.*)

SNORKEY: Miss, I say, Miss. (*Laura starts.*)—Sh—

LAURA: What do you want?

SNORKEY: Only one word—and perhaps it may be of service to you. I'd do any thing to serve you.

LAURA: And why me?

SNORKEY: I'm a blunt fellow, Miss, but I hope my way don't offend. Ain't you the lady that I brought a bouquet to on New Year's night—not here, but in a big house, all bright and rich—and who was so kind to a poor soldier?

LAURA: (*Faint and leaning against chair.*) Whoever you may be, promise to tell no one you saw me here.

SNORKEY: No fear, Miss! I promise.

LAURA: Sacredly!

SNORKEY: No need to do more than promise, Miss—I keeps my word. I promised Uncle Sam I'd stick to the flag—though they tore my arm off, and by darnation I stuck. I don't want to tell on you Miss. I want to tell on some one else.

LAURA: What do you mean?

SNORKEY: They're looking for you.

LAURA: Who?

SNORKEY: Byke. (*Laura utters a loud cry and sinks on chair.*) He's on it day and night. I've got his money in my pocket now, and you've got his letter in your hand this minute. (*Laura drops the letter in dismay.*)

LAURA: This?

SNORKEY: Yes, it's his writin'—looks like a woman's, don't it? Lord! the snuff that man's up to, would make Barnum sneeze his head off. He's kept me in hand, 'cause he thinks I know you, having seen you that once. Every day he reads the advertisements, and picks out a dozen or so and says to me: "Snorkey, that's like my little pet" and then he sits down and answers them and gets the advertisers to make appointments with him, which he keeps regularly, and regularly comes back cussing at his ill luck. See here Miss, I've a bundle of answers to deliver, as usual, to advertisers. I calls 'em Byke's Target Practice, and this time, you see, he's accidentally hit the mark.

LAURA: For Heaven's sake do not betray me to him! I've got very little money, I earn it hardly; but take it, take it—and save me. (*Offers money.*)

SNORKEY: No, Miss; not a cent of it. Though Byke is a devil and would kick me hard if he thought I would betray him.

LAURA: I don't want you to suffer for my sake, take the money.

SNORKEY: No, I stood up to be shot at for thirteen dollars a month, and I can take my chances of a kickin' for nothing. But Byke ain't the only one Miss, there's another's looking for you.

LAURA: (*Her look of joy changing to fear.*) Another! Who?

SNORKEY: (*Approaching smilingly and confidential.*) Mr. Trafford. (*Laura turns aside despairingly.*) He's been at me every day for more than six weeks. "Snorkey" says he, "do you remember that beautiful young lady you brought the bouquet to on New Year's night?" "Well," says I, "Capt'n, the young lady I slightly disremember, but the cakes and wine I got there that night I shall never forget." "Search for that young lady,"says he, "and when you find her"—

LAURA: No, no, no; not even he must know. Do you hear—not he—not anyone. You have served them well; serve me and be silent.

SNORKEY: Just as you please, Miss, but I hate to serve you by putting your friends off the track—it don't seem natural—Byke I don't mind; but the Capt'n wouldn't do you any harm. Just let me give him a bit of a hint. (*Laura makes an entreating gesture.*) Well I'm mum, but as I've only got one hand, it's hard work to hold my tongue. (*Going.*) Not the least bit of a hint? (*Laura appealingly and then turns away.*) They say when a woman says no, she means yes! I wonder if I dare tell her that he's not far off. Perhaps I'd better not. But I can tell him. (*Exit.*)

LAURA: How shall I ever escape that dreadful man? And Ray searching for me too! Our friends then remember us as well as our enemies. (*Peachblossom enters quickly shutting the door behind her, with basket which she places on table.*)

PEACHBLOSSOM: Miss Nina, whatever is into the people? There's a strange man coming down the entry. I heard him asking that red cap fellow about you.

LAURA: Byke! Fasten the door quick. (*Peachblossom runs to door, it is slightly opened, she pushes it against some one on the other side.*)

PEACHBLOSSOM: O dear! He is powerful strong, I can't keep it shut. Go away, you willin! (*The door is forced and Ray enters.*)

RAY: (*Advancing.*) Laura—It is I.

LAURA: Ray! (*Shrinks from him.*)

RAY: Dear Laura! (*He stops as he becomes conscious that Blossom with her basket on her arm and her bonnet hanging on her back is staring at him.*) I say, my girl, havn't you some particular business somewhere else to attend to?

PEACHBLOSSOM: (*Seriously.*) No, sir; I've swept the sidewalk and gone a marketing, and now I'm indoors and I mean to stay.

RAY: And wouldn't you oblige me by going for a sheet of paper and an envelope? Here's a dollar—try and see how slow you can be.

PEACHBLOSSOM: (*Firmly.*) You can't sheet of paper me, mister, I'm protecting Miss Nina, and I'm not going to be enveloped.

LAURA: Go as the gentleman asks you, Blossom.

PEACHBLOSSOM: Oh! (*Takes money, fixes her bonnet.*) First it's "Keep the man

out," now it's "Let him stay in alone with me." But I suppose she's like all of us
—it makes a great difference which man it is. (*Exit.*)

RAY: (*After watching Peachblossom out.*) Laura, when I approached you, you
shrank from me. Why did you so?

LAURA: Look around you and find your answer.

RAY: (*Shuddering.*) Pardon me, I did not come here to insult your misery. When
I saw you I forgot everything else.

LAURA: And now it's time for us to remember everything. I told you to look around
that you might understand that in such a place I am no longer Laura Courtland,
nor anything I used to be. But I did not ask your pity. There is no misery here.

RAY: Alone, without means, exposed to every rudeness, unprotected, is this not
misery for you?

LAURA: (*Laughing.*) Oh, it's not so bad as that.

RAY: Laura, don't trifle with me. You cannot have exchanged everything that
made you happy, for this squalid poverty, and not feel it deeply.

LAURA: I have not time to feel anything deeply. (*Takes basket up, goes to table,
busies herself about preparing dinner.*) I work from sunrise till night, and I sleep
so soundly that I have not even dreams to recall the past. Just as you came in I
was about to cook our dinner. Only think—lamp chops!

RAY: Lamb chops! It makes me shudder to hear you speak.

LAURA: Does it? Then wait till I get the gridiron on the fire, and you'll shiver. And
if you want to be transfixed with horror, stop and take dinner.

RAY: I will not hear you mock yourself thus, Laura. I tell you in this self-banish-
ment you have acted thoughtlessly—you have done wrong.

LAURA: Why?

RAY: Because, let the miserable creatures who slandered you say what they might,
you had still a home and friends.

LAURA: A home! Where the very servants would whisper and point. Friends who
would be ashamed to acknowledge me. You are mistaken. That is neither home
nor friendship.

RAY: And you are resolved to surrender the past forever.

LAURA: The past has forgotten me in spite of myself.

RAY: Look at me.

LAURA: (*Coming down.*) Well then, there's one who has not forgotten me, but I
desire that he may. You speak to me of bitterness. Your presence, your words,
cause me the first pang I have felt since the night I fled unnoticed from my
chamber, and began my life anew. Therefore I entreat you to leave me, to forget me.

RAY: Laura, by the tie that once bound us—

LAURA: (*Going up.*) Yes, *once*. It *is* a long time ago.

RAY: What have I said?—the tie which still—

LAURA: (*Sharply turning.*) Mr. Trafford must I remind you of that night, when all
arrayed themselves so pitilessly against me? When a gesture from you might
have saved me! And you saw me sink without stretching a finger to the woman
who had felt the beating of your heart. No, you made your choice then—the
world without me. I make my choice now—the wide, wide, world without you.

RAY: I have been bitterly punished, for we are never so humiliated as when we
despise ourselves. But, by the Heaven above us both I love you Laura, I have
never ceased to love you.

LAURA: I thank you. I know how to construe the love which you deny in the face of society, to offer me behind its back.

RAY: Will you drive me mad! I tell you Laura, your misery, your solicitude is as nothing to the anguish I have suffered. The maniac who in his mental darkness, stabs to the heart the friend he loved, never felt in returning reason the remorse my error has earned me. Every day it says to me: "You have been false to the heart that loved you, and you shall account for it to your conscience all your life. You shall find that the bitterest drops in the cup of sorrow, are the tears of the woman you have forsaken." And it is true. O, forgive me—have pity on me.

LAURA: (*Moved.*) I forgive you. Yes, and I pity you—and, so good-bye, forever.

RAY: Of course, I am nothing to you now. That is some comfort to me. I have only to be sorry on my account. But, I come to you on behalf of others.

LAURA: Whom?

RAY: My mother and Pearl. They ask for you. For them I have sought you, to urge you to return to them.

LAURA: Dear little Pearl.

RAY: Yes, she has been quite ill.

LAURA: She has been ill?

RAY: Think of those two hearts which you have caused to suffer and do not drive me from you. It is not only wealth, luxury and refinement which you have surrendered—you have also cast away those greater riches: loving and devoted friends. But they shall persuade you themselves. Yes, I'll go and bring them to you, you cannot resist their entreaties.

LAURA: No, no, they must not come here. They must never know where I hide my shame, and you must never reveal it.

RAY: I promise it, if you will go to them with me. Think, they will insist on coming unless you do.

LAURA: Poor Pearl! If I go with you, you promise not to detain me—to permit me to come back, and to trouble me and my poor life no more?

RAY: I promise; but I know you will release me from it when you see them. I will get a carriage. So that no one will meet you. Wait for me, I shall not be long. Is it agreed?

LAURA: (*Smiling.*) Yes, it is agreed.

(*Enter Peachblossom, with a sheet of paper, foolscap, and some enormous envelopes.*)

PEACHBLOSSOM: Here they are

RAY: That's a good girl, keep them till I come back. In half an hour. Laura be ready. (*Exit.*)

PEACHBLOSSOM: (*With an air.*) What's he going to do in half an hour?

LAURA: He's going to take me away with him for a little while Blossom, and while I'm gone, I wish you to be a good girl, and watch the house, and take care of it till I return.

PEACHBLOSSOM: I don't believe it. You won't return. (*Crying.*) That's what our Sal said when she went off with her young man, and she never came back at all. You shan't go; I hate him. He shan't take you away.

LAURA: Blossom! (*Who is getting ready, putting her hat on, etc.*)

PEACHBLOSSOM: I don't care. If you go away, I'll go away; I'd bit and scratch him if he comes back. (*Fiercely tearing up the paper and envelopes.*) Let him come back. Let him dare come back.

LAURA: Blossom, you're very wicked. Go into the corner this minute and put you apron over your head.

PEACHBLOSSOM: (*Crying at Laura's feet.*) O, please, Miss Nina, let me go with you. Let me ask him to let me go with you. (*Figure passes the window.*) Here he is, I see him coming.

LAURA: Run! run! open the door. (*Peachblossom runs to door; throws it open, disclosing Byke. Exclamation of horror from Laura.*)

BYKE: (*Advancing.*) Ah, my dear little runaway! Found you at last,—and just going out. How lucky! I wanted you to take a walk with me.

LAURA: Instantly leave this place!

BYKE: How singular! you are always ordering me out and I am always coming in. We want a change. I will go out and I request you to come with me.

LAURA: Blossom, go find an officer. Tell him this wretch is insulting me.

BYKE: Blossom? ah,—exactly! Here you, Judas! (*Judas appears at door. Peachblossom crosses to Laura.*)

JUDAS: O, Miss, save me!

BYKE: (*Throws Peachblossom over to Judas.*) Take care of that brat. And as for you, daughter—come with me.

LAURA: Daughter!

BYKE: Yes; it is time to declare myself. Paternal feeling has been long smothered in my breast. Come to my arms, my child, my long-estranged child! (*Takes out dirty handkerchief and presses his eyes with pretended feeling.*)

LAURA: God! is there no help coming? (*She attempts to escape. Byke seizes her.*)

BYKE: What, unfilial girl! You take advantage of a father's weakness, and try to bolt! (*Clutching her by the arm.*) Come, go with me; and cheer my old age. Aint I good, to take you back after all these years?

Picture—Quick Curtain

END OF ACT II

ACT III

SCENE I

The Tombs Police Court. Long high desk with three seats, across back from right to left on platform. Railing in front. Railing around with open center. In front of railing, a bench. Gate in center of railing. Judge Bowling and another Justice seated behind high desk with clerk. Justice is reading paper, with his feet upon desk. Policeman 9-9-9 at right and left. Policeman at gate. Hard-looking set of men and women on benches. Lawyer Splinter is talking to Rafferdi, an organ-man, who is in crowd. As the curtain rises noisy buzz is heard.

BOWLING: Smithers, keep those people quiet. (*9-9-9 handling people roughly.*) Here—easy, officer; treat those poor people decently. Well, whom have you got there?

9-9-9: (*Going to one and dragging urchin within railing.*) Pickpocket, your Honor. Caught in the act.

BOWLING: What's he got to say for himself? Nothing, eh? What's his name?

9-9-9-: (*Stooping down to boy as if asking him.*) Says his name is Peter Rich.

BOWLING: You stand a poor chance, Rich! Take him away. (*Bowling consults with other Justice, as the boy is taken off.*)

SPLINTER: (*To Rafferdi, who has his monkey and organ.*) So you want to get out, eh? How much money have you got?

RAFFERDI: Be jabers! half a dollar in cents is all the money I'm worth in the world.

SPLINTER: Give it to me. I thought you organ fellows were Italians.

RAFFERDI: Devil doubt it! Aint I got a monkey?

9-9-9: Here, you; come up here. (*Takes Rafferdi inside the railing.*)

BOWLING: Now, then; what's this officer?

9-9-9: (*Rafferdi takes stand.*) Complaint of disturbing the neighborhood.

BOWLING: What have you got to say for yourself?

SPLINTER: If your Honor please, I appear for this man.

BOWLING: Well what have you got to say for him?

SPLINTER: Here is an unfortunate man, your Honor—a native of Sunny Italy. He came to our free and happy country, and being a votary of music, he bought an organ and a monkey, and tried to earn his bread. But the myrmidons of the law were upon him, and the Eagle of Liberty drooped his pinions as Rafferdi was hurried to his dungeon.

BOWLING: Rafferdi!—You're an Irishman, ain't you? What do you mean by deceiving us?

RAFFERDI: Sure I didn't. It's the lawyer chap there. I paid him fifty pints and he's lying out the worth of it.

BOWLING: You fellows are regular nuisances! I've a great mind to commit you.

SPLINTER: Commit him! If the Court please—reflect—commit him—to prison—what will become of his monkey?

BOWLING: Well, I'll commit him too.

SPLINTER: You cannot. I defy the Court to find anything in the statutes authorizing the commital of the monkey.

BOWLING: Well, we'll leave out the monkey.

SPLINTER: And if the Court please, what is the monkey to do in the wide world, with his natural protector in prison? I appeal to those kindlier feelings in your honor's breast—which must ever temper justice with mercy. This monkey is perhaps an orphan!

BOWLING: (*Laughing.*) Take them both away, and don't let me catch you here again Mr. Rafferdi or you'll go to jail. (*Exit Rafferdi. Splinter goes down, Rafferdi exits.*)

9-9-9: (*Pulling Sam who is drunk out of a crowd.*) Get up here.

SAM: (*Noisily.*) Look yah—don't pull me around.

BOWLING: Silence there! what's all this noise about?

SAM: Whar's de Court? I want to see de Judge.

SPLINTER: (*Approaching him.*) My colored friend, can I assist you?

SAM: Am you a Counsellor-at-Law?

SPLINTER: Yes, retain me! How much money have you got?

SAM: I ain't got no money—but I've got a policy ticket. It bound to draw a prize.

SPLINTER: Got any pawn tickets?

SAM: Of course. (*Giving him a handful.*)

BOWLING: Well, what's the charge?

9-9-9: Drunk and disorderly.

BOWLING: Well, my man, what have you to say?

SAM: Dis here gemman represents me.

SPLINTER: We admit, if the Court please, that we were slightly intoxicated, but we claim the privilege, as the equal of the white man.

BOWLING: (*To Clerk.*) Very good! Commit him for ten days.

SPLINTER: But this is an outrage, your honor.

BOWLING: (*To Officer.*) Take him off! (*Motioning to Sam, who is very wroth.*)

SAM: What?

BOWLING: Take him away.

SAM: Look here, judge, hab you read the Civil Right Bill? You can't send dis nigger to prison while dat bill am de law of de land.

BOWLING: That'll do—remove him.

SAM: I ain't no gipsy, I'm one of de Eureau niggers, I am. Where am de law? Don't touch me, white man! Dis am corruption—dis am 'ficial delinquency.

9-9-9: (*Collars him and carries him off.*)

SAM: Mr. Stevens! Thaddeus! (*Exit.*)

BOWLING: Any more prisoners? (*Noise.*) What noise is that? (*Officer goes out. Byke enters, followed by the officer who escorts Laura.*)

BYKE: Where is the judge? O, where is the good, kind judge?

BOWLING: Well, my dear sir, what is the matter?

BYKE: O, sir, forgive my tears. I'm a broken-hearted man!

BOWLING: Be calm, my dear sir. Officer, bring this gentleman a chair. (*Officer hands chair.*)

BYKE: Ah, sir, you are very good to a poor distressed father whose existence has been made a desert on account of his child.

BOWLING: Repress your emotion, and tell me what you want.

BYKE: I want my child.

BOWLING: Where is she?

BYKE: She is here, sir—here—my darling, my beautiful child, and so unfilial—so unnatural.

BOWLING: How is this, young lady?

LAURA: (*Standing inside railing.*) It is all a lie. He is not my father.

BYKE: Not your father? Oh, dear, oh, dear, you will break my heart.

BOWLING: This needs some explanation. If not his child, who are you?

LAURA: I am—I dare not say it. I know not who I am, but I feel that he cannot be my father.

BYKE: O, dear—O—

BOWLING: (*Sharply.*) Silence! (*To Laura, sternly.*) You say you don't know who you are. Do you know this man?

LAURA: Yes.

BOWLING: Where, and with whom do you live?

LAURA: I have lived alone for four months.

BOWLING: And with whom did you live before that?

LAURA: O, forgive me, if I seem disobedient—but I cannot tell.

BOWLING: Then I must look to this gentleman for information.

BYKE: And I will gladly give it. Yes, sir, I will gladly tell. She was taken from me years ago, when she was but a little child, by rich people who wanted to adopt her. I refused—they paid me—I was poor—I was starving—I forebore to claim her—she was happy, but they turned her forth four months ago into the street. I could not see her suffer—my child—the prop of my declining days. I begged her to come—she refused. My enemies had poisoned my daughter's mind against *me*, her father. I am still poor. I taught school, but I have saved a little money, only for her.

BOWLING: How old is she?

BYKE: Nineteen.

BOWLING: (*To Laura.*) Your father is your legal guardian during your minority, and is entitled to your custody. Why are you so undutiful? Try to correct this.

BYKE: Oh, bless you, dear, good judge for those words.

LAURA: O, have I no friends, must I go with him?

BOWLING: Certainly.

LAURA: Anything then. Exposure! Disgrace, rather than that. (*Judges consult. Enter Snorkey—goes opposite to Laura and signals her.*)

BYKE: (*Aside.*) Snorkey! the devil!

SNORKEY: (*Crossing to Laura.*) Can I help you miss? Only tell me what to do, and if it takes my other arm off, I'll save you.

LAURA: Yes, yes, you can help me! (*To Judge.*) Will you let me send a message?

BOWLING: You may do that.

LAURA: Run to that house—not my house—but the one in which you saw me first. Do you remember it?

SNORKEY: Don't I, and the wine and cakes.

LAURA: Ask for Miss Pearl. Tell her where I am. Tell her to come instantly. (*Snorkey going.*) Stay—tell her to bring the ebony box in mother's cabinet. Can you recollect?

SNORKEY: Can I what? Gaze at this giant intellect and don't ask me! The ebony box—all right—I'm off. (*Exit.*)

BOWLING: It would have been as well, young lady, to have answered frankly at first.

BYKE: O, sir! Don't be harsh with her! Don't be harsh with my poor child!

BOWLING: Your father has a most Christian disposition.

LAURA: Sir, I have told you and I now solemnly repeat it, that this man is no relation of mine. I desire to remain unknown, for I am most unfortunate; but the injustice you are about to commit forces me to reveal myself, though in doing so I shall increase a sorrow already hard to bear. (*Splinter talks with Laura aside.*)

BOWLING: We sit here to do right, according to the facts before us. And let me tell you, young lady, that your obstinate silence has more than convinced us that your father's statement is correct. Further, unless the witnesses you have sent for can directly contradict him, we shall not alter our decision.

LAURA: Let it be so. He says he gave me into the care of certain wealthy people when I was a little child.

BYKE: I am willing to swear to it.

LAURA: (*Splinter watching effect of question.*) Then he will be able to describe the clothes in which I was dressed at the time. They were safely kept. I have sent for them.

BYKE: Let them be produced—and I will recognize every little precious garment. (*Aside.*) This is getting ferociously hot for me! Ha! (*Re-enter Snorkey with Ray hastily.*)

SNORKEY: (*Excitedly.*) Here's a witness! Here's evidence! (*9-9-9 admonishes him.*)

LAURA: (*Ray takes her hand through the rail.*) Ray?

BOWLING: Who is this?

RAY: I am a friend, sir, of this lady.

BYKE: He is a dreadful character—a villain who wants to lead my child astray! Don't—please don't let him contaminate her!

BOWLING: Silence! (*To Ray.*) Can you disprove that this young lady is his daughter?

RAY: His daughter? (*Looks at Laura.*)

LAURA: He knows nothing.

BOWLING: Let him answer. Come—have you any knowledge of this matter?

RAY: I had been told, sir, that—(*Laura looks at him.*) No—I know nothing.

LAURA: Have you brought the ebony box? It contained the clothes which I wore when—

RAY: I understand; but in my haste, and not knowing your peril I brought nothing. But can you not remember them yourself?

LAURA: Perfectly.

RAY: Write, then! (*Handling her a memorandum book. To Bowling.*) Sir, this lady will hand you a description of those articles which she wore when she was found, thirteen years ago. Then let this scoundrel be questioned—and if he fail to answer, I will accuse him of an attempted abduction.

BOWLING: That's the way.

BYKE: (*Aside.*) It will not be a great effort for me to remember.

BOWLING: (*Taking the book from Ray.*) Now, sir, I will listen to you.
(*Ray and Laura are eager and expectant.*)
BYKE: (*Deliberately.*) A soiled gingham frock, patched and torn. (*Laura gives a shudder and turns aside.*)
BOWLING: What kind of shoes and stockings?
BYKE: Her feet were bare.
BOWLING: And the color of her hood?
BYKE: Her dear little head was uncovered.
BOWLING: (*Handing book back.*) He has answered correctly.
LAURA: It is useless to struggle more! Heaven alone can help me!
RAY: You can see, sir, that this lady cannot be his daughter. Look at her and at him!
BOWLING: I only see that he has pretty well proven his case. She must go with him, and let her learn to love him as a daughter should.
RAY: She shall not! I will follow him wherever he goes.
BYKE: (*Taking Laura's hand.*) I appeal to the Court.
BOWLING: Officer, take charge of that person, until this gentleman is gone.
BYKE: (*Coming forward with Laura who is dumb and despairing.*) My child, try and remember the words of the good judge. "You must learn to love me as a daughter should." (*Leading her out.*)
SNORKEY: (*To Ray.*) Stay here, sir, I'll track him. No one suspects me!

(*Music. Tableau. Scene closes in.*)

SCENE II

Exterior of the Tombs, with ballads on strings upon the railings. Enter Judas followed by Peachblossom.

PEACHBLOSSOM: Only tell me where he has taken her, and I'll go with you—indeed I will.
JUDAS: We don't want you, we wouldn't be bothered with you; she's our game.
PEACHBLOSSOM: What are you going to do with her?
JUDAS: Do? why we'll coin her. Turn her into dollars. We've had it on foot for a long time.
PEACHBLOSSOM: What! Is she the rich young lady I heard you and Byke speak of so often before I got away from you?
JUDAS: (*Savagely.*) Heard me speak of! What did you hear?
PEACHBLOSSOM: (*Dancing off.*) O, I know! I know more than you suppose. When you used to lock me up in the back cellar for running away, you forgot that doors had key-holes.
JUDAS: (*Aside.*) This girl must be silenced.
PEACHBLOSSOM: What are you muttering about—don't you know how Byke used to throw you down and trample on you for muttering?
JUDAS: I'll have you yet, my beauty.
PEACHBLOSSOM: I think you are a great fool, Judas.
JUDAS: Likely, likely.
PEACHBLOSSOM: Why don't you give up Miss Nina to that handsome young gentleman? He'd pay you well for the secret. He'd give his whole fortune for her, I know, I saw it in his face. And he'd treat you better than Byke does.

JUDAS: Not yet my chicken; besides, what does he care for her now? Isn't he going to marry the other girl—she's the one will pay when the time comes—but we intend to hold the goods 'till the price is high.

PEACHBLOSSOM: Then, if you won't, I'll tell all as I knows. I'll tell him all I used to overhear about babies and cradles, and he'll understand it perhaps, if I don't.

JUDAS: (Aside.) Hang her—she'll make mischief. (Aloud.) Well, come along with me, my beauty, and I'll talk it over with you.

PEACHBLOSSOM: Don't touch me, I won't trust you with your hands on me. (Judas makes a dart at her.) I knew that was your game. But I'll be even with you yet. (Dancing off tantalizingly before Judas. Both exit.)

(Enter Snorkey.)

SNORKEY: (Despondent.) I'm no more use than a gun without a trigger. I tried to follow Byke, but he smoked me in a minute. Then I tried to make up with him, but he swore that I went against him in Court, and so he wouldn't have me at no price. Then I ran after the carriage that he got into with the lady, till a damned old woman caught me for upsetting her applestand and bursting up her business. What am I to do now? I'm afraid to go back to the Cap'n, he won't have me at any price either, I suppose. (Gazing at ballads, hand in his pockets— going from one to the other. Enter Bermudas with ballads in his hands and preparing to take others off the line as if to shut up shop.)

BERMUDAS: (After gazing at Snorkey.) What are you a-doing of—Sa-a-ay? (Snorkey takes no notice.) This here's one of the fellows as steals bread of the poor man. Reading all the songs for nothin, and got bags of gold at home. Sa-a-y!

SNORKEY: Well, youngster, what are you groaning about? Have you got the cholera?

BERMUDAS: Ah! What are you doing? Taking the bloom off my songs? You've read them 'ere ballads till they're in rags.

SNORKEY: I was looking for the "Prairie Bird."

BERMUDAS: Perary Bird! eh? There aint no perary bird. There's a "Perary Flower."

SNORKEY: Now don't go into convulsions. I'll find it. (Turns to the songs.)

BERMUDAS: Sa-a-y—you needn't look no further for that bird! I've found him, and no mistake. He's a big Shanghae with a red comb and no feathers.

SNORKEY: He's dropped on me.

BERMUDAS: Ain't you a mean cuss, sa-a-y? Why don't you come down with your two cents, and support trade?

SNORKEY: But I ain't got two cents. What's a fellow to do if he hasn't got a red?

BERMUDAS: (Toning down.) Haint you? Where's your messages?

SNORKEY: Havn't had one go to-day.

BERMUDAS: Where do you hang out?

SNORKEY: Nowheres.

BERMUDAS: My eye—no roost?

SNORKEY: No.

BERMUDAS: I tell you what, come along with us—we've got a bully place—no rent—no taxes—no nothin.

SNORKEY: Where is it?

BERMUDAS: Down under the pier!—I discovered it. I was in swimmin and seed a hole and I went in. Lots of room, just the place for a quiet roost. We has jolly times every night I tell you on the dock; and when it is time to turn in we goes below, and has it as snug as a hotel; come down with us.

SNORKEY: I will! These young rascals will help me track that scoundrel yet.

BERMUDAS: Now, help me to take in my show windows; it's time to shut up shop.

(*Enter Ray Trafford.*)

RAY: If what that crazy girl has told me can be true, Laura may yet be restored to her friends if not to me, for I have dispelled that dream for ever. But that villain must be traced immediately, or he will convey his victim far beyond our reach or rescue.

(*Snorkey helping to take down songs sees Trafford, who has crossed.*)

SNORKEY: Hollo! Cap'n!

RAY: The man of all I wanted. You tracked him?

SNORKEY: They was too much for me, sir—two horses was—but I saw them turn into Greenwich Street, near Jay.

RAY: This may give us a clue. I have learned from a girl who knows this fellow, that he has some hiding place over the river, and owns a boat which is always fastened near the pier where the Boston Steamers are.

SNORKEY: Well, Cap'n, if anything's to be done, you'll find me at Pier—what's the number of our pier, Shorty?

BERMUDAS: Pier 30!—Down stairs!

SNORKEY: Pier 30. That's my new home, and if you want me, say the word.

RAY: You will help me?

SNORKEY: You bet, Cap'n. I was on Columbia's side for four years and I'll fight for her daughters for the rest of my life, if you say so. If there's any fightin' count me in, Cap'n.

RAY: Thank you, brave fellow. Here take this—no nonsense—take it. Pier 30 is it?

SNORKEY: Pier 30. (*Exit Trafford.*)

BERMUDAS: (*Eyeing money.*) How much, Perary?

SNORKEY: One—two—three—four—four dollars.

BERMUDAS: Four dollars! Sa-a-y—Don't you want to buy a share in a paying business? I'm looking out for a partner with a cash capital, for the ballad business. Or I tell you what to do. Lay your money on me in a mill. I'm going to be a prize fighter, and get reported in the respectable dailies. "Rattling Mill, 99th round, Bermudas the victor, having knocked his antagonist into nowheres."

SNORKEY: Come along, you young imp. I could floor you with my own arm, and then the report would be: "25th round—Snorkey came up first, while his antagonist showed great signs of distress."

BERMUDAS: Say, Perary, what are you going to do with all that money?

SNORKEY: I won't bet it on you, sure.

BERMUDAS: I'll tell you what to do, let's go and board at the Metropolitan Hotel for an hour.

SNORKEY: What will we do for toothpicks?

BERMUDAS: Oh, go along. You can't get anything to eat for four dollars. (*Exit Snorkey, Bermudas squaring off.*)

SCENE III

Foot of Pier 30, North River. Sea cloth down and working—A pier projecting into the river. A large cavity in front. Bow of a vessel at back, and other steamers, vessels and piers in perspective on either side. The flat gives view of Jersey City and the river shipping by starlight. Music of distant serenade heard.

(Byke enters sculling a boat, and fastens his boat to the pier. Old Judas is on the pier, smoking pipe, looking down.)

JUDAS: Have you fixed everything across the river?

BYKE: Yes, I have a horse and wagon waiting near the shore to carry her to the farm. Has any one been around here.

JUDAS: Not a soul. I've been waiting here for an hour. What made you so long?

BYKE: I pulled down the river for a spell to throw any spies off the track. It was necessary after what you told me of that girl's threat to blab about the Boston pier.

JUDAS: Pshaw! she'd never dare.

BYKE: Never mind, it's best to be certain. Is the prize safe?

JUDAS: Yes, she was worn out, and slept when I came away. How her blood tells—she wouldn't shed a tear.

BYKE: Bah! if she'd been more of a woman and set up a screaming, we shouldn't have been able to get her at all. Success to all girls of spirit, say I.

JUDAS: Don't you think it might be worth while to treat with this young spark, Trafford, and hear what he has to offer?

BYKE: Satan take him! no. That'll spoil your game about the other girl, Pearl. He was making up to her all right, and if he gets this one back he'll upset the whole game by marrying her. I tell you he's got the old feeling for her, spite of her running away. Now you can judge for yourself, and do as you please.

JUDAS: Then I do as you do—get her out of the city. When Pearl is married to him we can treat for Laura's ransom, by threatening them with the real secret.

BYKE: Then that's settled. *(Taking out flask.)* Here's the precious infant's health. Do you think she'll go easy, or shall we drug her?

JUDAS: Just tell her it's to meet her beau and get her ransom, or give her a reason and she'll be as mild as a lamb.

BYKE: Ha! let me get hold of her, and I'll answer she goes across, reason or no reason. *(Bermudas calls outside.)* There's a noise.

JUDAS: It's only the market boys coming down for a swim.

BYKE: Softly then, come along. *(Music, exeunt.)*

(Enter Bermudas, Peanuts, and a couple other boys.)

BERMUDAS: Say, Peanuts, go down and see if any of the fellows is come yet. *(Peanuts scrambles down to hole in front on side of dock; comes out again.)*

PEANUTS: There's nobody there.

SNORKEY: *(Without.)* Hollo!

BERMUDAS: Hollo! That's our new chum. Hollo! follow your front teeth, and you'll get here afore you knows it. *(Enter Snorkey with more boys.)*

SNORKEY: What a very airy location.

BERMUDAS: It's a very convenient hotel. Hot and cold saltwater baths at the very door of your bedrooms, and sometimes when the tide rises we has the bath brought to us in bed—doesn't we, Peanuts?

PEANUTS: That's so.

SNORKEY: Come, what do you do before you go to bed?

BERMUDAS: We has a swarry. Say, one of you fellows, go down and bring up the piany forty. (*Peanuts goes into hole and gets banjo.*) What'll I give you?

SNORKEY: Something lively. (*Music, and dance by boys, ensue,—given according to capacity and talent. At the end of it, a general shout of jubilee; when—*)

SERGEANT OF PATROL: (*Outside.*) Here, boys! less noise.

BERMUDAS: It's Acton and the police. Let's go to bed. (*Bermudas and boys get down into hole.*)

SERGEANT: (*Entering in patrol boat.*) If you boys don't make less noise, I'll have to clear you out.

BERMUDAS: (*On the pier.*) It's an extra occasion, Mr. Acton;—we're having a distinguished military guest, and we're entertaining him. (*Boat passes out.*) Come along, Perary, let's go to bed. (*Snorkey is about to descend.*)

(*Enter Ray Trafford, on pier.*)

RAY: Is that you, Snorkey?

SNORKEY: (*Quickly whispering.*) Here, sir. Anything turned up?

RAY: Byke was overheard to say he intended crossing the river to-night; he will doubtless use that boat which he keeps by the Boston Pier. The river patrol are on the watch for him. But I will meet him before he can embark.

SNORKEY: Which Boston Pier is it, Cap'n? there are three on this river.

RAY: Three!

SNORKEY: Yes; one of them is two slips below. I tell you what, Cap'n: You get the officers, go by the shore way, search all the slips; I'll find a boat about here, and will drop down the river, and keep an eye around generally.

VOICES: (*Without.*) This way, sir.

RAY: That's the patrol calling me. Your idea is a good one. Keep a sharp eye down the stream. (*Exit.*)

SNORKEY: (*Alone.*) Now for my lay.

BERMUDAS: (*Popping his head up.*) Say, can't I do nothin? I'm the Fifth-Ward Chicken, and if there's any muss, let me have a shy.

SNORKEY: No; get in and keep quiet. (*Bermudas disappears.*) I wonder where I can find a boat. There ought to be plenty tied up about here. My eye! (*Discovering Byke's.*) Here's one for the wishin'; sculls too. I'm in luck. Say, Bermuda, whose boat is this?

BERMUDAS: Yours, if you like. Tie it loose. (*Jumps down, enters boat, pushes off.*)

BERMUDAS: (*Inside.*) Keep your toe out of my ear! (*Pause.*)

(*Byke, Laura, and Judas enter on pier.*)

LAURA: Is this the place? There's no one here; you have deceived me.

BYKE: Well, we have but we won't do so any longer.

LAURA: What do you mean?

BYKE: (*Drawing pistol.*) Do you see this? It is my dog Trusty. It has a very loud voice and a sharp bite; and if you scream out, I'll try if it can't outscream you. Judas, unfasten the boat.

LAURA: What are you about to do? You will not murder me?

BYKE: No; we only mean to take you to the other shore, where your friends won't think of finding you. Quick, Judas.

JUDAS: The boat's gone.

BYKE: Damn you, what do you mean? Where is it? Here, hold her. (*Judas clutches Laura.*) Where the devil is that boat?

SNORKEY: (*Re-appearing in boat.*) Here!

BYKE: Snorkey! We're betrayed. Come. (*Drags Laura towards exit.*)

SNORKEY: The police are there! Turn, you coward! Don't run from a one-armed man!

BYKE: Judas, take her! (*Snorkey strikes at him with oar. Byke takes oar from him and strikes him; he falls in boat. The boys hear the noise, and scramble up at back. The patrol boat appears with lights.*)

SNORKEY: Help! Bermudas!

BERMUDAS: Hi! Ninety-ninth round! first blood for Bermudas! (*Jumps at Byke.*)

BYKE: (*Flinging Bermudas off.*) Judas, toss her over!

(*Judas throws Laura over back of pier. Ray enters. Boys all get on pier and surround Byke, fighting him. Officers enter at left. Ray leaps into water after Laura.*)

Curtain. Moonlight on during scene.

END OF ACT III

ACT IV

SCENE I

Long Branch. Ground floor of an elegant residence—open windows from floor to ceiling at back—opening upon a balcony or promenade. Perspective of the shore and sea in distance. Door right and left. Sunset.

(As the curtain rises to lively music, enter Pearl, Mrs. Van Dam, Sue Earlie, and other ladies in summer costume, Demilt and Windel with them.)

PEARL: And so the distinguished foreigner is in love with me? I thought he looked excessively solemn at the hop last night. Do you know, I can't imagine a more serious spectacle than a French man or an Italian in love. One always imagines them to be sick. *(To Mrs. Van Dam.)* Do fasten my glove—there's a dear.

MRS. VAN DAM: Where's Ray?

PEARL: O, he's somewhere. I never saw such another. Isn't he cheerful? He never smiles, and seldom talks.

MRS. VAN DAM: But the foreigner does. What an ecstasy he was in over your singing; sing us a verse, won't you, while we're waiting for Ray?

ALL: It will be delightful—do.

PEARL: Well! *(Song introduced.)*

(Air; "When the War is Over, Mary.")

I.

Now the summer days are fading,
Autumn send its dreary blast
Moaning through the silent forest
Where the leaves are falling fast.
Soon dread winter will enfold us—
Chilling in its arms of snow,
Flowers that the summer cherished,
Birds that sing, and streams that flow.

II.

Say, shall all things droop and wither,
That are born this Summer day?
Shall the happy love it brought us—
Like the flowers fade away?
No; be still thou flutt'ring bosom—
Seasons change and years glide by,
They may not harm what is immortal—
Darling—love shall never die!

PEARL: Now, I've sung that to Ray a dozen times, and he never even said it was nice. He hasn't any soul for music; O, dear, what a creature!

MRS. VAN DAM: Yes, and what a victim you will be with a husband who has $60,000 per annum income.

PEARL: That's some comfort, isn't it?

RAY: (*Enters bowing to others.*) Going out, Pearl?

PEARL: Yes, we're off the Shrewsbury. Quite a party's going—four carriages—and we mean to stay and ride home by moonlight.

RAY: Couldn't you return a little earlier?

MRS. VAN DAM: Earlier! Pshaw! What's in you, Trafford? (*The ladies and gents go up.*)

RAY: (*To Pearl.*) You know that Laura will be quite alone and she is still suffering.

PEARL: Well, she'll read and read, as she always did, and never miss me.

RAY: But, at least, she ought to have some little attention.

PEARL: Dear, dear, what an unreasonable fellow you are. Isn't she happy now—didn't you save her from drowning, and havn't I been as good to her as I can be—what more do you want?

RAY: I don't like to hear you talk so, Pearl, and remember what she and you were once. And you know that she was something else once—something that you are now to me. And yet how cheerful, how gentle she is. She has lost everything and does not complain.

PEARL: Well, what a sermon! There, I know you're hurt and I'm a fool. But I can't help it. People say she's good-looking but she's got no heart! I'd give anything for one, but they ain't to be bought.

RAY: Well, don't moan about it, I didn't mean to reprove you.

PEARL: But you do reprove me. I'm sure I havn't been the cause of Laura's troubles. I didn't tell the big, ugly man to come and take her away, although I was once glad he did.

RAY: Pearl!

PEARL: Because I thought I had gained you by it. (*Ray turns away.*) But now I've got you, I don't seem to make you happy. But I might as well complain that you don't make me happy—but I don't complain, I am satisfied, and I want you to be satisfied. There, *are* you satisfied?

MRS. VAN DAM: (*Who with others has been promenading up and down the balcony.*) Here are the carriages.

PEARL: I'm coming. Can't you get me my shawl, Ray. (*Ray gets it from chair.*)

MRS. VAN DAM: And here's your foreign admirer on horseback.

(Sue Earlie, Demilt and Windel exit.)

PEARL: Bye, bye, Ray. *(Exit.)*
MRS. VAN DAM: Are you not coming, Trafford?
RAY: I? No!
MRS. VAN DAM: Do come on horseback, here's a horse ready for you.
PEARL: *(Without.)* Ray! Ray!
MRS. VAN DAM: Pearl's calling you. Be quick or Count Carom will be before you, and hand her in the carriage.
RAY: *(Taking his hat slowly.)* O, by all means, let the Count have some amusement.
MRS. VAN DAM: *(Taking Ray's arm.)* You're a perfect icicle. *(They exit.)*

(Noise of whips and laughter. Plaintive music as Laura enters and gazes out at them.)

LAURA: Poor Pearl. It is a sad thing to want for happiness but it is a terrible thing to see another groping about blindly for it when it is almost within the grasp. And yet she can be very happy with him. Her sunny temper, and her joyous face will brighten any home. *(Sits at table, on which are books.)* How happy I feel to be alone with these friends, who are ever ready to talk to me—with no longings for what I may not have—my existence hidden from all, save two in the wide world, and making my joy out of the joy of that innocent child who will soon be his wife.

(Peachblossom appears at back looking in cautiously, grotesquely attired.)

PEACHBLOSSOM: If you please.
LAURA: *(Aloud.)* Who is there?
PEACHBLOSSOM: *(Running in window.)* O, it's Miss Nina! O, I'm so glad; I've had such a hunt for you. Don't ask me nothing yet. I'm so happy. I've been looking for you so long, and I've had such hard luck. Lord what a tramp—miles on miles.
LAURA: Did any one see you come here? How did you find me?
PEACHBLOSSOM: I asked 'em at the hotel where Mr. Trafford was, and they said at Courtlands, and I asked 'em where Courtlands was, and they said down the shore, and I walked down lookin' at every place till I came here.
LAURA: Speak low, Blossom. My existence is a secret, and no one must hear you.
PEACHBLOSSOM: Well, Miss, I says to Snorkey—says I—
LAURA: Is he with you?
PEACHBLOSSOM: No, Miss, but we are great friends. He wants me to keep house for him some day. I said to him—"I want to find out where Miss Nina's gone," and so he went to Mr. Trafford's and found he was come to Long Branch, but never a word could we hear of you.
LAURA: And the others—those dreadful people?
PEACHBLOSSOM: Byke and old Judas? Clean gone! They hasn't been seen since they was took up for throwing you into the water, and let off because no one came to Court agin 'em. Bermudas says he's seen 'em in Barnum's wax-work show, but Bermudas is *such* a liar. He brought me up here.

LAURA: Brought you up here.

PEACHBLOSSOM: Yes, he sells papers at Stetson's; he's got the exclusive trade here, and he has a little wagon and a horse, and goes down to the junction every night to catch the extras from the Express train what don't come here. He says he'll give me lots of nice rides if I'll stay here.

LAURA: But you must not stay here. You must go back to New York this evening.

PEACHBLOSSOM: Back! No, I won't.

LAURA: Blossom!

PEACHBLOSSOM: I won't, I won't, I won't! I'll never let you away again. I did it once and you was took away and dragged about and chucked overboard and almost drowned. I won't be any trouble, indeed I won't. I'll hire out at the hotel, and run over when my work is done at night, when nobody can see me, to look up at your window. Don't send me away. You're the only one as ever was good to me.

LAURA: (*Aside.*) It's too dangerous. She certainly would reveal me sooner or later. I must send her back.

PEACHBLOSSOM: Besides, I've got something to tell you. Dreadful! dreadful! about old Judas and Byke—a secret.

LAURA: A secret! what in the world are you saying?

PEACHBLOSSOM: Is it wicked to listen at doors when people talk?

LAURA: It is very wicked.

PEACHBLOSSOM: Well, I suppose that's why I did it. I used to listen to Byke and Judas when they used to talk about a rich lady whom they called Mrs. Courtland.

LAURA: Ah!

PEACHBLOSSOM: Judas used to be a nurse at Mrs. Courtland's, and was turned off for stealing. And wasn't she and Byke going to make money off her! and Byke was to pretend to be some beautiful lady's father. Then, when they took you, Judas says to me: "Did you ever hear of children being changed in their cradles?"—and that you wasn't her child, but she was going to make money off the real one at the proper time.

LAURA: What do you tell me?

PEACHBLOSSOM: Oh! I'm not crazy. I know a heap, don't I? And I want you to think I'm somebody, and not send me away.

LAURA: (*To herself.*) She must speak the truth. And yet if I were to repeat her strange words here, I should be suspected of forging some tale to abuse the ear of society. No! better let it rest as it is. She must go—and I must go too.

PEACHBLOSSOM: You ain't mad with me?

LAURA: No, no; but you must go away from here. Go back to the hotel to your friend—anywhere, and wait for me; I will come to you.

PEACHBLOSSOM: Is it a promise?

LAURA: (*Nervously.*) Yes, go.

PEACHBLOSSOM: Then I'll go; for I know you always keep your word—you ain't angry, cause I came after you? I did it because I loved you—because I wanted to see you put in the right place. Honor bright, you ain't sending me away now? Well, I'll go; good bye! (*Exit.*)

LAURA: (*Animated.*) I must return to the city, no matter what dangers may lurk there. It is dangerous enough to be concealed here, with a hundred Argus-eyed women about me every day, but with this girl, detection would be certain. I must go—secretly if I can—openly if I must.

RAY: (*Outside.*) No, I shall not ride again. Put him up. (*Entering.*) Laura, I knew I should find you here.

LAURA: (*Sitting and pretending composure.*) I thought you had gone with Pearl?

RAY: I did go part of the way, but I left the party a mile down the road.

LAURA: You and Pearl had no disagreement?

RAY: No—yes; that is, we always have. Our social barometers always stand at "cloudy" and "overcast."

LAURA: (*Rising.*) And whose fault is that?

RAY: (*Pettishly.*) Not mine. I know I do all I can—I say all I can—but she—(*Crossing.*)

LAURA: But she is to be your wife. Ray—my friend—courtship is the text from which the whole solemn sermon of married life takes its theme. Do not let yours be discontented and unhappy.

RAY: To be my wife; yes. In a moment of foolishness, dazzled by her airs and teased by her coquettishness, I asked her to be my wife.

LAURA: And you repent already?

RAY: (*Taking her hand.*) I lost you, and I was at the mercy of any flirt that chose to give me an inviting look. It was your fault—you know it was! Why did you leave me?

LAURA: (*After conflict with her feelings.*) Ray, the greatest happiness I have ever felt, has been the thought that all your affections were forever bestowed upon a virtuous lady, your equal in family fortune and accomplishments. What a revelation do you make to me now! What is it makes you continually war with your happiness?

RAY: I don't know what it is. I was wrong to accuse you. Forgive me! I have only my own cowardice to blame for my misery. But Pearl—

LAURA: You must not accuse her.

RAY: When you were gone, she seemed to have no thought—no wish—but for my happiness. She constantly invited me to her house, and when I tried to avoid her, met me at every turn. Was she altogether blameless?

LAURA: Yes, it was her happiness she sought, and she had a right to seek it.

RAY: Oh! men are the veriest fools on earth; a little attention, a little sympathy, and they are caught—caught by a thing without soul or brains, while some noble woman is forsaken and forgotten.

LAURA: (*Ray throws himself into a seat.*) Ray, will you hear me?

RAY: (*Looking at her hopefully.*) Yes, speak to me as you used to speak. Be to me as you used to be.

LAURA: (*Smiling sadly.*) I cannot be that to you; but I can speak as the spirit of the Laura who is dead to you forever.

RAY: Be it as you will.

LAURA: (*Standing beside him.*) Let the woman you look upon be wise or vain, beautiful or homely, rich or poor, she has but one thing she can really give or refuse—her heart! Her beauty, her wit, her accomplishments, she may sell to you—but her love is the treasure without money and without price.

RAY: How well I have learned that.

LAURA: She only asks in return, that when you look upon her your eyes shall speak a mute devotion; that when you address her your voice shall be gentle, loving and kind. That you shall not despise her because she cannot understand, all at once, your vigorous thoughts and ambitious designs: for when misfortune and evil have defeated your greatest purposes—her love remains to console you. You look to the trees for strength and grandeur—do not despise the flowers, because their fragrance is all they have to give. Remember,—love is all a woman has to give; but it is the only earthly thing which God permits us to carry beyond the grave.

RAY: (*Rising.*) You are right. You are always right. I asked Pearl to be my wife, knowing what she was, and I will be just to her. I will do my duty though it break my heart.

LAURA: Spoken like a hero.

RAY: But it is to you I owe the new light that guides me; and I will tell her—

LAURA: Tell her nothing—never speak of me. And when you see her say to her it is she, and she alone, whom you consult and to whom you listen.

RAY: And you—

LAURA: You will see me no more.

RAY: You will leave me?

LAURA: Something of me will always be with you—my parting words—my prayers for your happiness. (*Distant music heard.*)

RAY: (*Falling on his knees.*) O, Laura, you leave me to despair.

LAURA: No; to the happiness which follows duty well performed. Such happiness as I feel in doing mine.

(*Picture. Scene closes in. During last of this scene the sun has set, and night come on. Stage dark.*)

SCENE II

Woods near Shrewsbury Station.

(*Enter Byke shabbily dressed.*)

BYKE: It's getting darker and darker, and I'm like to lose my way. Where the devil is Judas? It must be nine o'clock, and she was to be at the bend with the wagon half an hour ago. (*Rumble of wheels heard.*) Humph—at last.

JUDAS: (*Entering.*) Is that you Byke?

BYKE: Who did you suppose it was? I've been tramping about the wet grass for an hour.

JUDAS: It was a hard job to get the horse and wagon.

BYKE: Give me a match. (*Lights pipe and leans against a tree.*) Did you get the bearing of the crib?

JUDAS: Yes, it is on the shore, well away from the other cottages and hotels.

BYKE: That's good. Nothing like peace and quietness. Who's in the house?

JUDAS: Only the two girls and the servants.

BYKE: How many of them?

JUDAS: Four.

BYKE: It'll be mere child's play to go through that house. Have you spied about the swag?

JUDAS: They have all their diamonds and jewels there; Pearl wears them constantly; they're the talk of the whole place.

BYKE: We'll live in luxury off that girl all our lives. She'll settle a handsome thing on us, won't she? when she knows what we know, and pays us to keep dark;—if t'other one don't spoil the game.

JUDAS: Curse her! I could cut her throat.

BYKE: O, I'll take care of that!

JUDAS: You always do things for the best, dear old Byke!
BYKE: Of course I do. What time is it?
JUDAS: Not ten yet.
BYKE: An hour to wait.
JUDAS: But, Byke, you won't peach on me before my little pet is married, will you?
BYKE: What's the fool about now?
JUDAS: I can't help trembling; nothing is safe while Laura is there.
BYKE: I've provided for that. I've had the same idea as you—while she's in the way, and Trafford unmarried, our plans are all smoke, and we might as well be sitting on the hob with a keg of powder in the coals.
JUDAS: That we might. But what have you thought to do?
BYKE: Why, I've thought what an unfortunate creature Laura is—robbed of her mother, her home, and her lover; nothing to live for; it would be a mercy to put her out of the way.
JUDAS: That's it; but how—how—how—
BYKE: It's plain she wasn't born to be drowned, or the materials are very handy down here. What made you talk about cutting her throat? It was very wrong! When 'a thing gets into my head, it sticks there.
JUDAS: You oughtn't to mind me.
BYKE: Make your mind easy on that score.
JUDAS: (*Alarmed.*) Byke, I heard some one in the bushes just there. (*Points.*)
BYKE: (*Nervously and quickly.*) Who? Where?
JUDAS: Where the hedge is broken. I could swear I saw the shadow of a man.
BYKE: Stop here. I'll see. (*Exits.*)
JUDAS: (*Solus.*) I begin to shiver. But it must be done or we starve. Why should I tremble? it's the safest job we ever planned. If they discover us, our secret will save us:—we know too much to be sent to jail.

(*Re-enter Byke, slowly.*)

BYKE: There are traces, but I can see no one. (*Looking off.*)
JUDAS: Suppose we should have been overheard!
BYKE: (*Glaring at her.*) Overheard? Bah! no one could understand.
JUDAS: Come, let us go to the wagon and be off.
BYKE: (*Always looking off.*) Go you, I will follow. Bring it round by the station, and wait for me in the shadows of the trees and I will follow. (*Judas goes off. Byke, after a moment,—still looking,—buttons up his coat and hides behind wood.*) Heigho! I must be off.

(*Enter Snorkey, slowly.*)

SNORKEY: Tracked 'em again! We're the latest fashionable arrivals at Long Branch. "Mr. Byke and Lady, and Brigadier-General Snorkey, of New York;"— there's an item for the papers! With a horse and wagon, they'll be at the seaside in two hours; but in the train I think I'll beat 'em. Then to find Cap'n Trafford, and give him the wink, and be ready to receive the distinguished visitors with all the honors. Robbery; Burglary; Murder;—that's Byke's catechism:—"What's to be done when you're hard up? Steal! What's to be done if you're caught at it? Kill!" It's short and easy, and he lives up to it like a good many Christians don't live up to their laws. (*Looking off.*) They're out of sight. Phew! it's midsummer, but I'm chilled to the bone; something like a piece of ice has been stuck between my shoulders all day, and something like a black mist is always before me. (*Byke is behind tree.*) Just like old Nettly told me he felt, the night before Fredericksburg;—and next day he was past all feeling,—hit with a shell, and knocked into so many pieces, I didn't know which to call my old friend. Well, (*Slapping his chest.*) we've all got to go; and if I can save *them*, I'll have some little capital to start the next world on. The next world perhaps I shan't be the maimed beggar *there* that I am in this. (*Takes out pistol, examines cap; goes off, Byke gliding after him.*)

SCENE III

Railroad Station at Shrewsbury Bend. The station shed, platform around it, and door at side, window in front. Clump of shrubs and tree. The Railroad Track runs from left to right. View of Shrewsbury River in perspective. Night. Moonlight. The switch, with a red lantern and Signalman's coat hanging on it. The signal lamp and post beside it.

(*As the scene opens, several packages are lying about the stage, among them a bundle of axes. The Signalman is wheeling in a small barrel, whistling at his work. Enter Laura in walking dress, feebly.*)

LAURA: It is impossible for me to go further. A second time I've fled from home and friends, but now they will never find me. The trains must all have passed, and there are no conveyances till to-morrow. (*She sits at clump.*)
SIGNALMAN: Beg pardon, ma'am, looking for anybody?
LAURA: Thank you, no. Are you the man in charge of this station?
SIGNALMAN: Yes, ma'am.
LAURA: When is there another train for New York?
SIGNALMAN: New York? Not till morning. We've only one more train to-night; that's the down one; it'll be here in about twenty minutes—"Express Train."
LAURA: What place is that?
SIGNALMAN: That? That's the signal station shed. It serves for store-room, depot, baggage-room, and everything.
LAURA: Can I stay there to-night?
SIGNALMAN: There? Well it's an odd place, and I should think you would hardly like it. Why don't you go to the hotel?
LAURA: I have my reasons—urgent ones. It is not because I want money. You shall have this (*Producing portmonnaie.*) if you let me remain here.
SIGNALMAN: Well, I've locked up a good many things in there over night, but I never had a young lady for freight before. Besides, ma'm, I don't know anything about you. You know it's odd that you won't go to a decent hotel, and plenty of money in your pocket.
LAURA: You refuse me—well—I shall only have to sit here all night.
SIGNALMAN: Here, in the open air? Why, it would kill you.
LAURA: So much the better.
SIGNALMAN: Excuse me for questions, Miss, but you're a running away from some one, ain't you?
LAURA: Yes.

SIGNALMAN: Well, I'd like to help you. I'm a plain man you know and I'd like to help you, but there's one thing would go agin' me to assist in. (*Laura is interested.*) I'm on to fifty years of age, and I've many children, some on 'em daughters grown. There's a many temptations for young gals, and sometimes the old man has to put on the brakes a bit, for some young men are wicked enough to persuade the gals to steal out of their father's house in the dead of night, and go to shame and misery. So tell me this—it ain't the old man, and the old man's home you've left, young lady?

LAURA: No; you good, honest fellow—no—I have no father.

SIGNALMAN: Then, by Jerusalem! I'll do for you what I can. Anything but run away from them that have not their interest but yours at heart. Come, you may stay there, but I'll have to lock you in.

LAURA: I desire that you should.

SIGNALMAN: It's for your safety as much as mine. I've got a patent lock on that door that would give a skeleton key the rheumatism to fool with it. You don't mind the baggage. I'll have to put it in with you, hoes, shovels, mowing machines, and what is this—axes. Yes, a bundle of axes. If the Superintendent finds me out, I'll ask him if he was afraid you'd run off with these. (*Laughs.*) So, if you please, I'll first tumble 'em in. (*Puts goods in house, Laura sitting on platform looking at him. When all in, he comes towards her, taking up cheese-box to put it in Station.*) I say, Miss, I ain't curious—but, of course, it's a *young man* you're a going to?

LAURA: So far from that, it's a young man I'm running away from.

SIGNALMAN: (*Dropping box.*) Running away from a young man! Let me shake hands with you. (*Shakes her hand.*) Lord, it does my heart good! At your age, too! (*Seriously.*) I wish you'd come and live down in my neighborhood a while, among my gals. (*Shaking his head.*) You'd do a power of good. (*Putting box in station.*)

LAURA: I've met an excellent friend. And here at least I can be concealed until to-morrow—then for New York. My heart feels lighter already—it's a good omen.

SIGNALMAN: Now, Miss, bless your heart, here's your hotel ready. (*Goes to switch and takes coat off, putting it on.*)

LAURA: Thanks, my good friend; but not a word to any one—till to-morrow; not even—not even to your girls.

SIGNALMAN: Not a word, I promise you. If I told my girls, it would be over the whole village before morning. (*She goes in. He locks the door. Laura appears at window facing audience.*)

LAURA: Lock me in safely.

SIGNALMAN: Ah! be sure I will. There! (*Tries door.*) Safe as a jail. (*Pulls out watch, and then looking at track with lantern.*) Ten minutes and down she comes. It's all safe this way, my noisy beauty, and you may come as soon as you like. Good night, Miss!

LAURA : (*At window.*) Good night.

SIGNALMAN: Running away from young man. Ha! ha! ha! (*He goes to track, then looks down—lights his pipe and is trudging off when enter Snorkey.*)

SNORKEY: Ten minutes before the train comes. I'll wait here for it. (*To Signalman, who re-enters.*) Hollo, I say, the train won't stop here too long, will it?

SIGNALMAN: Too long? It won't stop here at all.

SNORKEY: I must reach the shore to-night. There'll be murder done, unless I can prevent it!

SIGNALMAN: Murder, or no murder, the train can't be stopped.

SNORKEY: It's a lie. By waving the red signal for danger, the engineer must stop, I tell you!

SIGNALMAN: Do you think I'm a fool! What! disobey orders and lose my place; then what's to become of my family? (*Exit.*)

SNORKEY: I won't be foiled. I will confiscate some farmer's horse about here, and get there before them somehow. (*Byke enters at back with loose coil of rope in his hand.*) Then when Byke arrives in his donkey cart he'll be ready to sit for a picture of surprise. (*Byke enters suddenly throwing coil over Snorkey.*)

BYKE: Will he?

SNORKEY: Byke!

BYKE: Yes, Byke. Where's that pistol of yours? (*Tightening rope round his arm.*)

SNORKEY: In my breast pocket.

BYKE: (*Taking it.*) Just what I wanted.

SNORKEY: You ain't a going to shoot me?

BYKE: No!

SNORKEY: Well, I'm obliged to you for that.

BYKE: (*Leading him to platform.*) Just sit down a minute, will you.

SNORKEY: What for? (*Laura appears horror struck at window.*)

BYKE: You'll see.

SNORKEY: Well, I don't mind if I do take a seat. (*Sits down. Byke coils the rope round his legs.*) Hollo! what's this?

BYKE: You'll see. (*Picks the helpless Snorkey up.*)

SNORKEY: Byke, what are you going to do!

BYKE: Put you to bed. (*Lays him across the railroad track.*)

SNORKEY: Byke, you don't mean to—My God, you are a villain!

BYKE: (*Fastening him to rails.*) I'm going to put you to bed. You won't toss much. In less than ten minutes you'll be sound asleep. There, how do you like it? You'll get down to the Branch before me, will you? You dog me and play the eavesdropper, eh! Now do it if you can. When you hear the thunder under your head and see the lights dancing in your eyes, and feel the iron wheels a foot from your neck, remember Byke! (*Exit.*)

LAURA: O, Heavens! he will be murdered before my eyes! How can I aid him?

SNORKEY: Who's that?

LAURA: It is I. Do you not know my voice?

SNORKEY: That I do; but I almost thought I was dead, and it was an angel's. Where are you?

LAURA: In the station.

SNORKEY: I can't see you, but I can hear you. Listen to me, Miss, for I've got only a few minutes to live.

LAURA: (*Shaking door.*) God help me! and I cannot aid you.

SNORKEY: Never mind me, Miss. I might as well die now, and here, as at any other time. I'm not afraid. I've seen death in almost every shape, and none of them scare me; but, for the sake of those you love, I would live. Do you hear me?

LAURA: Yes! yes!

SNORKEY: They are on the way to your cottage—Byke and Judas—to rob and murder.

LAURA: (*In agony.*) O, I must get out! (*Shakes window bars.*) What shall I do?

SNORKEY: Can't you burst the door?

LAURA: It is locked fast.

SNORKEY: Is there nothing in there?—no hammer?—no crowbar?

LAURA: Nothing! (*Faint steam whistle heard in the distance.*) O, heavens! The train! (*Paralysed for an instant.*) The axe!!!

SNORKEY: Cut the woodwork! Don't mind the lock—cut round it! How my neck tingles! (*A blow at door is heard.*) Courage! (*Another.*) Courage! (*The steam whistle heard again—nearer, and rumble of train on track. Another blow.*) That's a true woman! Courage! (*Noise of locomotive heard—with whistle. A last blow; the door swings open, mutilated—the lock hanging—and Laura appears, axe in hand.*)

SNORKEY: Here—quick! (*She runs and unfastens him. The locomotive lights glare on the scene.*) Victory! Saved! Hooray! (*Laura leans exhausted against switch.*) And these are the women who ain't to have a vote!

(*As Laura takes his head from the track, the train of cars rushes past with roar and whistle from left to right.*)

END OF ACT IV

ACT V

An elegant boudoir at Courtland's cottage, Long Branch; open window and balcony at back; moonlight exterior; tree overhanging balcony. Bed and toilette table; arm chair; door; lighted lamp on toilette table; dresses on chair by bed and by window. Music.

(Pearl is discovered en negligee brushing her hair out at table before mirror.)

PEARL: I don't feel a bit sleepy. What a splendid drive we had! I like that foreigner. What an elegant fellow he is! Ray is nothing to him. I wonder if I'm in love with him. Pshaw! What an idea! I don't believe I could love anybody much. How sweetly he writes!—(*Picks up letter and sits on chair.*) "You were more lovely than ever to-night; with one more thing, you'd be an angel!" Now, that's perfectly splendid: "with one more thing, you'd be an angel—that one thing is love. They tell me Mr. Trafford is your professed admirer. I'm sure he could never be called your lover—for he seems incapable of any passion but Melancholy." It's quite true. Ray does not comprehend me. (*Takes up another letter.*) "Pearl, forgive me if I have been cross and cold. For the future, I will do my duty, as your affianced husband, better." Now, did ever anyone hear such talk as that from a lover? Lover!—O, dear! I begin to feel that he can love, but not me. Well, I'd just as soon break—if he'd be the first to speak. How nice and fresh the air is!—(*She turns down lamp.*) It's much nicer here, than going to bed. (*Settles her self in tete-a-tete for a nap. Pause.*)

(Moonbeams fall on Byke, who appears above the balcony. He gets over the rail and enters.)

BYKE: Safely down! I've made no mistake—no, this is her room. What a figure I am for a lady's chamber. (*Goes to table, picks up delicate lace handkerchief, and wipes his face.*) Phew! Hot! (*Puts handkerchief in his pocket.*) Now for my bearings. (*Taking huge clasp-knife from his pocket.*) There's the bed where she's sleeping like a precious infant, and here—(*Sees Pearl in chair and steals round at back, looking down at her.*) It's so dark—I can't recognize the face. It's a wonder she don't feel me in the air and dream of me. If she does she'll wake sure—but it's easy to settle that. (*Takes phial of chloroform from his pocket, saturates the handkerchief he picked up, and applies it.*) So!—now my charmer—we'll have the ear-rings. (*Takes them out.*) What's here? (*Going to table.*) Bracelets—diamonds! (*Going to dresses, and feeling in the pockets.*) Money! That's handy. (*He puts all in a bag, and hands them over balcony.*) Now for the drawers, there's where the treasure must be. Locked? (*Tries them with bunch of keys.*) Patent lock, of course! It amuses me to see people buying patent locks, when there's one key will fit 'em all. (*Produces small crowbar, and just as he is about to force the drawer, a shout is heard, and noise of wagon.*) What's that? (*Jumps, catching at bureau, which falls over.*) Damnation!

PEARL: (*Starting up.*) Who's there? What's that?

BYKE: Silence, or I'll kill you!

PEARL: Help! Help!

BYKE: (*Running to bureau for knife.*) You will have it my pretty one. (*Pearl runs to door.*)

PEARL: Save me! Save me! (*Byke pursues her, the door bursts open and Ray and Laura enter. Byke turns and runs to balcony, and confronts Snorkey and Bermudas, who have clambered over.*)

LAURA: Just in time.

RAY: (*Seizing Byke.*) Scoundrel!

SNORKEY: Hold him, Governor! Hold him. (*Assists Ray to bind Byke in chair.*)

BERMUDAS: Sixty-sixth and last round. The big 'un floored, and Bermudas as fresh as a daisy.

PEARL: Dear, dear Laura, you have saved me.

RAY: Yes, Pearl; from more than you can tell.

LAURA: No, no, her saviors are there. (*Pointing to Bermudas and Snorkey.*) Had it not been for the one, I should never have learned your danger, and but for the other, we could never have reached you in time.

SNORKEY: Bermudas and his fourth editions did it. Business enterprise and Bermudas' pony express worked the oracle this time.

BERMUDAS: The way we galloped! Sa-a-y, my pony must have thought the extras was full of lively intelligence.

PEARL: Darling Laura, you shall never leave us again.

RAY: No! never.

SNORKEY: Beg pardon, Cap'n, what are we to do with this here game we've brought down?

RAY: The Magistrates will settle with him.

SNORKEY: Come, old fellow!

BYKE: One word, I beg. My conduct, I know, has been highly reprehensible. I have acted injudiciously, and have been the occasion of more or less inconvenience to every one here. But I wish to make amends, and therefore I tender you all in this public manner my sincere apologies. I trust this will be entirely satisfactory.

RAY: Villain!

BYKE: I have a word to say to you, sir.

SNORKEY: Come, that's enough.

BYKE: My good fellow, don't interrupt gentlemen who are conversing together. (*To Ray.*) I address you, sir—you design to commit me to the care of the officers of the law?

RAY: Most certainly.

BYKE: And you will do your best towards having me incarcerated in the correctional establishments of this country? (*Ray bows.*)

SNORKEY: How very genteel!

BYKE: Then I have to say if you will, I shall make a public exposure of certain matters connected with a certain young lady.

LAURA: Do not think that will deter us from your punishment. I can bear even more than I have—for the sake of justice.

BYKE: Excuse me, but I did not even remotely refer to you.

LAURA: To whom, then?

BYKE: (*Pointing to Pearl.*) To her.

RAY: Miss Courtland?

BYKE: O, dear! no, sir. The daughter of old Judas—the spurious child placed in *your* cradle, Miss Laura Courtland, when you were abducted from it by your nurse.

PEARL: What does he say?

BYKE: That you're a beggar's child—we have the proofs! Deliver me to prison, and I produce them.

RAY: Wretch!

PEARL: Then it's you, dear Laura, have been wronged—while I—

LAURA: You are my sister still—whatever befalls!

PEARL: Oh, I'm so glad it's so! Ray won't want to marry me, now—at least, I hope so; for I know h‿ loves you—he always loved you—and you will be happy together.

RAY: Pearl, what are you saying?

PEARL: Don't interrupt me! I mean every word of it. Laura, I've been very foolish, I know. I ought to have tried to reunite you—but there is time.

RAY: Dear Laura! Is there, indeed, still time? (*She gives her hand.*)

BYKE: Allow me to suggest that a certain proposition I had the honor to submit has not yet been answered.

RAY: Release him. (*Snorkey undoes his cords.*)

BYKE: Thank you—not so rough! Thank you.

RAY: Now, go—but remember, if you ever return to these parts you shall be tried, not only for this burglary, but for the attempt to kill that poor fellow.

BYKE: Thank you. Good-bye. (*To Snorkey.*) Good-bye, my dear friend; overlook our little dispute, and write to me. (*Aside.*) They haven't caught Judas, and she shall make them pay handsomely for her silence, yet.

(*Enter Peachblossom.*)

PEACHBLOSSOM: O Miss! O, such an accident—old Judas!

LAURA & BYKE: Well?

PEACHBLOSSOM: She was driving along the road away from here—just now, when her horse dashed close to the cliff and tumbled her down all of a heap. They've picked her up, and they tell me she is stone dead.

BYKE: (*Aside.*) Dead! And carried her secret with her! All's up. I'll have to emigrate. (*Aloud.*) My friends, pardon my emotion—this melancholy event has made me a widower. I solicit your sympathies in my bereavement. (*Exit.*)

BERMUDAS: Go to Hoboken and climb a tree! I guess I'll follow him and see he don't pick up anything on his way out. (*Exit Bermudas.*)

SNORKEY: Well there goes a pretty moment of grief. Ain't he a cool 'un? If I ever sets up an ice cream saloon, I'll have him for head freezer.

PEACHBLOSSOM: O, Miss Laura, mayn't I live with you now, and never leave no more.

LAURA: Yes, you shall live with me as long as you please.

SNORKEY: That won't be long if I can help it. (*Peachblossom blushes.*) Beg pardon. I suppose we'd better be going. The ladies must be tired, Cap'n, at this time of night.

RAY: Yes, it is night! It is night always for me. (*Moving towards door.*)

LAURA: (*Placing one hand on his shoulder, taking his hand.*) But there is a tomorrow. You see it cannot be dark forever.

PEARL: Hope for to-morrow, Ray.

LAURA: We shall have cause to bless it, for it will bring the long sought sunlight of our lives.

Curtain.

END

THE GIRL
OF THE GOLDEN WEST

David Belasco

"In those strange days, people coming from God knows where, joined forces in that far western land; and according to the rude custom of the camp became known as 'St. Louis Joe,' 'Noo Orleans Bill,' 'Handsome Jack,' 'Ace-high Jim,' etc.; and here, their real names lost and unrecorded, they struggled, laughed, gambled, cursed, killed, loved, and worked out their strange destinies in a manner incredible to us of to-day. Of one thing only are we sure—they lived!"

Early History of California

FIRST PICTURE: *In the Sierras. A glimpse of the home of the Girl on Cloudy Mountain.*

SECOND PICTURE: *At the foot of Cloudy Mountain, showing the Girl's place of business: the Polka Saloon.*

ACT I.—*In the Polka Saloon. Midnight.*
"The Girl and the Stranger."

ACT II.—*In the home of the Girl, one o'clock in the morning.*
"Two people who came from nothing."

ACT III.—*The dance-hall of the Polka. A few days later. Nine o'clock in the morning.*
"No star is ever lost we once have seen,
We always may be what we might have been."

ACT IV.—*The boundless prairies of the West. At the dawn of a day about a week later.*
"Oh, my beautiful West!
Oh, my California!"

THE CAST:

The Girl
Wowkle, the fox, Billie's Squaw
Dick Johnson, a stranger (Ramerrez, the Road-Agent)
Jack Rance, gambler and sheriff
Sonora Slim
Trinidad Joe
Nick, bartender at the "Polka"
The Sidney Duck, a faro-dealer
Jim Larkens
Happy Halliday
Handsome Charlie
Deputy Sheriff
Billy Jackrabbit, an Indian
Ashby, Wells-Fargo Agent
José Castro, ex-padroña of the bull-fights and horse-breaker, now with Ramerrez's Band
Rider of the Pony Express
Jake Wallace, a traveling-camp minstrel
Bucking Billy, from Watson's
The Lookout
A Faro-Dealer
The Boy from the Ridge
Joe
Concertina Player
Citizens of the Camp and Boys of the Ridge

TIME: During the days of the gold fever, 1849-50
PLACE: Cloudy Mountain, California, a mining camp

ACT I

The two scenes, which precede the dialogue of the play, are not drawn in detail but are merely a few lines and lights to show the steep snow-tipped Sierras, the trail, the silent California night, deep ravines, and cabins of the miners of '49 hid amongst the manzanitas and pines; in fact, the scene represents a little world by it-self, drawn in a few crude strokes, to explain more than the author could tell in a thousand pages.

The curtain rises to a glimpse of Cloudy Mountain, in the Sierras. The peak is white, the sky above very blue, and the moon, which seems strangely near, shines on the steep trail leading up to the cabin of the Girl. A lamp, placed in the cabin window by Wowkle, the squaw, shows that the Girl has not yet come home from her place of business, the Polka Saloon.

This scene shifts to an exterior view of the Polka Saloon and the miners' cabins at the foot of Cloudy Mountain. The cheerful glow of kerosene lamps, the rattle of poker chips, and an occasional "whoop," show that life in the Polka is in full swing. The strains of "Dooda Day" are heard from within, the singer accompanying himself on the concertina:

"Camp town ladies, sing this song, Dooda! Dooda!
Camptown race track, five miles long, Dooda! Dooda! Day.
G'wine to run all night,
G'wine to run all day,
Bet my money on a bob-tail nag,
Somebody bet on the bay."

(As the scene shifts to the interior of the Polka, we see a large square barroom, built of rough pine boards. A pair of scales for weighing gold-dust, and a dice-box used to "shake for drinks," are on the bar. Behind the bar on a shelf are liquors, cigars, and chewing tobacco.

The till contains one and two bit pieces, Mexican dollars, and slugs of gold ($50).

The safe is made out of an empty whiskey keg. Boxes and cans of provisions lie on the floor, and strings of red peppers hang from the rude rafters. A stuffed grizzly bear graces the scene, a small green parasol in one paw, a battered old silk hat on its head. An odd collection of hats and caps are stuck on the prongs of a pair of elk antlers on the wall, and several saddles lie on the floor under the antlers.

The furniture is composed of pine chairs, a faro table, a poker table, and an old whittled desk at which the miners write their rare letters to those at home.

A $5000 reward for the road-agent, Ramerrez, or information leading to his capture, signed by Wells-Fargo, is tacked to the back of the door. The platform on which a camp minstrel is singing "Dooda Day" is protected by a piece of sheet iron which the musician can lift as a shield to ward off stray bullets in case of a sudden quarrel. The room is heated by a blazing pine log fire in an adobe fireplace. A square opening in the wall leads to the dance-hall left; a ladder, resting against a balcony over the bar, enables the bartender to ascend in case of trouble and cast a quick glance over both rooms.

As the interior of the barroom is disclosed, Sonora Slim, a tall, lanky miner with an emphatic manner, and Trinidad Joe, his partner, are playing at faro. The dealer is "Sid," an Australian known as "Sidney Duck," fat, greasy, unctuous, and cowardly. He is an expert at fancy shuffling. His even voice is heard from time to time, murmuring below the dialogue, as the game goes on. A case-keeper and lookout complete the group at the faro table. Billy Jackrabbit, a full-blooded Indian, lazy, shifty and beady-eyed, wearing moccasins, odds and ends of a white man's costume, and a quantity of brass jewelry, is watching the game. He frequents the barroom, picking up cigar butts, and occasionally, when the opportunity presents itself, steals a drink.

Handsome Charlie, a big picturesque miner, is drinking at the bar with Happy Halliday, a long-legged fellow, high-booted and spurred. Nick, the bartender, is busy during the act carrying drink into the dance-hall and returning to those in the barroom. He wears 'Frisco trousers, very high-heeled boots, a flashy necktie, a gay velvet vest. He combs his hair over his forehead in a cowlick.)

SONORA: (*Joining the singer who is accompanying himself on the concertina.*) "Dooda! Dooda! Day!" (*To the faro-dealer.*) What did that last eight do?
SID: Lose.
SONORA: Well, let the tail go with the hide.

(*Nick, who has entered, sets a few fresh candles about and gives a drink to the concertina player who goes into the dance-hall.*)

TRINIDAD: How many times did the aces win?
SID: Three times.
BILLY JACKRABBIT: Give Billy Jackrabbit four two dolla—Mexican—chips.

(*Sid gives some chips to the Indian. As the music starts in the dance-hall, and the shuffling of feet is heard, Happy, unable to resist, gives a long whoop.*)

HAPPY: Root hog or die!

(*With another whoop, he joins the dancers. Handsome would follow him, but decides to remain to take another drink.*)

SONORA: (*Suspiciously.*) See here, gamboleer Sid, you're too lucky.
TRINIDAD: You bet! More chips, Australiar.

(*Sid gives some chips to Trinidad. The proprietor of a wheel-of-fortune, which is set up in the dance-hall, is heard to call in a professional voice.*)

PROPRIETOR OF THE WHEEL-OF-FORTUNE: And round goes the wheel!
HAPPY'S VOICE: (*Heard above the music.*) Git, you loafer!

(*A muffled shot is heard. The music stops abruptly.*)

A VOICE: (*From the dance-hall.*) Missed!

(*Nick hastens off, not forgetting to take a bottle and glasses with him. During the excitement, Billy Jackrabbit steals four cigars from a box on the bar.*)

THE PROPRIETOR OF THE WHEEL-OF-FORTUNE: The lone star now rises!

(*The music continues and Nick re-enters, giving the Indian a suspicious glance. Billy Jackrabbit decides to take himself off for a short time.*)

NICK: (*Explaining as loud whoops are heard.*) Boys from the Ridge—cuttin' up in the dance-hall. Hy're you, Jim?

(*Jim Larkens, shabby and despondent, a miner who has not struck it rich, returns Nick's greeting, gets paper, a pen and ink from the bar, and sits at the desk to write the usual sad letter to his family in the East.*)

SONORA: (*Looking towards the dancers with disgust.*) I don't dance with men for partners. When I chassay, Trinidad, I want a femi*nine* piece of flesh and blood—with garters on!
TRINIDAD: You bet!
SONORA: I say, Nick. (*Going to the bar, confidentially.*) Has the Girl said anything more about me to-day?
NICK: (*Lying as usual.*) Well, you got the first chance.
SONORA: (*Grinning.*) Yes? Cigars for the boys.

(*Nick brings a box of cigars to the far table, and the men smoke.*)

VOICE OF THE FIDDLER: (*Calling in time to the dance music*):
    "First lady swing with the right hand gent,
    With the left hand gent, with the right hand gent,
    First lady swing with the left hand gent,
    And—lady in the centre, and gents all around!"

(*During this, two men from the rival mining-camp at the Ridge enter—dancing up to the bar.*)

SID: Hello, boys! 'Ow's things at the Ridge?
ONE OF THE RIDGE MEN: (*Defiantly.*) Wipes this camp off the map.

(All jump to their feet, save Sid. The insult calls for immediate punishment.)

SONORA: What?
TRINIDAD: Say it again!

(Nick persuades the Ridge boys to retire to avert bloodshed, and they disappear with a final defiant whoop as Jake Wallace, a favorite camp minstrel, who journeys from one camp to another, is heard in the road outside, playing on his banjo and singing.)

JAKE:
"Wait for the wagon—wait for the wagon—
Wait for the wagon and we'll all take a ride.
Wait for the wagon, and we'll all take a ride."
NICK: *(Announcing in extravagant style.)* Aw! Here he is, boys—just up from the Ridge—Jake Wallace, the camp favorite!

(Jake Wallace enters, carrying a banjo, his face half blackened. He wears a long minstrel's duster over his heavy coat, flapping shoes, and a "stove-pipe" hat. He is the typical camp minstrel.)

SONORA: Howdy, Jake!
HANDSOME: Hello, Jake, old man! How be you?
TRINIDAD, SID and the CASE-KEEPER: Hello, Jake!
JAKE: *(Nods, smiling, seats himself on the musician's stand, in the musician's chair.)* Hello, boys! My first selection, friends, will be, "The little—"
SONORA: Aw—give us "Old Dog Tray," Jake. *(Jake tunes up.)*
TRINIDAD: *(Apart to Nick.)* Nick, have you saw the Girl?
NICK: *(Confidentially.)* Well, I gave her your message. You've got the best chance. *(Digs him playfully in the ribs and winks at him.)*
TRINIDAD: Whiskey for everybody.

(Nick sets out whiskey and glasses, and the men drink.)

JAKE: *(Strikes a chord, announcing impressively.)* "Old Dog Tray, or Echoes from Home."

(During the song, Billy Jackrabbit, who has followed Jake on, sits on the floor playing solitaire. The miners continue to gamble.)

"How often do I picture
Them old folks down to home:
And often wonder if they think of me!"

(Larkens, dropping his letter in the box on the floor, chokes back a sob.)

SONORA: Slug's worth of chips.

(Sid give chips to Sonora.)

JAKE:
"Would angel mother know me,
If back there I did roam?
Would old dog Tray remember me?"

(*The singer pauses to take a drink from Nick.*)

Now, boys!

(*All join in the chorus, keeping time with their feet.*)

ALL:
"Oh, mother, angel mother, are you a-waitin' there,
Beside the littul cottage on the lea?"
JAKE: (*Alone.*) "On the lea—"
ALL:
"How often would she bless me, all in them days so fair—
Would old dog Tray remember me?"
SONORA: "Remember me!"

(*Larkens breaks down and sobs. All stop playing and turn in their chairs, looking at him.*)

Why, Jim . . .
LARKENS: Say, boys,—I'm homesick and I'm broke, and I don't give a damn who knows it. I want to go home again . . . I'm tired o' drillin' rocks . . . I want to be out in the fields again . . . I want to see the grain growin' . . . I want the dirt in the furrows at home . . . I want old Pennsylvany . . . I want my folks . . . I'm done! I'm done! I'm done! (*He sobs on the bar, his face buried in his hands.*)
JAKE: (*Quite used to these scenes.*)
"Oh, mother, angel mother, are you a-waitin'—"
SONORA: (*Motions Jake to stop singing. Jake, understanding, smilingly makes a gesture as though touching an imaginary hat brim, and collects his money.*) Here, Jake. (*Tosses a coin to Jake.*) Boys, Jim Larkens allows he's goin' back East. Chip in. (*The miners and gamblers throw money on the table. When the cash is handed to Sonora, he gives it to Larkens.*) Here you are, Jim.
JIM: (*Deeply touched.*) Thank you, boys—thank you. (*Crying, he stumbles out of the room.*)
TRINIDAD: (*Who has suddenly made a lunge at Sid's card box.*) That ain't a square deal—he's cheating!

(*Billy Jackrabbit picks up a chair, and holds it up to protect himself; Jake hides behind the shield. The lookout steals out as though in league with Sid. Nick re-enters with a large tray of whiskey glasses. Handsome and the gambler seize Sid and bring him down in front of the table.*)

SONORA: Lift his hand!
TRINIDAD: Hist his arms! (*Taking up the deck of cards and throwing it on the table.*) There!

SONORA: String him up!

TRINIDAD: You bet!

SID: (*Whining.*) For 'eaven's sike!

NICK: Chicken lifter!

TRINIDAD: String him!

SID: Oh, boys! Boys!

RANCE: (*Who has come in, stands impassively watching the scene. He is the cool, waxen, deliberate gambler. His hands, almost feminine in their whiteness, are as waxen as his face. He has a very black moustache. He wears the beaver hat of the times, and an immaculate suit of broadcloth. His boots are highly polished, long and narrow with high heels, his trousers strapped over them. He wears a white puffed shirt, with a diamond stud held by side chains, and a large diamond flashes on his hand. He smokes the Spanish cigarros.*) Well, gentlemen, what's this?

SONORA: Ah! Here's Jack Rance.

TRINIDAD: (*Threatening Sid.*) The Sheriff!

RANCE: What's the matter with the cyards? (*He takes out his handkerchief, delicately unfolding it, and flicks it over his boots.*)

SONORA: The Sidney Duck's cheated.

TRINIDAD: String him! (*To Sid.*) Come on,—you!

RANCE: Wait a minute. Don't be hasty, gentlemen. I've got something to say about this. I don't forget, although I am Sheriff of Manzanita County, that I'm running four games. It's men like him cast reflections on square-minded sporting men like myself; and worse—he casts reflections on the Polka, the establishment of the one decent woman in Cloudy.

NICK: (*Indignant.*) You bet!

SONORA: A lady, damn it! (*Turning on Sid.*) You lily-covered skunk!

TRINIDAD: String him up!

HANDSOME: Come on!

(*There is general movement towards Sid.*)

RANCE: Hold on! Hold on! After all, gents, what's death? A kick and you're off. I've thought of a worse punishment. Give him his coat. (*Handsome gives a coat to Sid, who puts it on.*) Stand him over here. (*Sid is pushed forward.*) Hand me the deuce of spades. (*Sonora gives Rance the card. Rance takes a pin from Sid's cravat, and pins the card over Sid's heart.*) I place it over his heart as a warning. He can't leave the camp, and he never plays cyards again. Handsome, pass the word to the boys.

(*Handsome goes into the dance-hall to spread the news.*)

SID: (*Sniffs imploringly.*) Ow—now! Don't say that! Don't say that!

NICK: (*Pointing to the door.*) Git! Git!

(*Sid leaves the room hurriedly, followed by Billy Jackrabbit, who is never quite comfortable when the Sheriff is laying down the law. Jake, one eye on the would-be lynchers, is softly playing "Pop Goes the Weasel."*)

RANCE: (*Cooly, as though nothing had occurred.*) Well, gentlemen, a little game of poker, just for social recreation? Nick, chips.

SONORA: Ha! I'm your Injun! (*Goes to the poker table as Nick brings down the poker chips.*)

TRINIDAD: (*Joining Rance.*) That's me!

(*But before the game can proceed, a Deputy Sheriff enters, a gaunt, hollow cheeked, muscular man, with a heavy, sweeping moustache, his hair in a cowlick—wearing a pale, faded beaver hat and a heavy overcoat, his pistol and powder flask in his belt.*)

DEPUTY: (*To Rance.*) Sheriff, Ashby, of Wells-Fargo, just rode in with his posse.

RANCE: Ashby? Why, what's he doing here?

DEPUTY: He's after Ramerrez.

RANCE: Ramerrez? Oh, that polite road-agent that's been visitin' the other camps?

DEPUTY: Yes, they say he has just turned into our county.

(*Nick gives the Deputy a drink.*)

SONORA: (*Apprehensively.*) What? Our county?

(*Ashby enters,—a man to remember,—nervous, dogged, white and closely-cropped hair, very black eyebrows—thin lips. He wears 'Frisco clothing, which shows the wear and tear of the road. He is suave in his greetings, but quick in action and speech. He is never sober, never drunk, but continually drinking.*)

ASHBY: (*Greeting Rance.*) Hello, Sheriff!

RANCE: Boys, Mr. Ashby, of Wells-Fargo.

(*Ashby shakes hands with Trinidad and Sonora, then makes for the bar.*)

ASHBY: Hello, Nick!

NICK: Hello, Ash!

ASHBY: (*To the Deputy.*) How are you, sir? (*Deputy returns Ashby's greeting and passes off, as Ashby shakes hands warmly with Nick.*) Nick, give us a drink.

NICK: Sure. (*Takes four glasses and a bottle of whiskey to the poker table and then hastens off into the dance-hall.*)

ASHBY: Everybody'll have the same. (*The camp minstrel joins the group as Rance pours the whiskey.*) Well, gentlemen, I trust the Girl who runs the Polka is well?

SONORA: Fine as silk, Mr. Ashby. How long you been chasin' up this here road-agent?

ASHBY: Oh, he only took to the road three months ago. Wells-Fargo have had me and a posse busy ever since. He's a wonder.

SONORA: Must be, to evade *you*.

ASHBY: Yes, I can smell a road-agent in the wind; but, Rance, I expect to get that fellow right here in your county.

RANCE: Is this Ramerrez a Spaniard?

ASHBY: No, can't prove it. Heads a crew of greasers and Spaniards. His name's assumed.

RANCE: They say he robs you like a gentleman.

ASHBY: (*Lifting his glass.*) Well, look out for the greasers up the road!

(All drink.)

RANCE: We don't let 'em pass through here.
ASHBY: Well, boys, I've had a long ride. Wake me up when the Pony Express goes through. (*Takes off his coat, goes up to a table, and, setting a bottle of whiskey in a convenient spot, lies down on the table.*)
NICK: (*Bringing in a kettle of hot water and glasses containing whiskey and lemon.*) Regards of the Girl. Hot whiskey with lemming extract. (*He pours the hot water into the glasses.*)
RANCE: (*Accepting a glass.*) Gentlemen, the Girl! The only girl in the Camp—the girl I mean to make Mrs. Jack Rance!

(Nick catches Sonora's eye, also Trinidad's.)

SONORA: That's a joke, Rance. She makes you look like a Chinaman.
RANCE: (*Rising, at white heat.*) You prove that!
SONORA: In what particular spot will you have it?

(Instantly Rance's right hand creeps towards his pistol as Sonora, anticipating his movement, has reached for his weapon. Trinidad runs to the bar and drops behind it as Nick crouches out of sight at one end of it. Jake hides behind the shield.)

NICK: (*Seeing the Girl coming in through the dance-hall.*) The Girl . . . (*Coaxingly.*) Aw—take your drinks.

(Trinidad and Jake venture to peep out. The quarrel is over.)

RANCE: Ha! Ha! Ha! Once more, friends,—the Girl!
ALL: The Girl! (*They drink. Ashby snores peacefully.*)

(The Girl enters. The character of the Girl is rather complex. Her utter frankness takes away all suggestion of vice—showing her to be unsmirched, happy, careless, untouched by the life about her. Yet she has a thorough knowledge of what the men of her world generally want. She is used to flattery—knows exactly how to deal with men—is very shrewd—but quite capable of being a good friend to the camp boys. Handsome follows her and stands leaning against the bar, watching her admiringly.)

GIRL: Hello, boys! How's everything? Gettin' taken care of?
SONORA: (*Who melts whenever he sees her.*) Hello, Girl!
GIRL: Hello, Sonora!
TRINIDAD: Hello, Girl!
GIRL: Hello, Trin.
SONORA: Mix me a prairie oyster.
GIRL: I'll fix you right up, Sonora. (*As shots are heard in the dance-hall.*) Say, Nick—you quiet things down. (*Nick leaves the room.*) They've had about enough. Look here, Sonora: before I crack this egg, I'd like to state that eggs is four bits apiece—only two hens left. (*Giving a little push to Handsome, who has been leaning on the bar.*) Oh, run away, Handsome. (*Handsome sits, watching the Girl.*)

SONORA: Crack the egg—I'll stand it.

NICK: (*Re-entering, grinning, pouring out a drink, going to the Girl.*) Regards of Blond Harry.

GIRL: (*Taking it.*) Here: give it to me—(*Pouring it back into the bottle.*)—and say it hit the spot.

NICK: (*Whispering.*) Say, Min: throw around a few kind words—good for the bar.

GIRL: (*Good-naturedly.*) Oh, you! (*Exit Nick to deliver the Girl's message to Blond Harry.*) Ha! Ha! (*As Ashby awakens.*) Hello, Mr. Ashby!

ASHBY: (*Rousing and gallantly picking up his glass, goes to the bar to toast the Girl.*) Compliments of Wells-Fargo!

GIRL: Thank you. (*Shaking Sonora's drink.*) You see we live high shouldered here in Cloudy.

SONORA: You bet!

ASHBY: What cigars have you?

GIRL: Regalias, Auroras and Eurekas.

ASHBY: Any'll do.

NICK: (*Entering hurriedly.*) Man jest come in threatin' to shoot up the furniture.

GIRL: (*Quietly, giving Ashby a cigar.*) Who is it?

NICK: Old man Watson.

GIRL: Leave him shoot. He's good for it.

VOICE: (*From the inner room.*) Nick! Nick!

(*Nick hastens off as several shots are heard. In the excitement, Billy Jackrabbit, who has re-entered, quietly steals down to the faro table and drains a glass of whiskey which has been left standing there.*)

GIRL: Here, you Billy Jackrabbit: what are you doing? Did you marry my squaw yet?

BILLY JACKRABBIT: Not so much married squaw yet.

GIRL: No so much married? Come here, you thieving redskin—(*Billy Jackrabbit goes up to the bar.*) with a pocketful of my best cigars! (*She takes the cigars from him.*) You git up to my cabin and marry my squaw before I get there. Git! (*Billy Jackrabbit goes out.*) With a papoose six months old—it's awful! Here, Sonora: (*Bringing him the drink.*) here's your prairie oyster. Hello, Rance!

RANCE: Hello, Girl!

SONORA: Here, Girl: clear the slate out of that. (*Giving her a bag of gold-dust.*)

NICK: (*Re-entering with a bottle.*) Say, they's a fellow in there wants to know if we can help out on provisions.

GIRL: Sure. What does he want?

NICK: Bread. (*Putting the cigar-box and bottle back on the shelf.*)

GIRL: (*Behind the bar.*) Bread! Does he think we're runnin' a bakery?

NICK: Then he asked for sardines.

GIRL: Sardines! Great Gilead! You tell him we have nothing but straight provisions here: we got pickled oysters, smoking tobacco, an' the best whiskey he ever saw.

NICK: Yes'm.

TRINIDAD: You bet!

GIRL: Sonora. (*Gives him his change. Cleaning the slate on which she keeps the record of the drinks.*) Mr. Ashby,—change. (*She hands Ashby some coins.*)

ASHBY: (*Throws the money back on the bar.*) Keep the change. Buy a ribbon at the Ridge. Compliments of Wells-Fargo.

GIRL: (*Sweeping it into the drawer.*) Thank you.

SONORA: Girl: (*Going up to the bar.*) buy *two* ribbons at the Ridge. (*Throwing down a stack of silver dollars on the bar and facing Ashby. Insinuatingly.*) Fawn's *my* color! . . .

GIRL: Thank you.

RANCE: Play cyards.

ASHBY: (*Changing—raising his finger warningly.*) You, Girl! You must bank with us oftener, and then if this road-agent, Ramerrez, should drop in, you won't lose so much.

SONORA: The devil!

TRINIDAD: (*Thoughtfully.*) Ha!

GIRL: Oh, go on! I keep the specie in an empty keg now, but personally I've took to banking in my stocking.

NICK: (*Who has brought in an armful of wood and mended the fire.*) Say, we've got an awful pile this month—makes me sort o' nervous. Why, Sonora alone has got ten thousand in that keg fer safe keepin'. (*Pointing to a keg at the end of the bar.*)

ASHBY: And Ramerrez' band everywhere!

GIRL: Bet if a road-agent come in here, I could offer him a drink an' he'd treat me like a perfect lady.

SONORA: You bet he would, the darned old halibut!

NICK: Tobacco.

GIRL: Solace of Honeydew?

NICK: Dew. (*He takes it and is about to exit when the Deputy enters wildly.*)

DEPUTY: Boys! Boys! Pony Express!

(*The sound of the approaching pony has grown louder, and now stops quickly.*)

DRIVER OF THE PONY EXPRESS: (*Heard off.*) Hello!

(*Nick runs out.*)

DEPUTY'S VOICE: (*Outside.*) Hello!

DRIVER OF THE PONY EXPRESS: (*Unseen, speaking through the open door as though on horseback.*) Big hold-up last night at the Forks.

TRINIDAD: Hold-up?

DRIVER OF THE PONY EXPRESS: Ramerrez!

(*Enter Nick with several letters and one newspaper. He gives the mail to the Girl and goes to the bar.*)

SONORA: Ramerrez!

ASHBY: (*To the Girl.*) You see?

DRIVER OF THE PONY EXPRESS: (*Still out of sight.*) Look sharp! There's a greaser in the trail.

RANCE: A greaser? Deputy, go find him.

GIRL: (*Looking over the mail.*) Sonora, you got a newspaper. (*Sonora receives it joyously.*)

DRIVER OF THE PONY EXPRESS: So long!

ASHBY: (*Going to the door—calls.*) Pony Express: I want you.

HANDSOME: (*Leaning over Sonora—enviously.*) Sonora's got a newspaper.
SONORA: Yes—damn thing's two months old.
HANDSOME: (*Wistfully.*) Still, he *did* get a newspaper.

(*The Driver of the Pony Express enters, coming quickly towards Ashby. He is a thin young fellow of twenty—his skin deeply tanned by the wind—smooth-faced but unshaven. His clothing is weather-beaten and faded by wind, rain, dust and alkali. A leather patch is stitched over the seat of his breeches. His shabby leather gloves proclaim hard service. He is booted and spurred, and has a pistol in his belt. He carries a mail pouch.*)

ASHBY: You drop mail at the greaser settlement?
DRIVER OF THE PONY EXPRESS: Yes, sir—tough place.
ASHBY: Know a girl there named Nina Micheltoreña?
GIRL: (*Laughs.*) Nina Micheltoreña? Oh, they all know her. Whoo! She's one of them Cachuca girls, with droopy Spanish eyes. Oh, ask the boys about her! (*She slaps Handsome and Trinidad on the back.*)

(*The music starts in the dance-hall and the Girl runs off to see that her patrons are enjoying the evening. Handsome, Sonora, and Trinidad follow her off.*)

ASHBY: (*To the Driver of the Pony Express.*) Hold her letters.
DRIVER OF THE PONY EXPRESS: Yes, sir. (*He hastens off to ride to the next camp.*)
ASHBY: (*To Rance.*) Sheriff: I expect to see this Nina Micheltoreña tonight—here—in the Polka.
RANCE: You do? Well, the boys better look out for their watches. I met that lady once.
ASHBY: She wrote about that five thousand reward I offered for Ramerrez.
RANCE: What! She's after that? (*Shuffling the cards.*)
ASHBY: She knows something. (*Getting his coat. To the Girl who has re-entered and gone behind the bar.*) Well, I'll have a look at that greaser up the road. He may have his eye on the find in that stocking of yours.
GIRL: (*Good-naturedly.*) You be darned! (*Ashby goes out.*)
RANCE: Say, Minnie—
GIRL: (*Polishing glasses.*) H'm?
RANCE: Will you marry me?
GIRL: Nop.
RANCE: (*Going to the bar.*) Why not?
GIRL: 'Cause you got a wife in Noo Orleans—or so the mountain breezes say.
RANCE: Give me some cigars.
GIRL: (*Handing him cigars from a certain box.*) Them's your kind, Jack.
RANCE: (*Putting the cigars in his case.*) I'm stuck on you.
GIRL: (*Lightly.*) Thank you.
RANCE: I'm going to marry you.
GIRL: Think so?
RANCE: H'm . . . (*Lighting a cigar.*)
GIRL: They ain't a man here goin' to marry me.
NICK: (*Entering hurriedly.*) One good cigar.
GIRL: (*Handing a cigar to Nick.*) Here's your poison. Three bits. (*To Rance.*) Why, look at 'em! There's Handsome: got two wives I know of somewhere East—

(*Turning suddenly to Nick.*) Who's that cigar for?

NICK: Tommy!

GIRL: Give it back. He don't know a good cigar when he's smoking it. (*She puts the cigar back in the box, takes another and hands it to Nick.*) Same price. (*Nick goes off with the cigar.*) And Trin with a widder in Sacramento; and you—Ha! Not one of you travellin' under your own name.

NICK: (*Comes back, grinning.*) One whiskey.

GIRL: (*Pouring out the whiskey and giving it to Nick.*) Here you be.

NICK: With water.

GIRL: (*Putting the bottle back.*) No, no, you don't: no fancy drinks here.

NICK: Feller just rode in from the Crossin'—says he wants it with water.

GIRL: He'll take it straight, or git!

NICK: But he won't git.

GIRL: You send him to me—I'll curl his hair for him!

NICK: Yes'm. (*Exit.*)

RANCE: (*Earnestly.*) Give you a thousand dollars on the spot for a kiss.

GIRL: Some men invite bein' played.

RANCE: Well, what are men made for? (*Putting down a gold piece.*)

GIRL: (*Taking it.*) That's true.

RANCE: You can't keep on running this place alone—it's getting too big for you. Too much money circulating through the Polka. You need a man behind you. Marry me.

GIRL: Nop.

RANCE: My wife won't know it.

GIRL: Nop.

RANCE: Now, see here, Min—

GIRL: (*Firmly.*) No—take it straight, Jack—nop! Ah, come along: start your game again, Jack. Come along. (*Going to the faro table, Rance following her.*) Whoop la! Mula! Good Lord, look at that faro table!

RANCE: Listen: we may not have another chance.

GIRL: Look here, Jack: let's have it right now. I run this Polka alone because I like it. My father taught me the business, and—well, don't worry about me—I can look after myself. I carry my little wepping—(*Touching her pocket to show that she has a pistol.*). I'm independent—I'm happy—the Polka's paying an'—ha!—it's all bully! Say, what the devil do you mean proposin' to me with a wife in Noo Orleans? Now, this is a respectable saloon—an' I don't want no more of that talk.

RANCE: I didn't say nothin'.

GIRL: (*Tidying the faro table.*) Push me that queen. (*Rance slowly hands the card to her and, going to the table, leans thoughtfully against a chair.*) Thank you, Jack. No offense, Jack; but I got other idees of married life from what you have.

RANCE: Aw! Nonsense!

GIRL: (*Leaning against the faro table, facing Rance.*) I dunno about that. You see I had a home once, and I ain't forgot it. A home up over our little saloon in Soledad. Ha! I ain't forgot my father an' mother an' what a happy married couple they was. Lord! How they loved each other—it was beautiful!

SID: (*Entering, snivelling.*) Ow, Miss . . .

GIRL: Say—I've heard about you—you git! (*Sid hastily takes his departure. To Rance.*) I can see mother now . . . fussin' over father an' pettin' him, an' father dealin' faro—Ah, but he was square . . . and me, a kid as little as a kitten, under the table sneakin' chips for candy. Talk about married life! That was a little heaven. I guess everybody's got some remembrance of their mother tucked away. I always see mine at the faro table with her foot snuggled up to Dad's an' the light of lovin' in her eyes. Ah, she was a lady! No; (*Getting up from the table and going behind the bar.*) I couldn't share that table an' the Polka with any man—unless there was a heap o' carin' back of it. I couldn't, Jack, I couldn't.

RANCE: (*Restraining his anger.*) Oh, the boys were right! I *am* a Chinaman! (*Following her up to the bar.*)

GIRL: No, you're not, Jack.

RANCE: (*Following her.*) But once when I rode in here, it was nothing but Jack—Jack—Jack—Jack—Jack Rance! God! I nearly got you then.

GIRL: (*With playful sarcasm.*) Did you?

RANCE: Then you went on that trip to Sacramento and Monterey . . . and you changed . . . Who's the man?

GIRL: Ha! Ha! Ha! Ha! Ha!

RANCE: One of them high-toned Sacramento shrimps? (*As she laughs.*) Do you think he'd have *you*?

GIRL: (*Suddenly serious.*) What's the matter with me? Anythin' about me a high-toned gent would object to? Look here, Jack Rance, ain't I always been a perfect lady?

RANCE: Oh, Heaven knows your character's all right. (*He goes back to the faro table.*)

GIRL: (*Sarcastically.*) Well, that ain't your fault. Adios. (*She starts to leave the room, then pauses and looks at him.*) Jack . . . (*As he will not look at her, she turns again to go into the dance-hall, but, looking off, she sees an unexpected guest and exclaims in surprise.*) H'mp! Utopia! (*She goes behind the bar.*)

(*Mr. Johnson enters the room from the dance-hall. He is a young man of about thirty—smooth-faced, tall. His clothing is bought in fashionable Sacramento. He is the one man in the place who has the air of a gentleman. At first acquaintance, he bears himself easily but modestly, yet at certain moments there is a devil-may-care recklessness about him. He is, however, the last man in the world one would suspect of being the road-agent, Ramerrez.*)

JOHNSON: Where's the man who wanted to curl my hair?

(*Rance turns to look at the stranger.*)

GIRL: (*Who remembers Johnson as a man she met on the road to Monterey.*) Hello—er—stranger. (*Johnson looks at the Girl.*)

RANCE: We're not much on strangers here.

JOHNSON: I'm the man who wanted water in his whiskey.

GIRL: You, eh? (*To Nick who comes back with a bottle and glasses.*) Oh,—er—Nick, this gentleman takes his whiskey as he likes it.

NICK: Moses!

JOHNSON: (*Coming to the bar.*) In the presence of a lady—I will take—nothing. (*Bows to her with formality.*) Pardon me, but you seem to be almost at home here. (*Nick laughs softly.*)

GIRL: (*Amused.*) Who—me? (*Leaning on the bar.*)

NICK: (*Laughing.*) Why, she's the Girl who runs the Polka. (*He passes off, still laughing.*)

JOHNSON: (*Staring at the Girl.*) You?

GIRL: Yep.

JOHNSON: (*Meditating.*) The Girl who runs the Polka . . .

(*There is a merry twinkle in the Girl's eye as she looks at Johnson, but he is disconcerted. This news interferes with Johnson's plans.*)

GIRL: Yes.

RANCE: You're from the Crossing, the bartender said. I don't remember you.

JOHNSON: You're mistaken: I said that I rode over from the Crossing. (*Turning to the Girl again.*) So you are the Girl?

GIRL: Yes.

RANCE: (*Aggressively.*) No strangers allowed in this camp. (*A pause. The Girl and Johnson speak in such low tones that Rance is unable to hear them.*) Perhaps you're off the road. (*A pause. The Girl and Johnson are still talking. Sneeringly.*) Men often get mixed up when they're visiting Nina Micheltoreña on the back trail.

GIRL: Rance!

JOHNSON: (*Sharply to Rance.*) I merely stopped in to rest my horse—and perhaps try a game of—(*Coming to the table.*) er—poker. (*Picking up a pack of cards.*)

GIRL: Nick, bring in his saddle.

(*As Nick goes for the saddle, Rance rises, annoyed.*)

RANCE: A game, eh? I haven't heard your name, young man.

GIRL: (*Laughs.*) Oh! Names out here!

JOHNSON: My name's Johnson. (*Throwing down the cards.*)

GIRL: (*Cynically.*) Is—how much?

JOHNSON: Of Sacramento.

GIRL: Of—how much? (*Coming to Johnson and shaking hands—not believing a word he says.*) I admire to know you, Mr. Johnson, of Sacramento.

JOHNSON: Thank you.

RANCE: (*Angrily.*) Say, Minnie,—I—

GIRL: (*Aside to Rance, lightly.*) Oh,—set down. (*Turning to Johnson as Rance indignantly sits on the end of the faro table.*) Say, do you know what I think of you? I think you staked out a claim in a etiquette book. So you *think* you can play poker?

JOHNSON: That's my conviction.

GIRL: Out of every fifty men who *think* they can play, one ain't mistaken.

JOHNSON: (*Following the Girl to the bar.*) You may be right.

GIRL: Say, try a cigar.

JOHNSON: Thank you.

GIRL: Best in the house—my compliments. (*She lights a match.*)

JOHNSON: Thank you—you're very kind. (*In a lower tone.*) So you remember me?

GIRL: If you remember me.

RANCE: (*Muttering to himself, glancing over his shoulder.*) What the devil are they talking about, anyway?

JOHNSON: I met you on the road to Monterey—

GIRL: Goin' an' comin'. You passed me up a bunch of wild syringa over the wheel. You asked me to go a-berryin', but I didn't see it.
JOHNSON: I noticed that.
GIRL: And when you went away, you said—(*Embarrassed.*) Oh, I dunno . . .
JOHNSON: Yes, you do—yes, you do. I said: "I'll think of you all the time!" Well, I've thought of you ever since.
GIRL: Ha! Somehow I kinder thought you might drop in, but as you didn't . . . of course (*With a sense of propriety.*) it wasn't my place to remember you—first.
JOHNSON: But I didn't know where you lived . . . I—
GIRL: (*Confidentially.*) I got a special bottle here. Best in the house. Will you?
JOHNSON: Why—
GIRL: (*Gets a bottle and a glass.*) My compliments.
JOHNSON: You are *very* kind. Thanks.

(*Rance rises and, going up to the bar, proceeds to dash the glass to the floor as Johnson is about to take it.*)

RANCE: (*Livid.*) Look here, Mr. Johnson: your ways are offensive to me—damned offensive. My name's Rance—Jack Rance. Your business here—your business! (*Calling.*) Boys! Boys! Come in! (*Trinidad, Handsome, Sonora, and Happy come in.*) There's a man here who won't explain his business—he—
SONORA, TRINIDAD, HAPPY, HANDSOME: (*At the same time.*) What? Won't he? Oh, we'll see! Guess we'll make him.
GIRL: Wait a minute. I know him.
THE BOYS: (*As one man.*) Eh?
GIRL: (*To Rance.*) Yes, I didn't tell you, but I know him.
RANCE: (*To himself.*) The Sacramento shrimp, by God!
GIRL: (*Comes from behind the bar.*) Boys: I vouch to Cloudy for Mr. Johnson.

(*All the men except Rance salute Johnson, who makes a sweeping gesture.*)

JOHNSON: Boys . . .
THE BOYS: Hello, Johnson.
SONORA: Boys: Rance ain't runnin' the Polka yet.

(*A waltz is played as Nick enters.*)

NICK: (*To the Girl.*) The boys from the Ridge invites you to dance with them.
JOHNSON: May I have the honor of a waltz?

(*Trinidad, Sonora and Handsome are overcome by the manners of Johnson.*)

NICK: Moses! (*Retreats to dance-hall.*)
GIRL: Me waltz? Me? Ha! Oh, I can't waltz. Ha!—but I can polky.
JOHNSON: Then may I have the pleasure of the next polka?
SONORA: (*To the boys.*) He's too flip.
GIRL: Oh, I dunno. Makes me feel kind o' foolish,—you know—kind o' retirin' like a elk in summer.
JOHNSON: (*Amused.*) Yes, they *are* retiring.
GIRL: (*Unconsciously wipes her hands on her dress.*) Well . . . I don't like every-

body's hand on the back of my waist; but somehow—(*She looks at Rance recklessly. Johnson offers her his arm. Unused to this formality, she looks at his proffered arm two or three times, half ashamed, then she looks at the boys, who stand watching her with twinkling eyes.*) Oh, Lord, must I? (*Then making up her mind.*) Oh, come along.

JOHNSON: Thanks.

GIRL: (*Dances off with Johnson, calling to the Fiddler.*) A polky!

(*In the dance-hall, they are acclaimed by loud whoops.*)

SONORA: (*To Rance.*) Chink!

RANCE: Ha! Ha! Cleaned out, by God! by a high-toned, fine-haired dog named Johnson. Well, I'll be damned! (*As Nick comes in with a saddle.*) What's that?

NICK: Johnson's saddle.

RANCE: (*Knocking the saddle out of Nick's hands.*) You know, Nick—I've got a great notion to walk out of this door, and—

NICK: (*Scenting the loss of a good customer.*) Aw, she's only kiddin' him. (*He removes the saddle to a place of safety.*)

ASHBY: (*Outside.*) Boys!

RANCE: What's that?

TRINIDAD: Why, that's—

NICK: That's Ashby.

ASHBY: (*Outside.*) Come on—you!

TRINIDAD: What's the matter?

DEPUTY SHERIFF: (*Is heard to call.*) Run him in. (*He enters with Ashby and several men. They bring in José Castro. Billy Jackrabbit follows them on. Castro is an oily, greasy, unwashed Mexican greaser of a low type. His clothing is partly Mexican. He is yellow, sullen, wiry, hard-faced, tricky and shifty-eyed. He has the curved legs of a man who lives on a broncho. Ashby is completely transformed. His hat is on the back of his head, his hair is ruffled and falls over his forehead in straggling locks; his coat is thrown open and his face is savage and pitiless.*)

ASHBY: The greaser in the trail.

RANCE: (*Takes Castro by the hair, throwing him over and forcing his head back.*) Here, you—give us a look at your face.

ASHBY: Nick, come—give us a drink. (*Going to the bar.*)

RANCE: Tie him up.

(*Billy Jackrabbit goes to the fireplace, gets the lariat as Rance pushes Castro to the floor.*)

ASHBY: (*Inviting all to drink.*) Come on, boys.

(*The boys, with the exception of Sonora, join Ashby at the bar.*)

CASTRO: (*Seeing Johnson's saddle on the floor—to himself.*) Rammerez' . . . (*He pauses—overcome.*) Taken . . .

ASHBY: (*To Sonora, who is watching the Girl dance.*) Say, my friend, don't you drink?

SONORA: Oh, occasionally. (*He joins Ashby.*)

RANCE: (*Looking off at the Girl.*) Polkying!

(*Nick lets down the pelts which screen off the dance-hall, as Billy Jackrabbit and the Deputy throw Castro into a chair. Castro, who has caught a glimpse of Johnson dancing with the Girl, is relieved.*)

ASHBY: (*Having tasted his drink—going to Castro.*) Come now, tell us what your name is.
HAPPY: You bet!
ASHBY: Speak up! Who are you?
SONORA and HANDSOME: Speak up! What's your name?

(*Rance, eyeing Castro, sits at the faro table, his legs crossed.*)

CASTRO: José Castro, ex-padroña of the bull-fights.
RANCE: But the bull-fights are at Monterey. Why do you come to this place?
CASTRO: To tell the Señor Sheriff I know where ees—Ramerrez.

(*The men would surround Castro to question him, but Rance motions to them to stand back.*)

RANCE: You lie! (*Raises his hand for silence.*)
CASTRO: Nay, plaanty Mexican vaquero—my friends Peralta—Vellejos—all weeth Ramerrez—so I know where ees.
RANCE: (*Pointing at him quickly to take him off his guard.*) You're one of his men yourself!
CASTRO: (*Quickly with childlike innocence.*) No—no . . .
RANCE: (*Pointing to Ashby.*) That's Ashby—the man that pays out that reward you've heard of. Where is Ramerrez' camp?
CASTRO: Come weeth me one mile, and, by the soul of my mother,—the blessed Maria Saltaja,—we weel put a knife into hees back.
RANCE: One mile, eh?
SONORA: If I thought . . .
RANCE: Where is this trail?
CASTRO: Up the Madroña Canyada.
A MAN: (*Entering from the dance-hall.*) Hello, boys! What's—
ALL: (*Warning the new-comer to silence.*) Sh! Git! Git out! Shut up! Git!
RANCE: Go on.
CASTRO: Ramerrez can be taken, if many men come weeth me . . . forty minute there and back—
RANCE: What do you think?
ASHBY: Curious . . . This is the second warning we have had from here.
RANCE: (*To Ashby.*) This Nina Micheltoreña's letter to you? You say she is coming here tonight? (*As Ashby nods.*) Looks as though he was known around here.
ASHBY: All the same, I wouldn't go.
SONORA: What! Risk losin' him?
RANCE: Boys, we'll take the chance. (*He rises.*)
NICK: Want a drink? (*He goes up to the bar, clearing off the bottles and glasses.*)

(*Ashby has gone out. The men put on their overcoats, hats, etc., and prepare to leave in search of the road-agent. They exclaim:* "Ready, Sheriff!" "Come on, boys!" "Come on, Happy!" "Careful, boys!" *etc.*)

RANCE: (*At the open door, sniffing the air.*) I don't like the smell of the air. Snow. (*He goes out.*)
DEPUTY: Load up.
TRINIDAD: Get out the horses.
HAPPY: We'll git this road-agent.
SONORA: (*As he passes Castro.*) Come on, you oily, garlic-eating, red-peppery, dog-trottin' sun-baked son of a skunk!

(*The men hasten off, followed by Billy Jackrabbit, leaving Castro, Nick and the Deputy in the barroom.*)

DEPUTY: Come on, you!
CASTRO: (*His teeth chattering.*) One dreenk—I freeze—
DEPUTY: Give him a drink, Nick. Watch him. (*He goes out.*)
NICK: (*Contemptuously.*) What'll you have?
CASTRO: (*Rises.*) Geeve me—(*Loudly, suddenly facing the dance-hall and speaking so that his voice may be heard by Johnson.*) aguardiente.
NICK: Set down!

(*Castro, looking off, seeing that Johnson has seen him, sits, as Johnson hastens on from the dance-hall.*)

JOHNSON: So—you did bring my saddle in, eh, Nick?
CASTRO: (*In a low voice.*) Rammerez! . . . Master . . .
JOHNSON: Don't talk . . .
CASTRO: I let them take me, according to your beeding.
JOHNSON: (*Looking toward Nick.*) Careful, José . . . (*Puts the saddle on the table.*)
NICK: (*Coming down with a drink for Castro, who bolts it.*) Here.
VOICES: (*From the dance-hall.*) Nick! Nick!
NICK: Oh—the Ridge boys goin'. (*Goes back to the bar with the glasses—then speaks to Johnson.*) Say—keep your eye on him a minute, will you?
JOHNSON: Certainly. You tell the Girl you pressed me into service, will you? (*Touches his pistol pocket.*)
NICK: Sure. Say, she's taken an awful fancy to you.
JOHNSON: No!
NICK: Yes. Drop in often—great bar.
JOHNSON: It certainly is. (*Nick hastens off.*) Ha! Ha! Ha! (*To Castro.*) Go on . . .
CASTRO: Bueno! Our men lie in the bushes near, I lead the sheriff far off . . . then I slip away. Queeckly rob thes place now and fly. It is death for you to linger. Ashby ees here.
JOHNSON: (*Without looking.*) Ashby! Wait a minute. (*As Nick sticks in his head to cast a watchful glance at Castro.*) All right, Nick. Yes, everything's all right. (*Nick goes out again as a cachuca is gaily played.*)
CASTRO: By to-morrow twilight, you must be safe in your rancho.
JOHNSON: No—we'll raid on.
CASTRO: An hundred men on your track—
JOHNSON: One minute's start of the devil does me, José.

CASTRO: I fear the woman, Nina Micheltoreña . . . teeribly I fear. Close at hand . . . knowing all . . . fresh from your four week's quarrel with her . . still loving you.

JOHNSON: Loving me? Oh, no. Like you, Nina loves the spoils, not me. No, I raid on.

SONORA: (*Heard outside.*) Bring along the greaser, Dep.

(*The boys are heard off stage and the glare of torches is seen through the window.*)

DEPUTY: (*Heard outside.*) All right.

CASTRO: (*To Johnson.*) We start. Queeckly give the signal.

GIRL: (*Calling in the dance-hall.*) Good-night, boys—good-night. (*The music ends.*) Remember me to the Ridge.

VOICES OF THE RIDGE BOYS: (*Off stage.*) You bet! So long! Whoop! Whoopee!

CASTRO: All gone. Only the woman there—and her servant . . . Antonio waits your signal.

DEPUTY: (*Entering.*) Come on.

CASTRO: Adios.

JOHNSON: Adios.

DEPUTY: Come on.

(*He drags Castro off. We hear the boys moving away. Johnson takes up his saddle.*)

GIRL: (*Entering from the dance-hall.*) Nick, you can put the light out. (*Nick puts out the candle over the table.*) Put the lights out here, too. Oh, you ain't going'?

JOHNSON: Not yet, no, but . . .

GIRL: I'm glad of that. Don't it feel funny here? It's kind of creepy. I suppose that's because I never remember seeing the bar so empty before. (*Putting a chair in place.*)

NICK: (*Putting out the candle on the mantelpiece.*) I'm goin' to close the shutters. (*He closes the shutters.*)

GIRL: (*Crossing to the table.*) What for—so early?

NICK: (*In a half whisper.*) Well, you see, the boys is out huntin' Ramerrez—and they's too much money here.

GIRL: Oh, all right. Cash in. Don't put the head on the keg. I ain't cashed in m'self yet.

NICK: (*Rolling out the keg.*) Say, Min . . .

GIRL: Huh?

NICK: (*Looking uneasily at the keg, and then darting a glance towards Johnson.*) Know anything about—him?

GIRL: Oh, sure.

NICK: All right, eh?

GIRL: Yes. (*Nick blows out the lights at the door, and goes into the empty dancehall.*) Well, Mr. Johnson: it seems to be us a-keepin' house here to-night, don't it?

JOHNSON: Strange how things come about . . . Strange to be looking everywhere for you, and to find you at last at the Polka. (*Sitting on the table.*)

GIRL: Anything wrong with the Polka?

JOHNSON: Well, it's hardly the place for a young woman like you.

GIRL: How so?

JOHNSON: It's rather unprotected, and—

GIRL: Oh, pshaw! I said to Ashby only to-night: "I bet if a road-agent come in here, I could offer him a drink an' he'd treat me like a perfect lady." Say, won't you take something? (*Going back of the bar for a bottle.*)

JOHNSON: No, thank you. I'd like to ask you a question.

GIRL: I know what it is—every stranger asks it, but I didn't think *you* would. It's this: am I decent? Yep, I am—you bet!

JOHNSON: Oh, Girl: I'm not blind—that was not the question.

GIRL: (*Leaning over the bar, looking at him.*) Dear me suz!

JOHNSON: What I meant to say was this: I am sorry to find you here almost at the mercy of the passer-by . . . where a man may come, may drink, may rob you if he will; and where I daresay more than one has even laid claim to a kiss.

GIRL: They's a good many people claimin' things they never git. (*She is putting her money in a cigar-box.*) I've got my first kiss to give.

JOHNSON: (*Studying her.*) You're clever. Been here long?

GIRL: Yep.

JOHNSON: Live in the Polka?

GIRL: Nop.

JOHNSON: Where do you live?

GIRL: Cabin up the mountain a little ways.

JOHNSON: You're worth something better than this.

GIRL: What's better'n this? I ain't boastin', but if keepin' this saloon don't give me a sort of position round here, I dunno what does. Ha! Look here: say, you ain't one of them exhorters, are you, from the missionaries' camp?

JOHNSON: My profession has its faults, but I am not an exhorter.

GIRL: You know I can't figger out jest exactly what you are.

JOHNSON: Try.

GIRL: (*Getting a chair from behind the poker table.*) Well—you ain't one of us.

JOHNSON: No?

GIRL: Oh, I can tell—I can spot my man every time. I tell you, keepin' a saloon is a great educator. (*Sitting.*) I dunno but what it's a good way to bring up girls. They git to know things. Now, I'd trust you.

JOHNSON: You would trust me?

GIRL: Notice I danced with you to-night?

JOHNSON: Yes.

GIRL: I seen from the first you was the real article.

JOHNSON: I beg pardon.

GIRL: Why, that was a compliment I handed to you.

JOHNSON: Oh . . .

GIRL: (*Confidentially.*) Your kind don't prevail much here . . . I can tell—I got what you call a quick eye.

JOHNSON: I'm afraid that men like me—prevail, as you say, almost everywhere.

GIRL: Go on! What are you giving me? Of course they don't. Ha! Before I went on that trip to Monterey, I thought Rance here was the genu*ine* thing in a gent—but the minute I kind o' glanced over you on the road—I—I seen he wasn't. Say—take your whiskey—and water. (*She rises.*)

JOHNSON: No.

GIRL: (*Calling.*) Nick? (*Changing her mind.*) No, I'll help you to a drink myself.

JOHNSON: No, thank you.

GIRL: (*Leaning against the bar, studying him.*) Say, I've got you figgered out:

you're awful good, or awful bad . . .

JOHNSON: (*Half amused.*) Now what do you mean by that?

GIRL: Well, so good that you're a teetotaler—or so bad that you're tired of life an' whiskey.

JOHNSON: (*Rising and going up to her.*) On the contrary, although I'm not good—I've lived, and I've liked life pretty well, and I am not tired of it: it's been bully! (*Leaning on the bar.*) So have you liked it, Girl, only you haven't lived—you haven't lived. (*He attempts to take the Girl's hand, but she retreats.*) Not with *your* nature. You see, I've got a quick eye, too.

(*Nick enters slowly and prepares to seat himself in a chair back of the poker table.*)

GIRL: Nick, git! (*Nick casts an inquisitive glance at the pair and hastens out.*) Say, what do you mean by—I haven't lived?

JOHNSON: (*Insinuatingly, half under his breath.*) Oh, you know.

GIRL: No, I don't.

JOHNSON: Yes, you do.

GIRL: Well, say it's an even chance I do and an even chance I don't.

JOHNSON: (*In a low voice.*) I mean life for all it's worth . . . to the utmost . . . to the last drop in the cup . . . so that it atones for what's gone before, or may come after.

GIRL: No, I don't believe I do know what you mean by them words. Is it a—(*She crosses to the poker table and sits down on her revolver which is in her pocket. She rises hastily.*) Oh, Lord! Excuse me—I set on my gun. (*Impulsively.*) I can't pass you on the road. I take your dust. Look here: I'm goin' to make you an offer.

JOHNSON: An offer?

GIRL: It's this: if you ever need to be staked—

JOHNSON: Eh?

GIRL: Which of course you don't,—name your price—jest for the style I'll git from you an' the deportment.

JOHNSON: Deportment? Me?

NICK: (*Re-entering.*) Oh, er—I'd like to say—

GIRL: (*Annoyed.*) Oh! (*Nick goes off hurriedly.*)

JOHNSON: Well, I never heard before that my society was so desirable. Apart from the financial aspect of the matter—I—

GIRL: (*Admiringly, half to herself.*) Ain't that great? Ain't that great? Oh, you got to let me stand treat. (*Calls.*) Nick? (*She slips down from the table where she has been seated.*)

JOHNSON: No, really. Say, Girl: you're like finding some new kind of flower.

GIRL: You know the reason I made you that offer is—we're kind of rough up here, but we're reaching out. Now, I take it that what we're all put on this earth for—every one of us—is to rise ourselves up in the world—to reach out.

JOHNSON: (*With a change of manner.*) That's true—that's true. I venture to say there isn't a man who hasn't thought seriously about that. I have. If only a man knew how to reach out for something he hardly dare even hope for. It's like trying to catch the star shining just ahead.

GIRL: That's the cheese. You've struck it.

(*Nick enters.*)

NICK: I *have* been a-tryin' to say—
GIRL: What *is* it, Nick?
NICK: I jest seen an ugly lookin' greaser outside the winder.
GIRL: (*Going up to the door.*) A greaser? Let me look.
JOHNSON: (*Who knows that it is his man, awaiting the signal—speaking with an air of authority.*) I wouldn't.
GIRL: Why not?
NICK: I'll bolt all the winders. (*He goes off.*)

(*A whistle is heard outside. Johnson recognizes the signal.*)

GIRL: Don't that sound horrid? (*Getting behind the counter.*) I'm awful glad you're here. Nick's so nervous. He knows what a lot of money I've got. Why, there's a little fortune right in that keg.
JOHNSON: (*Crossing over to the keg and looking at it.*) In that keg?
GIRL: The boys sleep round it nights.
JOHNSON: But when they're gone—isn't that a careless place to leave it?
GIRL: (*Coming down to the keg.*) Oh, they'd have to kill me before they got it.
JOHNSON: I see—it's *your* money.
GIRL: No, it belongs to the boys.
JOHNSON: Oh, that's different. Now, I wouldn't risk my life for that.
GIRL: (*Putting the bags of gold-dust in the keg, and closing the keg and standing with her foot on it.*) Oh, yes, you would—yes, you would—if you seen how hard they got it. When I think of it—I—I nearly cry. You know there's something awful pretty in the way the boys hold out before they strike it—awful pretty—in the face of rocks and clay and alkali. Oh, Lord, what a life it is, anyway! Why, they eat dirt—an' they sleep dirt, an' they breathe dirt till their backs are bent, their hands twisted, their souls warped; they're all wind-swept an' blear-eyed—an' some of 'em just lie down in their own sweat beside the sluices, an' they don't never rise again. I've seen 'em there. I got some money of old Brownie's. (*Pointing to the keg.*) He was lyin' out in the sun on a pile of clay two weeks ago an' I guess the only clean thing about him was his soul—an' he was quittin'—quittin' right there on the clay—an' quittin' hard . . . (*Remembering the scene with horror.*) Oh, he died—jest like a dog . . . you wanted to shoot him to help him along quicker. Before he went, he sez: "Girl, give it to my old woman," and he—left. She'll git it. (*Slight pause.*) An' that's what aches you. They ain't one of these men working for themselves alone. The Almighty never put it in no man's heart to make a beast or pack-horse of himself—except for some woman, or some child. Ain't it wonderful? Ain't it wonderful, that instinct, ain't it?—What a man'll do when it comes to a woman. Ain't it wonderful? Yep, the boys use me as a—ha—sort of lady bank. (*She wipes her eyes.*) You bet I'll drop down dead before anyone'll get a dollar of theirs outer the Polka!
JOHNSON: (*After a short pause.*) That's right. (*Taking the Girl's hand.*) I'm with you. I'd like to see anyone get *that*. (*They shake hands over the keg—not heroically, but very simply.*) Girl, you make me wish I could talk more with you, but I can't. By daybreak I must be a long way off. I'm sorry. I should have liked to call at your cabin.
GIRL: (*Wistfully.*) Must you be movin'—so—soon?
JOHNSON: I'm only waiting till the posse gets back and you're safe. (*Listening.*) There . . . They're coming now . . .

GIRL: I'm awful sorry you got to go. I was goin' to say: (*Rolling the keg up stage, she takes a lantern off the bar and sets it on the keg.*) if you didn't have to go so soon, I'd like to have you come up to the cabin to-night, and we would talk of reaching out up there. You see, the boys will come back here . . . We close the Polka at one—any time after that.

JOHNSON: I—I should ride on now—but—I'll come.

GIRL: Oh, good! (*Giving the lantern to Johnson.*) You can use this lantern. It's the straight trail up—you can't miss it. Say, don't expect too much of me—I've only had thirty-two dollars' worth of education. (*Her voice breaks, her eyes fill with tears.*) P'raps if I'd had more—why you can't tell what I might have been. Say, that's a turrible thought, ain't it? What we—might have been? And I know it when I look at you.

JOHNSON: (*Touched.*) God knows it is! What we might have been—and *I* know it when I look at *you*, Girl—I know it—when I look at you.

GIRL: (*Wipes away a tear.*) You bet! (*Suddenly collapses, burying her face on her arm on the bar, sobbing, speaking through her tears.*) Oh, 'tain't no use—I'm ignorant—I don't know nothin' and I never knowed it till to-night. The boys always told me I knowed so much—but they're such damned liars.

JOHNSON: (*Comes up and leans on the bar. Earnestly, with a suggestion of tears in his voice.*) Don't you care—you're all right, Girl—you're all right. Your heart's all right—that's the main thing. As for your looks,—to me you've got the face of an angel. I—I'll just take a glance at my horse. (*He takes up his saddle, crosses to the door, then turns back. To himself.*) Johnson, what the devil's the matter with you? (*He goes out hastily, carrying the lantern and slamming the door behind him.*)

(*The Girl stands immovable for a moment, then calls suddenly.*)

GIRL: Nick! Nick! (*Nick enters quickly. She turns her face away, wiping off a tear.*) You run over to the Palmetter rest'rant an' tell 'em to send me up two charlotte rusks an' a lemming turnover—jest as quick as they can—right up to the cabin for supper. (*Nick goes off.*) Ha! (*She crosses to the poker table and sits on the edge, the light above shining down on her face. Strumming on a guitar and mandolin is heard as though the musicians were tuning up for the boys.*) He says . . . He says . . . (*Sentimentally.*) I have the face of an angel. (*A little pause, then turning her face away.*) Oh, Hell!

Curtain.

END OF ACT I

ACT II

"Two people who came from nothing."

SCENE:*The home of the Girl on Cloudy Mountain. One o'clock in the morning. The interior of the cabin has but one room, square, and made of logs. It is half papered as though the owner had bought wall-paper in camp and the supply had given out.*

There is but one door, and that leads to the trail. This door, in the center at back, is double boarded and fastened by a heavy bar. It opens on a rough vestibule, built to keep out the storms and cold. The windows, at which are calico curtains, are provided with heavy wooden shutters and bars. The barred door and windows give an air of security to the room as though it could be made into a little fortress.

The furniture is rather primitive. A bed, screened off by calico curtains, stands at the right side of the room. Below the bed is a bureau covered by a Navajo blanket on which a few crude toilet articles are set about. A cheap black framed mirror, decorated with strings of Indian beads and white cambric roses, hangs over the bureau. A wash-stand, backed by a "splasher" of white oilcloth, is near the bed. On the opposite side of the room, a pine wardrobe, rudely painted by a miner, contains most of the Girl's clothing. A sunbonnet and shawl hang on a peg driven into the side of the wardrobe. A gay hat-box from Monterey and a small basket grace the top of the wardrobe. A calico curtain covers a few garments hanging on pegs. In an angle, formed by a fireplace, is a row of shelves, holding tin cups, Indian baskets, two plates, a tin can, knives, forks and spoons. A rocking-chair, made of a barrel, set on rockers and dyed with blueing, is embellished with calico cushions and an antimacassar. There are four other chairs in the room. A pine table is almost in the center of the room. It is covered with a red cloth and over this a white table-cloth. Three dishes are on the table; one contains the charlotte "rusks," one the "lemming" turnover, and the other holds biscuit and chipped beef. A sugar bowl with brown sugar is placed in the center of the table. A fire burns in a fireplace which has an iron hood, a big back log and a smaller log in front. A pile of wood lies on the floor close at hand. A kettle hangs over the fire and a coffee-pot is set on a log. A few china ornaments, a bunch of winter berries stuck in a glass jar, and a bottle of whiskey with two glasses, are on the mantel. A box is nailed on the wall to form a bookshelf for a few well-worn old books. A wolf skin and moccasins are in front of the bureau, a large bear-skin rug is on the floor opposite the fireplace. A few pictures taken from "Godey's Lady's Book," one or two old prints, and a large sombrero hat hang on the wall. A horse-shoe over the door and the head of a small antelope, an old pair of snowshoes over the window and a lady's night-dress on a peg, complete the decorations in the lower part of the room. Above is a loft reached by a ladder which is swung up out of the way. By standing on a chair and reaching up, the ladder may be pulled down to the floor. Some old trunks and a few little boxes are neatly piled on the floor of the loft. Blankets screen off one end of the attic. A lamp hangs from an arm (swinging from the loft above) and shines down on the table. The winter is now beginning, and, although there is no evidence of snow in the early part of the act, the cabin windows are heavily frosted. When the curtain rises, the scene is lighted by the lamps and the glow from the fireplace. The moon is shining brightly through the window.

At the rise of the curtain, Wowkle, a squaw, is seated on the floor, singing, her papoose on her back. She is dressed in a long cloth skirt, a short red calico skirt hanging over it. She wears moccasins. Her hair is parted in the middle and drawn into two tight little blue-black braids, crossed in the back, low in the neck. She wears a number of glass bead necklaces and small silver hoops in her ears. She is young, beady-eyed, sweet-faced, and rather plump,—the lax, uncorseted, voluptuous type of squaw. She is perfectly good-natured, at times quizzical, but utterly unreliable and without any ideas of morality.

Billy Jackrabbit enters.

BILLY JACKRABBIT: Ugh!

WOWKLE: Ugh! (*As Billy Jackrabbit comes towards Wowkle, he sees the food on the table, looks at it greedily, picks up a plate and is about to stick his finger into the contents.*) Charlotte rusk—Palmetto rest'rant. Not take.

BILLY JACKRABBIT: (*Putting the plate back on the table.*) H'm . . . H'm . . . Me honest.

WOWKLE: Huh! (*Billy stoops and picks up a piece of paper to which some of the food, which has been wrapped in it, still clings. He rubs his fingers over the paper and licks them during the following conversation.*)

BILLY JACKRABBIT: (*Grunting, sitting down beside Wowkle.*) Send me up from Polka—say p'raps me marry you . . . Huh?

WOWKLE: (*Impassively.*) Me don't know. (*Pause.*)

BILLY JACKRABBIT: Me don't know. (*A slight pause. They are sitting side by side on the floor—unlike lovers—just two Indians.*) Me marry you, how much me got give fatha—Huh?

WOWKLE: (*Indifferently with a black look.*) Huh! Me don't know.

BILLY JACKRABBIT: Me don't know. (*Pause.*) Me give fatha four dolla—(*Indicating with his fingers—licking one as he speaks.*)—and one blanket.

WOWKLE: Betta me keep um blanket for baby.

BILLY JACKRABBIT: (*Grunts.*) Me give fatha three dolla and baby.

WOWKLE: We keep um baby.

BILLY JACKRABBIT: Tawakawa. (*Tearing off a piece of the sticky paper and handing it to Wowkle.*)

WOWKLE: Toanimbutuc. (*Billy offers to let the baby lick the paper, but Wowkle draws the child away.*) Aie! Missionary woman at Battla Ridge him say marry first—then baby.

BILLY JACKRABBIT: (*Who has licked the paper clean, and is now smoking his pipe.*) Huh!

WOWKLE: Me say baby first . . . him say all right, but marry—get plenty bead.

BILLY JACKRABBIT: (*Eyeing her beads and giving his pipe to Wowkle who takes a puff.*) You sing hymn for get those bead?

WOWKLE: Me sing—(*Singing softly but in a fairly high pitched voice with a slight nasal quality of tone.*)
"My days are as um grass—"

BILLY JACKRABBIT: (*Recognizing the air, gives a grunt and joins in with Wowkle.*)
"Or as um faded flowa—
Um wintry winds sweep o'er um plain,
We pe'ish in—um—ow-a—"
(*Taking his pipe from Wowkle.*)
By Gar, to-morrow we go missionary—sing like Hell—get whiskey. (*Rises.*)
"pe'ish in um ow-a"
(*He goes up to the door and stands there.*)
Al-right—go missionary to-morrow—get marry—huh?

WOWKLE: Billy Jackrabbit: (*She rises.*) p'haps me not stay marry with you for long time.

BILLY JACKRABBIT: (*Unimpressed.*) Huh! How long—seven monse?

WOWKLE: Six monse.

BILLY JACKRABBIT: (*Taking a red handkerchief from his pocket, and sticking it between the papoose and the board.*) Um . . . for baby. (*Nudging Wowkle with his elbow.*) You come soon?

WOWKLE: Girl eat suppa first—me come.

BILLY JACKRABBIT: (*Nudging her again—then going into the vestibule.*) Huh! Girl come.

(*The Girl appears outside the door, holding up a lantern. There is a certain suppressed excitement in her manner as she enters, yet she shows a new thoughtfulness and speaks quietly. She looks about as though to see what effect this little cabin will have on Johnson.*)

GIRL: Turn up the lamps—quick. (*She hangs her lantern on the outer door. Wowkle turns up the lamp on the table.*) Hello, Jackrabbit: fixed it?

BILLY JACKRABBIT: Me fix.

GIRL: (*Who is seated.*) That's good. Now git! (*Rising—going to the table.*) Wowkle it's for two to-night.

WOWKLE: Ugh!

GIRL: Yep.

WOWKLE: Come anotha? Neva before come anotha.

GIRL: Never you mind. He's coming—he's coming: Pick up the room. What time is it, Wowkle? (*She has hung up her coat and now shakes Wowkle. Wowkle gets plates, cups, etc.*) Wowkle, what did you do with them red roses?

WOWKLE: Ugh. (*Pointing to the bureau.*)

GIRL: Good. (*She finds the roses and arranges them in her hair.*) No offense—but

I want you to put your best foot forward (*Takes a pistol out of her pocket and puts it on the lower end of the bureau.*) when you're waitin' on table to-night. This here comp'ny of mine is a man of idees. Oh, he knows everything—sort of a damn-me style. Wowkle, how's the papoose. Father really proposed to you?

WOWKLE: Yep—get marry.

GIRL: (*Taking a ribbon from a drawer.*) Here: you can have that to fix the baby up for the weddin'. Hurry, Wowkle. I'm going to put them on, (*She sits on the floor and puts on a pair of new slippers which she has taken from the bottom drawer.*)—if I can git 'em on. Remember what fun I made of you when you took up with Billy Jackrabbit? "What for?" sez I. Well, perhaps you was right. Perhaps it's nice to have someone you really care for—who really belongs to you. Perhaps there ain't so much in the saloon business for a woman, after all—an' you don't know what livin' really is. Ah, Wowkle: it's nice to have someone you can talk to, someone you can turn your heart inside out to—(*As a knock sounds on the window.*) Oh, Lord! here he is, Wowkle! (*She tries to conceal herself behind the foot of the bed—one slipper in her hand. Sid opens the window and peers in.*)

WOWKLE: Ugh!

GIRL: (*Disgusted at seeing Sid.*) What are you doin' here, you Sidney Duck? You git!

SID: Beg pardon, Miss. I know men ain't allowed up here.

GIRL: No.

SID: But I'm in grite trouble. The boys are 'ot. They missed that road-agent, Ramerrez—and now they're tiking it out on me. (*Sniffs.*) If you'd only speak a word for me, Miss.

GIRL: No! Wowkle, shut the winder.

SID: (*Pleading.*) Ow, don't be 'ard on me.

GIRL: Now, look here: they's one kind of men (*Gesticulating with her slipper.*) I can't stand—a cheat and a thief, an' you're it. You're no better than that road-agent, Ramerrez. (*Putting on the other slipper.*) Wowkle, close the winder. Close the winder.

SID: Public 'ouse jide! (*He slams the window and disappears.*)

GIRL: I got 'em on! (*Rising with difficulty.*) Say, Wowkle: do you think he'll like 'em? How do they look? Gosh! They're tight. Say, Wowkle: I'm going the whole hog. (*She has taken a lace shawl from the bureau drawer and puts it on; then she sprinkles some perfumery over a large lace handkerchief and starts to draw on a pair of one-button gloves.*) Look here, Wowkle: does it look like an effort?

WOWKLE: (*Understanding at last.*) H'm! Two plate . . .

(*There is a knock on the door. The Girl hastily adjusts her belt, pulls up her stocking and opens the door.*)

JOHNSON: (*Surprised.*) Hello!

GIRL: (*Embarrassed.*) Hello, Mr. Johnson . . .

JOHNSON: (*Noticing her gloves.*) Are you—going out?

GIRL: Yes—no—I don't know. Oh, come on in.

JOHNSON: (*Setting his lantern on the table.*) Thank you. (*Attempting to put his arms around her.*)

WOWKLE: Ugh! (*She shuts the door which Johnson left open.*)

JOHNSON: (*Eyeing Wowkle.*) I beg your pardon. I didn't see—

GIRL: You stop jest where you are, Mr. Johnson.

JOHNSON: I—I apologize. But seeing you standing there, and looking into your lovely eyes—well, the temptation to take you in my arms was so great—that I—I took it.

(*Wowkle, blowing out Johnson's lantern, goes into the cupboard with her papoose.*)

GIRL: You must be in the habit of taking things, Mr. Johnson. I seen you on the road to Monterey, goin' an' comin'—I seen you once since, and passed a few words with you; but that don't give you no excuse to begin this sort of game. Besides, you might have prospected a bit first, anyway.

JOHNSON: I see how wrong I was. May I take off my coat? (*She does not answer.*) Thank you. (*He lays his coat on a chair.*) What a bully little place you have here—awfully snug. And I've found you again! Oh, the luck! (*Holding out his hands.*) Friends, Girl?

GIRL: (*Withholding her hand.*) Are you sorry?

JOHNSON: No, I'm not sorry.

GIRL: (*Bashfully—half to herself.*) That damn-me style! Well, look here: (*Going towards the chair at the table.*) down to the saloon to-night, you said you always got what you wanted. Well, of course I've got to admire you for that—I guess women always do admire men for gettin' what they want. But if huggin' me is included, cut it out, Mr. Johnson.

JOHNSON: (*Facing her across the table.*) That was a lovely day, Girl, on the road to Monterey, wasn't it?

GIRL: Was it? Oh, take a chair an' set down.

JOHNSON: Thanks. (*But he does not sit.*)

GIRL: Say, look here: I been thinkin' . . . You didn't come to the saloon to see me to-night. What brought you?

JOHNSON: It was Fate.

GIRL: Was it Fate—or—the back trail?

JOHNSON: (*Coming up to the table and attempting to embrace the Girl.*) It was Fate.

GIRL: (*Retreating to a corner.*) Wowkle: git the coffee. Oh, Lord, take a chair. (*Starts up to place a chair near the table, but Johnson intercepts her before she can pick up his coat which lies across the back of the chair.*)

JOHNSON: Careful, please! Careful!

GIRL: (*Peering at the revolvers in his coat pockets.*) How many guns do you carry?

JOHNSON: (*Hangs his coat on the peg.*) Oh, several—when travelling through the country.

GIRL: (*Apprehensively.*) Set down. (*He sits.*)

JOHNSON: Ha! It must be strange, living all alone way up here in the mountain. Isn't it lonely?

GIRL: Lonely? Mountains lonely? Ha! Besides—(*Sitting in the barrel rocking-chair.*) I got a little pinto, an' I'm all over the country on him—finest little horse you ever throwed a leg over. If I want to, I can ride right down into the summer at the foothills, with miles of Injun pinks just a-laffin'—an' tiger lilies as mad as blazes. There's a river there, too—the Injuns call it a 'water road'— an' I can git on that an' drift an' drift, an' I smell the wild syringa on the banks—M'm! And if I git tired o' that, I can turn my horse up grade an' gallop right into the winter an' the lonely pines an' firs a-whisperin' an' a-sighin'. Oh, my mountains! My beautiful peaks! My Sierras! God's in the air here, sure. You can see Him layin' peaceful hands on the mountain tops. He seems so near, you want to let your soul go right on up.

JOHNSON: (*Who has been listening, nodding his head slightly in appreciation.*) When you die, you won't have far to go, Girl.

GIRL: (*After a pause.*) Wowkle, git the coffee.

(*The Girl and Johnson sit at the table. Wowkle pours the coffee into the cups, and sets the pot back in the fireplace.*)

JOHNSON: But when it's cold up here—very cold and it snows?

GIRL: Oh, the boys come up an' dig me out of my front door—ha—like—a—(*Spearing a biscuit with her fork.*)

JOHNSON: Little rabbit, eh?

GIRL: I git dug out nearly every day when the mines is shet down an' the Academy opens.

JOHNSON: (*In surprise.*) Academy? Here? Who teaches in your Academy?

GIRL: Me. I'm her. I'm teacher.

JOHNSON: You teach? Oh—

GIRL: Yep. I learn m'self—(*Putting sugar in Johnson's coffee.*) an' the boys at the same time. But, of course, Academy's suspened when they's a blizzard on—

JOHNSON: (*Seeing that she is continuing to put sugar in his coffee.*) Hold on . . . hold on . . .

GIRL: —'Cause no girl could git down the mountain then.

JOHNSON: Is it so very severe here when there's a blizzard on?

GIRL: Oh, Lordy! They come in a minute—all of a sudden—and you don't know where you are. It's awful! (*Offering a dish with an air of pride.*) Charlotte Rusks!

JOHNSON: (*Surprised.*) No!

GIRL: And lemming turnovers!

JOHNSON: Well!

GIRL: Will you have one?

JOHNSON: You bet! Thank you. Let me send you some little souvenir of to-night—something you'd love to read in your course of teaching at the Academy. What have you been reading lately?

GIRL: Oh, it's an awful funny book, about a couple. He was a classic an' his name was Dant.

JOHNSON: He was a classic and his name was Dant. Oh, Dante! Yes, I know. And did you find it funny? Dante funny?

GIRL: I roared. You see, he loves a lady—(*Rising to get the book.*)

JOHNSON: Beatrice—

GIRL: How?

JOHNSON: Go on.

GIRL: He loves a lady. It made me think of it what you said down to the saloon to-night about livin' so you didn't care what come after. Well, he made up his mind—this Dant—Dantee—that one hour of happiness with her was worth the whole da—(*Correcting herself.*) outfit that come after. He was willin' to sell out his chances for sixty minutes with her. Well, I jest put the book down and hollered!

JOHNSON: Of course you did. All the same, you knew he was right.

GIRL: I didn't. (*Putting the book back on the shelf.*)

JOHNSON: You did.

GIRL: Didn't.

JOHNSON: You did.

GIRL: Didn't.

JOHNSON: You know he was right!

GIRL: I don't.

JOHNSON: Yes, you do. You do.

GIRL: I don't. That a feller could so wind himself up as to say: (*Sitting at the table.*) "Jest give me one hour of your sassiety—time ain't nothin'—nothin' ain't nothin'—only to be a da—darn fool over you." Ain't it funny to feel like that? Yet I suppose there are folks who feel like that; folks that love into the grave, and into death—and after. Golly! It jest lifts you right up by your boot-straps to think of it, don't it?

JOHNSON: (*Looks at her intently, not smiling. One can see that he is fascinated.*) It does have that effect.

GIRL: Yet p'raps he was ahead of the game. Ha—I dunno. Oh, say, I just love this conversation with you. I love to hear you talk. You give me idees. Wowkle, bring the candle. (*Wowkle gives the candle to Johnson.*) Say, look here: one of your real Havanas.

(*Wowkle knows now that Johnson is the chosen man. She eyes him with great curiosity.*)

JOHNSON: No, I—

GIRL: (*Handing him the cigar.*) Go on.

JOHNSON: (*Looking at her through and through, his eyes half closed.*) Thank you. How I would love to know you, Girl!

GIRL: You do know me.

JOHNSON: (*Lights his cigar.*) Not well enough.

GIRL: What's your drift?

JOHNSON: To know you as Dante knew the lady. To say: "One hour for me—one hour—worth the world" . . .

GIRL: He didn't git it, Mr. Johnson. (*Drinking her coffee.*)

JOHNSON: All the same, there are women we can die for . . .

GIRL: How many times have you died?

JOHNSON: (*Lays the cigar down on the table.*) That day on the road to Monterey, I said: "Just that one woman for me." (*Taking the Girl's hand.*) I wanted to kiss you then.

(*She rises, pulls her hand away and starts to clear the table.*)

GIRL: Wowkle, hist the winder. (*Wowkle goes to the window and stands there.*) Mr. Johnson: some men think so much of kisses, that they don't never want a second kiss from the same girl.

JOHNSON: That depends on whether they love her or not. All loves are not alike.

GIRL: No, but they all have the same aim—to git her, if they can.

JOHNSON: You don't know what love is.

GIRL: Nop, I don't. My mother used to say, Mr. Johnson, "Love's a tickling sensation at the heart that you can't scratch." (*Johnson rises and goes up to the door, laughing heartily.*) We'll let it go at that.

JOHNSON: (*Turns to embrace the Girl.*) Oh, Girl, you're bully!

(*Wowkle clears the table.*)

GIRL: (*Retreating.*) Look out or you'll muss my roses.

JOHNSON: Hadn't you better take them off, then?

GIRL: Give a man an inch, an' he'll be at Sank Hosey before you know it.

JOHNSON: (*Following the Girl.*) Is there anyone else?

GIRL: (*Taking off her roses.*) A man always says: "Who was the first one?" But the girl says: "Who'll be the next one?"

JOHNSON: But the time comes when there never will be a next one.

GIRL: No? (*Takes off one of her gloves, blows into it and puts it in the bureau drawer.*)

JOHNSON: No.

GIRL: I'd hate to stake my pile on that! Git to your wigwam, Wowkle.

(*She takes off the other glove. Wowkle, who has put the dishes in a pail, grunts, hangs the papoose on her back and puts on her blanket.*)

JOHNSON: Must I go, too?

GIRL: Mm—not just yet. You can stay—a—a hour or two longer.

JOHNSON: Yes? Well, I'm like Dante; I want the world in that hour, because I'm afraid the door of this little paradise may be shut to me afterwards. Let's say that this is my one hour—the hour that gives me that kiss.

GIRL: Go long . . .

(*Wowkle has reached the door and opened it. A gust of wind, and a little snow blows in. The wind has been rising for some time, but the Girl and Johnson have not noticed it.*)

WOWKLE: Ugh—come snow.

(*The Girl and Johnson do not hear her. All through the following scene, they are so engrossed in each other, that they don't notice Wowkle.*)

GIRL: (*To Johnson.*) You go to grass.

JOHNSON: (*Embracing her—trying to kiss her.*) Listen . . .

WOWKLE: Ugh! It snow . . . See . . .

GIRL: Why, if I let you have one, you'd take two.

JOHNSON: No, I wouldn't.

WOWKLE: Very bad.

JOHNSON: I swear I wouldn't.

WOWKLE: Ugh! (*She is disgusted and goes out closing the door.*)

GIRL: (*Retreating.*) Oh, please . . .

JOHNSON: (*Steps back a little and stands with his arms open.*) One kiss—only one.

GIRL: 'Tain't no use. I lay down my hand to you. (*She runs into his arms.*)

JOHNSON: (*Embracing and kissing her.*) I love you! (*The wind blows the snow against the windows. The vestibule doors slam. The curtains of the bed flap in the wind. A small basket on the wardrobe blows down. A flower-pot topples over. The blankets in the loft flap. The lamps flicker. Suddenly the wind dies down. The clock on the mantel strikes two. The wind begins to rise again. The Girl and Johnson are absolutely oblivious to the storm. After a little pause Johnson speaks, still holding her in his arms.*) What's your name, Girl—your real name?

GIRL: Min—Minnie. My father's name was Smith.

JOHNSON: Oh, Minnie Sm—

GIRL: But 'twasn't his right name.

JOHNSON: No?

GIRL: His right name was Falconer—

JOHNSON: Minnie Falconer. That's a pretty name. (*He kisses her hand.*)

GIRL: I think that was it,—I ain't sure. That's what he said it was. I ain't sure of anything—only—jest you. (*She snuggles closer.*)

JOHNSON: I've loved you ever since I first saw you . . . So you're sure of me—sure. (*He gently puts her away, remembering what he is.*) You turn your head away, Girl, and don't you listen to me, for I'm not worth you. Don't you listen. You just say, "No—no—no!" (*He turns away.*)

GIRL: Say, I know I ain't good enough for you, but I'll try hard. If you see anything better in me, why don't you bring it out? I've loved you ever since I saw you first . . . 'cause I knowed that you was the right man.

JOHNSON: (*Conscience-smitten.*) The right man. Ha, ha!

GIRL: Don't laugh.

JOHNSON: (*Seriously.*) I'm not laughing.

GIRL: Of course, every girl kind o' looks ahead.

JOHNSON: Yes.

GIRL: And figgers about—bein'—Well—Oh, you know—

JOHNSON: Yes, I know. (*He is standing so that she cannot see his face.*)

GIRL: She figgers about being settled . . . and when the right one comes—why, she knows him—just as we both knew each other standin' in the road to Monterey. I said that day: "He's good—he's grand—he can have me!"

JOHNSON: (*Meditatively, with longing—turning to her.*) I could have you . . . (*With sudden resolve.*) I have looked into your heart, Girl, and into my own, and now I realize what this means for us both—for you, Girl, for you—and knowing that it seems hard to say good-bye—as I should . . . and must . . . and will. (*He kisses her, then turns to go.*)

GIRL: What do you mean?

JOHNSON: (*Collecting himself.*) I mean it's hard to go—and leave you here. The clock reminded me that long before this, I should have been on the way. I shouldn't have come up here at all. God bless you, dear,—I love you as I never thought I could.

GIRL: (*Troubled.*) But it ain't for long you're goin'?

JOHNSON: For long? (*Resolving not to tell her the truth.*) No—no; but I've got to go now while I have the courage. (*Taking her face in his hands—kissing her.*) Oh, Girl! Girl! (*Kissing her hands.*) Good-bye . . . (*Getting his hat and coat and opening the door, he looks out.*) Why, it's snowing!

(*As the door opens, all the sounds of the storm-swept woods are heard—the whis-*

*pering and rocking of the storm-tossed pies, and the winds howling through a
deep cañon. The Girl runs up and closes the outside and inside doors, goes to the
window, pulls back the curtain, wipes the frost from the window-pane, trying to
peer out.*)

GIRL: Snowing . . . It's the first snow this winter. You can't see an inch ahead.
That's the way we git it up here. Look! Look!

JOHNSON: (*Looking through the window.*) This means—No . . . it can't mean that
I can't leave Cloudy to-night. I must.

GIRL: (*Turning to him.*) Leave Cloudy? You couldn't keep to the trail. It means
you can't get off this mountain to-night.

JOHNSON: (*Thinking of the posse.*) But I must!

GIRL: You can't leave this room to-night—you couldn't find your way three feet
from this door—you, a stranger . . . You don't know the trail anyway, unless
you can see it.

JOHNSON: (*Apprehensively.*) But I can't stay here.

GIRL: Why not? It's all right. The boys'll come up an' dig us out to-morrow or
day after. Plenty of food here—and you can have my bed.

JOHNSON: I couldn't think of taking it.

GIRL: I never use it cold nights. I always roll up in my rug in front of the fire.
(*Amused.*) Think of it storming all this time, an' we didn't know it!

JOHNSON: (*Pre-occupied—gravely.*) But people coming up and finding me here,
might . . .

GIRL: Might what?

(*Two shots, fired in quick succession, are heard in the distance at the foot of the
mountain.*)

JOHNSON: What's that? . . . What's that?

GIRL: Wait . . . (*More shots are heard in the distance, fired at intervals.*) They've
got a road-agent . . . It's the posse. Perhaps they've got Ramerrez or one of his
band. (*Johnson rushes to the window, vainly trying to look out.*) Whoever it is,
they're snowed in—couldn't git away. (*Another shot is heard.*) I guess that time
another thief crept into camp. (*Meaning eternity.*)

JOHNSON: (*Wincing.*) Poor devil! But, of course—as you say—he's only a thief.

GIRL: (*Who has thrown her pillow in front of the fire.*) I ain't sorry for him.

JOHNSON: (*After a slight pause.*) You're right! (*Then, as though he had made up
his mind, he takes down his overcoat and puts it on.*) Girl, I've been thinking
. . . I've got to go—I've got to go. I have very important business at dawn—im-
perative.

GIRL: Ever sample one of our mountain blizzards? In five minutes you wouldn't
know where you was. Your important business would land you at the bottom of
a cañon—about twenty feet from here. You say you believe in Fate: well, it's
caught up with you. You got to stay here.

(*She puts the tablecloth in the cupboard as though putting the house in order for
the night.*)

JOHNSON: Well, it is Fate—my Fate—(*Throwing down his coat.*) that has always
made it easy for me to do the thing I shouldn't do. As you say, Girl, if I can't go,

I can't . . . (*Looking at her intently.*) but I know now as I stand here, that I'll never give you up.

GIRL: (*Not quite understanding.*) Why, what do you mean?

JOHNSON: (*Deliberately—speaking above the crying of the wind.*) I mean . . . suppose we say that's an omen—(*Pointing as though to the falling snow.*) that the old trail is blotted out and there's a fresh road . . . Would you take it with me, a stranger—who says: "From this day I mean to be all that you would have me"? Would you take it with me? Far away from here—and—forever?

GIRL: Well, show me the girl who would want to go to Heaven alone. (*Johnson kisses her hand.*) I'll sell out the saloon. I'll go anywhere with you—you bet!

JOHNSON: You know what that means, don't you? (*He sits by the table, looking at the Girl.*)

GIRL: Oh, yes. They's a little Spanish Mission Church here . . . I pass it 'most every day. I can look in an' see the light burnin' before the Virgin—an' all the saints standin' round with glassy eyes an' faded satin slippers—an' I often thought: what'd they think if I was to walk right in to be made—well, some man's wife. That's a great word, ain't it—wife? It makes your blood like pin-points thinkin' about it. There's somethin' kind o' holy about love, ain't there? Say: did you ever ask any other woman to marry you?

(*She sits down on the floor, leaning towards Johnson, in his arms.*)

JOHNSON: No.

GIRL: Oh, I'm glad! Ah—take me—I don't care where—as long's it's with you. Jest take me.

JOHNSON: So help me Heaven, I'm going to, Girl. You're worth something better than me, Girl; but they say love works miracles every hour: it weakens the strong and strengthens the weak. With all my soul I love you . . . (*He notices that she is dozing.*) Why, Minnie . . . Minnie . . .

GIRL: (*Waking with a start.*) I wasn't asleep . . . I'm jest happy an' let down, that's all. Say, I'm awful sorry—I've got to say good-night.

JOHNSON: Good-night. (*He kisses her.*)

(*They rise.*)

GIRL: That's your bed over there.

JOHNSON: I hate to take it. Hadn't you better take the bed and let me sleep by the fire?

GIRL: Nop. (*She moves the barrel rocking-chair away from the fireplace.*)

JOHNSON: Are you sure you will be more comfortable there?

GIRL: You bet I will—don't worry.

JOHNSON: Very well. (*He throws his coat and hat on the bed.*)

GIRL: (*As she spreads rugs on the floor in front of the fire.*) This beats a bed any time. There's one thing—(*Reaching up and pulling down a quilt from the loft.*)— you don't have to make it up in the morning. (*She puts a lighted candle on the hearth, blows out the lamps on the mantel, the stand and the bureau. She climbs up on the table, turns down the hanging lamp, steps to the floor, notices that she has turned it too low, glances at Johnson, making sure that he does not see her, gets up on the table again, turns the wick higher, then goes into the wardrobe where she make her toilet for the night.*) Now, you can talk to me from your bunk, and I'll talk to you from mine.

JOHNSON: Good-night.

GIRL: Good-night.

JOHNSON: (*Starts to go to bed—turns quickly—listens—then goes towards the bed —pauses—runs to the door and listens. His face is full of resolve. He shows the desperado's ability to meet all emergencies. He speaks quietly—in fact, the scene between these two, from this moment until the door is opened, must be done in the lowest audible tones — to convey the impression that those outside do not hear.*) What's that?

GIRL: That's snow slidin' . . . Good-night.

JOHNSON: God bless you, Girl. Thank you. (*He goes behind the curtains of the bed. A pause.*) H'm . . . there is something out there . . . sounded like someone calling.

GIRL: That's only the wind. (*She comes out of the wardrobe.*) It's gettin' colder, ain't it? (*She sits on the floor, takes off her slippers and puts on moccasins, then rises and comes down to the fire, arranges the rugs and pillow, says a brief prayer, lies down and tucks herself in.*) Good-night again.

JOHNSON: Good-night.

GIRL: (*Lifting up her head.*) Say, what's your first name?

JOHNSON: Dick.

GIRL: (*Sentimentally.*) So long, Dick.

(*She snuggles down again in the folds of the rug.*)

JOHNSON: So long, Girl.

GIRL: (*Half rising.*) Say, Dick, are you sure you don't know that Nina Micheltoreña?

JOHNSON: (*After a slight pause.*) Sure.

GIRL: (*With a satisfied air.*) Good-night. (*She lies down again.*)

JOHNSON: Good-night.

(*Suddenly a voice is heard to call and some one knocks on the door. The Girl rises and sets the candle on the table. Johnson throws open the curtains and pulls his revolvers from his pockets.*)

GIRL: There *is* some one calling.

NICK: Hello!

GIRL: Listen! What could that—

JOHNSON: (*In a low voice.*) Don't answer.

GIRL: Who can it be?

JOHNSON: You can't let anybody in here—they wouldn't understand.

GIRL: Understand what?

(*She goes to the window. It never occurs to her that the situation is compromising.*)

JOHNSON: Sh!

GIRL: It's the posse. How did they ever risk it in this blizzard? What can they want?

JOHNSON: (*Low, but very distinctly, above the rising wind, his hands on his pistols.*) Don't answer.

NICK: (*Outside.*) Min! Minnie! Girl!

GIRL: (*Calling off through the door.*) What do you want? (*Turning quickly to Johnson.*) What did you say?

JOHNSON: Don't let them in.

SONORA'S VOICE: Are you all right, Girl?

GIRL: (*Calling loudly through the door.*) Yes, Sonora, I'm all right. (*Turning again to Johnson.*) Jack Rance is there . . . If he was to see you here—he's that jealous—I'd be afraid of him. (*Listening at the door.*) And Ashby's there and—

JOHNSON: (*Now sure that they are after him.*) Ashby!

NICK: (*Outside.*) We want to come in.

JOHNSON: No.

GIRL: (*Glibly, calling.*) You can't come in. (*To Johnson.*) What will I say?

JOHNSON: (*Quietly.*) You've gone to bed.

GIRL: Oh, yes. (*To Nick, outside.*) I've gone to bed—I'm in bed now.

ASHBY: (*Outside.*) We've come to warn you.

GIRL: They've come to warn me.

NICK: (*Outside.*) Ramerrez . . .

GIRL: (*Calling through door.*) What?

NICK: Ramerrez is on the trail.

GIRL: Ramerrez is on the trail. (*To Johnson.*) I got to let 'em in. (*Johnson gets behind the curtains of the bed where he is entirely concealed.*) I can't keep 'em out such a night. (*Calling to the men outside.*) Come on in, boys. (*She opens the door, and the men enter—Rance first.*)

(*Rance, wearing a luxurious fur overcoat, his trousers tucked into his high-heeled boots, goes to the candle, warming his hands over it, taking off his gloves, brushing the snow off with his handkerchief. Sonora, wearing a buffalo overcoat, cap, ear muffs, and high boots, comes down to the fireplace. Ashby follows with a lighted lantern; he is dressed as before, but wears an overcoat over the one in which he first appeared. Nick comes down to the Girl, then crosses to the fire; he has pieces of blanket tied round his legs and feet. Rance turns up the wick of the hanging lamp. All are snow-covered.*)

SONORA: (*As he goes to the fireplace.*) Ow! Glad you are safe. I'm froze! (*He stamps his feet and rubs his hands together.*)

NICK: The Polka has had a narrow squeak, Girl.

GIRL: (*Seated.*) Why, what's the matter, Nick?

RANCE: (*Suspiciously.*) It takes you a long time to get up,—and you don't seem to have so much on you, either.

GIRL: (*Indignantly.*) Well, upon my—(*She rises and, picking up a rug from the floor, wraps it round her knees and sits. The wind rises and falls, crying in the cañons.*)

SONORA: We thought sure you was in trouble. My breath jest stopped . . .

GIRL: Me—in trouble?

RANCE: See here—that man Johnson—

SONORA: Fellow you was dancin' with—

RANCE: (*With a grimace of pleasure, spreading his stiffened fingers before the blaze.*) Your polkying friend Johnson is Ramerrez.

GIRL: (*Blankly.*) What'd you say?

ASHBY: I warned you. Bank with us oftener.

GIRL: (*Dazed.*) What did you say?

RANCE: We say—Johnson was a—

GIRL: What?

RANCE: Are you deef? The fellow you've been polkying with is the man that has been asking people to hold up their hands.

GIRL: (*Lightly, yet positively.*) Go on! You can't hand me out that.

RANCE: You don't believe it yet, eh?

GIRL: (*Imitating his "yet."*) No, I don't believe it yet, eh! I know he isn't.

RANCE: Well, he *is* Ramerrez, and he *did* come to the Polka to rob it.

GIRL: But he didn't rob it.

SONORA: That's what gits me—he didn't.

GIRL: I should think it would git you.

ASHBY: We've got his horse.

SONORA: I never knew one of these men to separate from his horse.

RANCE: Oh, well, if we've got his horse, with this storm on, we've got him. The last seen of Johnson he was heading this way. You seen anything of him?

GIRL: Heading this way?

SONORA: So Nick said.

(*The Girl gives Nick a glance.*)

NICK: He was. Sid says he saw him, too.

RANCE: But the trail ends here—and if she hasn't seen him—(*He looks at the Girl.*)—where was he going?

(*Nick spying Johnson's cigar, recognizes it as one of their rare dollar Havanas. The Girl's eyes follow Nick's glance. Unseen by Rance, there is a glance between Nick and the Girl.*)

NICK: (*To himself.*) Oh, my God!

SONORA: (*Answering Rance's question.*) Yes, where was he going?

(*Rance looks at the Girl, now intercepting Nick's glance.*)

NICK: Well, I thought I seen him—I couldn't swear to it. You see, it was so dark. Oh, that Sidney Cove's a liar, anyway. (*Nick puts the tell-tale cigar in his pocket, looking furtively about to make sure that he is not seen.*)

ASHBY: He's snowed under. Something scared him off, an' he lit off without his horse.

GIRL: (*Sitting down.*) Ha! How do you know that man is a road-agent?

SONORA: (*Warming his hands and breathing on his fingers.*) Well, two greasers jest now was pretty positive of it before they quit.

GIRL: (*With scorn.*) Greasers! Oh!

RANCE: But the woman knew him—she knew him. (*Sitting on the table.*)

GIRL: (*Quietly, for the first time impressed.*) The woman? What'd you say?

SONORA: It was the woman who first told us that Ramerrez was here—to rob the Polka.

RANCE: She's down at the Palmetto now.

ASHBY: It will cost us the reward.

RANCE: But Ramerrez is trapped.

GIRL: Who is this woman?
RANCE: (*As though to excite her jealousy.*) Why the woman from the back trail—that damn—
GIRL: Nina Micheltorena?
RANCE: H'm, h'm.
GIRL: Then she knows him. She *does* know him . . . (*She rises again.*)
RANCE: He was the sort of man who polkas with you first—then cuts your throat.
GIRL: (*Turning on Rance.*) It's my throat, ain't it?
RANCE: Well, I'll be—
NICK: (*Going to Rance and speaking to him in a low voice.*) Say, she's cut up because she vouched for him. Don't rub it in.
GIRL: Nina Micheltoreña . . . How did she know it?
SONORA: Why, from what she said—
RANCE: She's his girl. She's—
GIRL: His girl?
RANCE: Yes, she gave us his picture—(*Taking a picture from his pocket, and turning it over.*) — with "Love" on the back.
GIRL: (*Takes the picture, looks at it, and laughs.*) Nina Micheltoreña, eh? Ha! I'm sorry I vouched for him, Mr. Ashby.
RANCE: Ah!
GIRL: (*So that Ashby shall not suspect.*) I suppose they had one of them little lovers' quarrels that made her tell you, eh? He's the kind of man that sort o' polkys with every girl he meets. Ha! Ha! Ha! Ha!
RANCE: What are you laughing at?
GIRL: (*Turning to Rance again.*) Oh, nothing—only it's kind o' damn funny how things come out,—ain't it? Took in! Nina Micheltoreña! Nice company he keeps. One of them Cachuca girls with eye-lashes at half mast, ha! And she sold him out—for money. Ah, you're a better guesser than I am, Jack.
RANCE: (*Grimly.*) Yes.
GIRL: Well, it's gittin' late. Thank you. Good-night, boys.
SONORA: Hell, boys! Come on and let a lady go to bed. Good-night, Girl.

(*He goes to the door, followed by the other men, Ashby following Sonora, then Rance, and last, Nick. When the door opens, all the lamps flicker in the wind.*)

GIRL: Good-night, Sonora. Good-night, Mr. Ashby. Good-night, Jack.
SONORA: Lordy! Will we ever git down again?
NICK: (*As the others are outside, looking at her meaningly.*) You want *me* to stay?
GIRL: (*Going to the door.*) No. Good-night. (*The men all go off calling "good-night," etc. The Girl shuts the door, and stands with her back against it. With a change of manner, her eyes blazing.*) Come out of that—step out there! (*Johnson appears between the curtains of the bed.*) You came here to rob me.
JOHNSON: (*Quietly.*) I didn't.
GIRL: (*Viciously.*) You lie!
JOHNSON: I don't.
GIRL: You do.
JOHNSON: I—I admit that every circumstance points to—
GIRL: Stop! Don't you give me any more of that Webster dictionary talk—but git to cases. If you didn't come here to steal—you came to the Polka to rob it, didn't you?

JOHNSON: (*With sudden determination.*) Yes, I did, but when I knew it was you who—(*He goes towards her.*)

GIRL: Wait! Wait! (*Johnson pauses.*) Don't you take a step—look out, or I'll—A road-agent . . . a road-agent! . . . Well, ain't it my luck? Wouldn't anybody know to look at me that a gentleman wouldn't fall my way? A road-agent . . . Oh! Oh! Oh! (*Then with a revulsion of feeling.*) You can git now—git! You—you thief! You imposer on a decent woman. I ought to have told the boys—but I wasn't goin' to let on I could be so took in. I wasn't goin' to be the joke of the world, with you behind the curtain, an' me eatin' charlotte rusks and lemming turnovers and a-polkering with a road-agent. Ha! But now you can git! Now you can git! (*She sits on the table, looking straight before her as though to forget the sight of the man.*)

JOHNSON: (*In a low voice.*) One word—only one word . . . I'm not going to say anything in defense of myself. It's all true—everything is true, except that I would have stolen from you. I am called Ramerrez—I have robbed—I am a vagabond—a vagabond by birth—a cheat and a swindler by profession. I'm all that—and my father was all that before me. I was born, brought up, educated, thrived on thieves' money—but until six months ago, when he died, I didn't know it. I lived in Monterey—Monterey where we met. I lived decently. I wasn't the thing I am to-day. I only learned the truth when he died and left me with a rancho and a band of thieves—nothing else—nothing for us all—and I . . . I was my father's son—no excuse . . . it was in me—in the blood . . . I took to the road. I didn't mind much after—the first time. I only drew the line at killing. I wouldn't have that. And that's the man I am—the blackguard I am. (*With feeling.*) But, so help me God, from the moment I kissed you to-night, I meant to change. I meant to change.

GIRL: (*Sniffling.*) The devil you did!

JOHNSON: (*Advancing a step.*) I did, believe me—I did. I meant to go straight and take you with me—but honestly . . . when I could do it honestly. I meant to work for you. Every word you said to me to-night about being a thief, cut me like a knife. Over and over again, I said to myself: "She must never know." Now . . . (*A slight pause.*) Well,—I've finished.

GIRL: Is that all?

JOHNSON: No. Yes. What's the use? That's all.

GIRL: (*Half crying.*) Well, there's jest one thing you've overlooked explainin', Mr. Johnson. It shows jest exactly what you are. It wasn't so much bein' a road-agent I got against you—it's this: you kissed me. You kissed me. You got my first kiss.

JOHNSON: Yes, damn me!

GIRL: You said you'd been thinkin' of me ever since you saw me at Monterey—an' all the time you'd walked straight off and been kissing that other woman. You've got a girl. It's that I've got against you. It's my first kiss I've got against you. It's that damned Nina Micheltoreña that I can't forgive. But now you can git—you can git! (*Rushing to the door and opening it.*) If they kill you, so much the better. I don't care—I don't care—I don't care!

JOHNSON: You're right. You're right. By God! You're right. (*He takes out a pistol, but not much caring whether he lives or dies, he looks at the pistol, then puts it back in his pocket and goes out empty-handed—his head bowed.*)

GIRL: That's the end of that—that's the end of that. (*She goes to the door, closes it.*) I don't care—I don't care. I'll be like the rest of the women I've seen. I'll give

American Melodrama/226

that Nina Micheltoreña cards and spades. (*Wipes her nose.*) There'll be another huzzy around here. (*At that moment, we hear a shot outside, close at hand.*) They've got him . . . (*With a bravado toss of her head.*) Well, I don't care—I don't care.

(*Johnson falls against the door outside. The Girl, with a revulsion of feeling, rushes to the door, opens it, and he staggers in, her arms about him. Johnson leans against the wall. The Girl closes the door.*)

JOHNSON: (*Holding his hand to his right side.*) . . . Don't lock the door . . . I'm going out again . . . I'm going out . . . (*He swings round, lurches and nearly falls as the Girl pushes him onto a chair.*) Don't bar the door. Open it . . . Open it . . . By God! I won't hide behind a woman.

GIRL: (*Leaning over Johnson.*) I love you an' I'm goin' to stand by you. You asked me to go away with you. (*Crosses for the whiskey bottle and a glass.*) You get out of this, an' I will. If you can't save your own soul—(*There is a rap on the window. Rance is peering through, but he cannot see Johnson. The Girl sets down the bottle and glass and pauses. She looks up at the ladder to the loft, gets on a chair and lets it down. Rance goes from the window to the door.*)—I'm goin' to save it for you. You're the man that had my first kiss. Go up there! (*In a lower voice, never pausing, she urges Johnson to the loft.*)

JOHNSON: (*His handkerchief pressed to his side.*) No—no—no—no—Not here.

GIRL: Do you want them to see you in my cabin? Hurry . . . Hurry . . .

JOHNSON: No—No—

(*There is a rap on the door. She gives him a push, and with an effort, Johnson gradually climbs up the ladder, reeling as he goes.*)

GIRL: Yes, you can do it—you can—you're the man I love. You've got to show me the man that's in you. Go on . . . Go on . . . (*There is a second rap on the door.*) Just a step—a step.

JOHNSON: I can't . . . I can't. (*He reaches the loft, collapses, falling to his knees. He lies on the floor of the loft, one outstretched hand holding the handkerchief. The Girl swings the ladder up.*)

GIRL: (*Looks up, calls softly.*) You can. Don't move. (*There is another rap on the door.*) The cracks are wide—take that handkerchief away. (*He draws the handkerchief out of sight.*) That's it. (*There is another knock. The Girl calls off.*) Yes, yes, in a minute. (*In a whisper to Johnson.*) Don't move. (*The door opens and Rance appears. He slams the door behind him.*) Well, what do you want now? You can't come in here, Jack Rance.

RANCE: No more Jack Rance. It's the Sheriff after Mr. Johnson.

GIRL: What?

RANCE: I saw him coming in here. (*He cocks his revolver.*)

GIRL: It's more than I did— (*Rance glances at the bed, opening the curtains.*) and the door was barred. Do you think I want to shield a man who tried to rob me? If you doubt my word, go on—search the place; but that ends your acquaintance with the Polka. Don't you ever speak to me again—we're through!

RANCE: Wait a minute . . . What's that? (*He listens—the wind is calling. After a slight pause, Rance comes down to the table. The Girl is leaning against the *bureau. Rance uncocks his revolver, puts it in the holster, takes off his hat, shakes the water from it, and drops it on the table. His eyes never leave the Girl's face.*) I saw someone standing outside—there—(*He crosses to the fireplace.*) against the white snow. (*Taking off his overcoat.*) I fired. (*Shaking the coat.*) I could have sworn it was a man.

GIRL: Go on—go on— finish your search,—then never speak to me again.

RANCE: (*Seeing that he has gone too far—turning to her.*) Say, I—I don't want to quarrel with you.

GIRL: Go on—go on—and then leave a lady to herself to git to bed. Go on and git it over. (*She goes up to the bureau, her back to Rance.*)

RANCE: I'm crazy about you. I could have sworn I saw—You know it's just you for me—just you—and damn the man you like better! I—I—Even yet I—I can't—(*Starting to put on his coat.*) get over the queer look on your face when I told you who that man really was. You don't love him, do you? (*A pause. He throws the coat down on the floor and advances towards her.*) Do you?

GIRL: (*Lightly.*) Who? Me? (*With a forced laugh, she eyes Rance disdainfully.*)

RANCE: (*His feelings somewhat relieved, takes a step towards her.*) Say, was your answer to-night final about marrying me?

GIRL: (*Coyly, flirting with him.*) I might think it over, Jack. (*With another somewhat artificial laugh.*)

RANCE: Minnie . . . (*Coming close to her.*) I love you . . . (*Putting his arms about her, kissing her.*) I love you. (*She struggles to escape from him, and, picking up the bottle from the table, raises it to strike him, then sinks to the floor, sobbing.*)

GIRL: (*Nervously.*) Oh, my God, I—(*Rance stands looking down at her.*)

RANCE: (*With the nasty laugh of a man whose vanity is hurt.*) Ha! Ha! Ha! God! I—I didn't think it was that bad,—I didn't. I am much obliged to you. Thank you. (*Taking his cap from the table and going up towards the door.*) Good-night. (*Taking up his coat and starting to put it on.*) Good-night. Much obliged. Can't you—can't you even say good-night? (*He has his coat in his left hand, his cap in his right. The Girl rubs her hands on her dress and comes reluctantly towards him. He drops his cap.*)

GIRL: Yes. Good-night, Jack Rance. Good-night, Jack Rance. I—(*As he holds out his hand, a drop of blood from the loft falls on it.*)

RANCE: (*Slowly, after a pause.*) Look at my hand . . . (*Pulls out his handkerchief and wipes his hand.*) . . . my hand. (*Looking at the blood.*) That's blood.

GIRL: Yes, I must have scratched you just now. I'm awful sorry.

RANCE: There's no scratch there. There isn't a mark. (*More blood falls on the outstretched hand, holding the handkerchief.*)

GIRL: (*Quickly.*) Yes, but there will be in the morning, Jack. You'll see in the morning.

RANCE: (*Looks towards the loft. Placing his hand on his pistol, he puts his handkerchief in his pocket.*) He's up there.

GIRL: (*Holding his hand which grasps the revolver.*) No, he isn't, Jack. No, he isn't. No, he—

RANCE: You go straight to the devil. (*He picks up a chair to climb up—then sees the ladder.*)

GIRL: (*Trying to stop Rance.*) No, he isn't, Jack. Not there, Jack. Not there, Jack. He is not there—(*Drawing down the ladder.*)

RANCE: Mr. Johnson, come down.

GIRL: Wait a minute, Jack . . . Wait a minute . . .

RANCE: (*As Johnson moves towards the top of the ladder.*) Come down, or I'll—

GIRL: Wait jest a minute, Jack—jest a minute . . .

RANCE: (*His revolver levelled at Johnson.*) Come down here!

(*Step by step, Johnson comes down the ladder, his eyes fastened on Rance. The Girl stands watching Johnson. Johnson's hands, which are up, slowly fall, and, with unseeing eyes, he lurches to the chair behind the table, falls forward, his head resting on the table—unconscious, half in shadow. Rance puts his revolver in the holster.*)

GIRL: Don't you see he can't hold up his hands? Oh, Jack don't make him. Don't you see he can't? Oh, Jack, don't make him. No, no, wait, Jack, jest a minute—wait!

RANCE: (*Leaning over Johnson.*) Wait a minute? What for? (*Laughs—a low, unctuous laugh.*) So you dropped into the Polka, Mr. Johnson, to play me a little game of poker to-night? Ha! Ha! Ha! Funny how things change about in an hour or two. You think you can play poker? That's your conviction, is it? Ha! Ha! Ha! Well, you can play freeze-out as to your chances, Mr. Johnson, of Sacramento! It's shooting or the tree. Speak up—which will you have?

GIRL: (*Who has picked up her pistol—in a low voice, quiet but tense.*) You better stop that laughing, or you'll finish it in some other place where things ain't quite so funny. (*Something in her voice strikes Rance and he stops laughing.*) He doesn't hear you. He's out of it. But me—me—I hear you—I ain't out of it. You're a gambler—he was, too—so am I. (*Having engaged Rance's attention, she throws the pistol back into the drawer.*) I live on chance money—drink money—card money—saloon money. We're gamblers—we're all gamblers. (*Leaning over towards Rance.*) You asked me to-night if my answer to you was final. Now's your chance. I'll play you a game—straight poker. It's two out of three for me. Hatin' the sight of you—it's the nearest chance you'll ever git for me.

RANCE: Do you mean—

GIRL: With the wife in Noo Orleans—all right. If you're lucky, you git him an' me; but if you lose, this man settin' between us is mine—mine to do with as I please—an' you shut up and lose like a gentleman.

RANCE: (*Looking in her eyes.*) You must be crazy about him.

GIRL: (*Briefly.*) That's my business.

RANCE: Do you know you're talking to the Sheriff?

GIRL: I'm talkin' to Jack Rance, the gambler.

RANCE: (*Quietly and cooly.*) You're right. (*Standing upright.*) And I'm just fool enough to take you up. (*Looks for a chair.*) Ah! (*Brings the chair down, placing it before the table.*) You and the cards have got into my blood. I'll take you. (*He pulls off the table-cover and throws it on the floor.*)

GIRL: Your word?

RANCE: I can lose like a gentleman. (*She starts to draw back her hand, but he grasps it.*) But, my God! I'm hungry for you—and, if I'm lucky, I'll take it out on you so long as God lets you breathe.

GIRL: (*Draws away from him.*) Fix the lamp. (*Rance, his eyes still on her, reaches up to the lamp, does not find it at first, looks up, turns up the wick.*) Wait jest a minute—jest a minute. (*She goes into the wardrobe with the candle.*)

RANCE: What are you waiting for? (*He takes a pack of cards from his pocket, sits at the table and shuffles them.*)

GIRL: (*In the closet.*) I'm jest gettin' the cards, an' kind o'—steadyin' my nerves.

RANCE: I've got a deck here.

GIRL: (*Coming out of the wardrobe, blowing out the candle, and throwing it on the floor.*) We'll use a fresh deck. (*Laying a fresh pack of cards on the table.*) There's a good deal dependin' on this, Jack Rance. (*The Girl sits. Rance looks at her, then lays aside his own cards and takes hers.*) Are you—ready?

RANCE: Ready? Yes, I'm ready. Cut for deal. (*She cuts. Rance shuffles.*) This is a case of show-down.

GIRL: Show-down.

RANCE: Cut. (*Begins to deal.*) The best two out of three.

GIRL: Best two out of three.

RANCE: (*As he glances over the cards he has drawn—in a low voice—colloquially.*) What do you see in him?

GIRL: What do you see in me, Jack? (*Taking up her cards.*) What have you got?

RANCE: King high.

GIRL: King high.

RANCE: (*Showing her the hand.*) Jack next.

GIRL: (*Showing her hand to Rance.*) Queen next.

RANCE: You've got it. (*Throws down his hand. She shuffles.*) You've made a mistake on Johnson.

GIRL: (*Dealing.*) If I have, Jack, it's my mistake. What have you got?

RANCE: One pair—aces. (*Showing her the cards.*)

GIRL: Nothing. (*Throwing down her cards.*)

RANCE: (*Shuffles the cards.*) We're even. We're even.

GIRL: It's the next hand that tells, Jack, ain't it?

RANCE: Yes.

GIRL: I'm awful sorry it's the next hand that tells. I—I— want to say that no matter how it comes out—

RANCE: Cut. (*She cuts the cards and he picks them up and deals.*)

GIRL: —that I'll always think of you the best I can, and I want you to do the same for me.

RANCE: You heard what I said.

GIRL: (*Starts to draw her cards towards her. He reaches across, places his hand over hers and over the cards.*) Yes.

RANCE: But I have got a feeling that I win—that in one minute I'll hold you in my arms. (*He spreads out his cards, still holding her hand and looking at her. Then, as though resolved to face the consequences, he looks at his cards. She is leaning forward and her hand is being drawn towards him. As he sees his cards, he smiles. The Girl collapses with a shudder. He leans forward. Very calmly.*) I win.

GIRL: (*Very anxiously.*) Think so?

RANCE: Three Kings and it's the last hand. (*Showing his cards to the Girl.*)

GIRL: Oh, Jack, quick—get me something—I'm fainting!

RANCE: (*Throws the cards face down on the table.*) Where? Where?

GIRL: There.

RANCE: (*Finds the bottle, but not the glass.*) Oh, yes, here it is—here's the bottle. Where's a glass? Where's that damn glass?

(*As Rance turns away, she puts her cards in the bosom of her dress and draws five cards from her stocking.*)

GIRL: Hurry . . . Hurry . . .
RANCE: (*Dropping the bottle, turning and leaning forward as if to impress her, his arm round her neck.*) You're fainting because you've lost.
GIRL: (*Rises, laying down her hand on the table.*) No, Jack—it's because I've won—three aces and a pair! (*He looks at her hand. There is a slight pause.*)
RANCE: Good-night. (*Always the gambler, he picks up his hat and coat and goes.*)

(*The Girl drops the cards and takes Johnson in her arms.*)

Curtain.

END OF ACT II

ACT III

The interior of a typical mining-camp dance-hall of the period. The walls are of
rough boards nailed across upright beams.

The mines are closed on account of the weather, and the hall is decorated in honor
of the opening of the "Academy." Garlands of pine and wreaths of red berries hang
over the doors and windows. Yellow curtains hang at the windows. Eagles' wings
as well as wings of smaller birds, are tacked to the wall. Antlers (on which the
miners hang their hats when the "Academy" is in session) are fastened to the wall,
also birds' wings and a motto, painted on an old weather-beaten piece of wood,
"Live and Learn." A stuffed game-cock and a candle lamp with a reflector are over
a door at right. A horseshoe is fastened over the door to the exterior. A lamp hangs
from the center of the ceiling, and stuck in its cheap iron brackets are flags whose
stars indicate the number of States of that period. At the back, towards the right, is
a platform on which the teacher's home-made desk stands. It is decorated with a
garland of pine. A bunch of red and white berries, a ruler, chalk, a whiskey bottle,
glass and bell are on the desk. A box is used for the teacher's seat. A black-board
is at the back, standing on the floor and resting against the table. An old sheet-iron
stove, heavily dented, is below the desk. The fire is burning brightly. The stove has
an iron railing fastened to the base, on which the miners rest their feet. The stove-
pipe goes up through the ceiling. Whittled benches are arranged about the room
and two or three chairs. Sonora's coat is lying on a chair, and Trinidad's jacket is on
the bench against the wall at back. Doors lead to the bar-room, which we saw in
the first act, and a glimpse of the bar is shown. Fastened to the frame of one of these
doors is a large hand, rudely painted, the index finger pointing to the words, "To
the bar!" A red curtain cuts off the balcony on this same side of the room. Another
door, on the opposite side of the room, leads to a lean-to in which there is a door
leading to the exterior. A door at back opens directly upon the trail, and, when this
door is ajar, one sees the snow-covered country and the green firs of Cloudy Mountain heavily weighted by snow. It is a bright winter's morning.

At the rise of the curtain, Jack Rance is sitting near the fire,—worn, pale and wax-
en. He has not slept, and his eyes are red and half closed as he sits thinking. He is no
longer immaculate in dress,—his necktie is partly undone, his waist-coat is un-
fastened, his boots unpolished, his hair is ruffled and his cigar (in his hand) has
gone out. Nick, standing near the foot of the platform, seems troubled as he looks
through the window as though towards the Girl's cabin.)

NICK: I'd be willin' to lose the profits of the bar, if we could git back to a week ago,
  before Johnson walked into this room. (*He pours out a drink.*)
RANCE: (*Showing feeling.*) Johnson! By—(*Taking off his hat.*)—week—a week
  . . . A week in her cabin—nursed and kissed . . .
NICK: (*Remonstrating.*) Oh, say, Rance!
RANCE: You bet she kissed him, Nick. It was all I could do to keep from telling the
  whole camp he was up there.
NICK: But you didn't. If I hadn't been let into the game by the Girl, I'd a-thought
  you were a level Sheriff, looking for him. Rance, you're my 'deal of a perfect
  gent.
RANCE: What did she see in that Sacramento shrimp to love?
NICK: (*Puts his foot on a chair, hands the drink to Rance.*) Well, you see, I figger
  it out this way, boss: love's like a drink that gits a-holt on you, and you can't quit
  . . . it's a turn of the head, or a touch of the hands, or it's a half sort of
  smile—and you're doped—doped with a feelin' like strong liquor runnin'
  through your veins—(*Rance drops the hand which holds the glass.*) an' there
  ain't nothin' on earth can break it up, once you've got the habit. That's love. I've
  got it—you've got it—the boys've got it—the Girl's got it—the whole damn
  world's got it! It's all the Heaven there is on earth, and, in nine cases out of ten,
  it's Hell.

(*There is a pause. Rance, deep in thought, lets his glass tip and his whiskey drip to*
the floor. Nick touches Rance's arm, points to the whiskey. Rance takes out his
watch, glances at it, hands the glass back to Nick, who goes towards the door
leading to the bar.)

RANCE: Well, Nick, her road-agent's got off by now. (*Looking at his watch.*)
NICK: Left Cloudy at three o'clock this morning—five hours off.

(*Rance takes out a match, strikes it on the stove, then lights his cigar. Suddenly we*
hear a voice calling.)

RIDER OF THE PONY EXPRESS: (*Outside.*) Hello!
NICK: Pony Express! Got through at last! (*Goes to the bar-room.*)

(*The Rider of the Pony Express comes in from the bar-room, muffled up to his*
eyes.)

RIDER OF THE PONY EXPRESS: Hello, boys! (*Giving a letter to the Deputy*
  Sheriff, who comes in from the lean-to.) Letter for Ashby. Well, boys, how'd
  you like bein' snowed in for a week?
RANCE: Ashby ain't up yet. Dep: call Ashby. (*The Deputy Sheriff goes off.*)
RIDER OF THE PONY EXPRESS: (*At the stove.*) Boys: there's a rumor up at the

Ridge that you all let Ramerrez freeze, an' missed a hangin'. Say: they're roaring at you, boys. So long!

(*Sonora and Trinidad, who have appeared from the bar-room, give the Rider a hard glance as he goes out through the bar.*)

SONORA: (*Calling after the Pony Express Rider.*) Wait! Says you to the boys at the Ridge as you ride by—the Academy at Cloudy is open to-day—says you—full blast. (*We hear a door slam as the Rider goes on his way.*)

TRINIDAD: (*Calling after the Rider.*) Whoopee! Whoop! They ain't got no Academy at the Ridge.

NICK: (*Bringing in whiskey for Trinidad and Sonora.*) Here, Sonora.

RANCE: (*With a sneer.*) Academy! Ha! Ha! Academy!

SONORA: What's the matter with you, Rance, anyway? We began this Academy game together—we boys an' the Girl—an' there's a—(*Spits on the floor.*)—pretty piece of sentiment back of it. She's taught some of us our letters and—

TRINIDAD: He's wearin' mournin' because Johnson didn't fall alive into his hands.

SONORA: Is that it?

TRINIDAD: (*To Rance.*) Ain't it enough that he must be lyin' dead down some cañon with his mouth full of snow?

SONORA: You done all you could to git him. The boys is all satisfied he's dead. (*Nick gives Sonora a sharp look, then turns guiltily to Rance.*)

RANCE: (*Rising, walking about restlessly.*) Yes—he's dead. The matter with *me* is, I'm a "Chink." (*He goes up to the window and glances out.*)

ALL: Ha! Ha! Ha! Ha!

RANCE: Boys: it's all up with the Girl and me.

TRINIDAD: (*Self-consciously.*) Throwed him!

SONORA: (*In a low voice to Nick, who has picked up the empty glasses and is standing near the window.*) As sure's you live, she throwed him over for me. (*Nick hastily leaves the room with the glasses—coming back at once.*)

TRINIDAD: (*Singing in his glee.*) "Will old dog Tray remember me."

SONORA: (*Crossing to the door at the left.*) The percession will now form to the Academy wood-pile, to finish splittin' wood for teacher.

TRINIDAD *and* SONORA: (*Singing.*) "Old dog Tray remember me."

SONORA: (*Chuckling to himself.*) For me! (*They go out to the lean-to.*)

DEPUTY: (*Entering excitedly.*) Ashby's out with a posse. (*Rance turns quickly.*) Got off just after three this morning. (*Closes the door.*)

NICK: What?

RANCE: (*Aside to Nick, with much excitement.*) He's after Johnson!

NICK: Help yourself, Dep. (*The Deputy goes into the bar-room.*)

RANCE: Ashby's after Johnson! He was watching that horse—took him ten minutes to saddle up. Johnson has ten minutes' start. (*Hopefully.*) Oh, God! (*Going towards the bar.*) They'll never get him. Johnson's a wonder on the road. You got to take your hat off to the damn cuss. (*He passes off.*)

(*We hear the whoop of approaching miners coming to school. Sonora enters with an armful of wood, which he puts on the floor near the stove. Trinidad enters, runs to the door at the back and opens it, then puts on his jacket. The Deputy strolls in from the bar.*)

SONORA: Boys gatherin' for school.

(*Handsome, Happy, Joe, a gambler, and a miner, come into the room, playing leap-frog as they enter, talking and laughing. Their boots are covered with snow. Happy goes up to the teacher's desk and picks up a book tied in a red handkerchief.*)

HAPPY: Here, Trin,—here's the book. (*He throws it to Trinidad, who throws it to Sonora, Sonora to Joe, Joe to Handsome, Handsome to Sonora. Bucking Billy, a new scholar from Watson's Camp, comes in.*)

THE DEPUTY SHERIFF: Sh, boys! Noo scholer from Watson's. (*Indicating Bucking Billy.*)

(*Billy is a large, awkward miner, wearing an overcoat, muffler and top boots with brass tips. He carries a dinner pail which contains a sandwich and whiskey flask. He has a slate under his arm.*)

SONORA: (*As all stare at Billy.*) Did you ever play lame soldier, m'friend?
BUCKING BILLY: No.
SONORA: We'll play it after school. You'll be the stirrup. (*To the others—with a wink.*) We'll initiate him.
NICK: (*Up at the window.*) Boys, boys, here she is.
HAPPY: (*Looking out of the window.*) Here comes the Girl.
SONORA: Fix the seats.

(*All save Nick, Trinidad and one miner hasten off.*)

TRINIDAD: (*Confidentially.*) Here, Nick: you don't think to-day'd be a good time to put the splice question to her?
NICK: (*Dubiously.*) I wouldn't rush her. You got plenty of time.

(*He hangs the blackboard on the wall. Sonora enters with a cask. The Miner gets another cask, Handsome enters with a plank, which he lays across the two casks. This forms a long table for the students. Sonora picks up his coat, which is lying on a chair, and puts it on hurriedly. Happy, the Deputy, and the Miner arrange more benches.*)

TRINIDAD: Hurry up, boys—hurry up! Git everything in order.

(*The Girl enters. She is carrying a small book of poems. The men take off their hats.*)

BOYS: (*All speaking together.*) Hello, teacher!
GIRL: Hello!

(*Sonora crosses to the Girl and hands her a bunch of berries.*)

TRINIDAD: Hello, teacher! (*He hands her an orange.*) From 'Frisco.
HAPPY: (*Comes down with a bunch of berries which he gives to the Girl.*) Regards! (*Nick takes off her moccasins.*)

GIRL: (*Quietly.*) Hello, boys! How's everything? (*With a guilty look, she glances from one to another, to see if they suspect her.*)

HAPPY: Bully!

SONORA: Say—we missed you. Never knew you to desert the Polka for a whole week before.

GIRL: (*Who has gone up to the desk.*) No, I—I—(*She lays the berries and the orange on the desk.*)

HAPPY: Academy's opened.

GIRL: Yes . . . I see . . . (*She takes off her gloves.*)

SONORA: Here's a noo pupil—Bucking Billy from Watson's. (*Bucking Billy comes forward.*)

GIRL: How do you do, Bucking Billy?

BUCKING BILLY: (*Shyly.*) How do!

GIRL: (*Starting and looking out of the window.*) What's that?

NICK: Log fell in the stove.

GIRL: Oh . . . (*Pulling herself together.*) I guess I'm kind of nervous today. (*She exchanges glances with Nick as she takes off her coat and hands it to him.*)

SONORA: No wonder. Road-agent's been in camp . . . and we missed a hangin'. I can't get over that!

GIRL: Well, come on, boys, and let me see your hands. (*Emphatically.*) Let me see them! (*After looking at the outstretched hands.*) Git in there and wash them.

SONORA: Yes'm. Been blackenin' my boots. (*He points to his boots.*)

GIRL: Yes, and look at them boots—and them boots—and them boots! Git in there, the whole lot of you, and clean up—and leave your whiskey behind. (*The boys go into the lean-to. Untying the strings of her cap, she takes it off and hands it to Nick.*) Have you heard anything? Did he git away safe?

NICK: Yes.

GIRL: I was watchin' an' I seen him go . . . but suppose he don't git through . . . suppose . . .

NICK: He'll git through, sure. We'll hear he's out of this country before you know it. (*He hangs up the Girl's wraps. Rance enters.*)

GIRL: Jack Rance: I want to thank you.

RANCE: Oh, don't thank me that he got away. (*In a low voice.*) It was them three aces and the pair you held.

GIRL: (*In confidence.*) About them three aces—I want to say—

RANCE: But he better keep out of my country. (*The Girl and Rance look intently at one another.*)

GIRL: Yes . . .

(*She rings the bell. The boys enter. Rance sits down by the stove, paying no attention to the others. Happy enters, carrying the slates which are in a very bad condition—some have no frames, some have very little slate left—one or two have sponges hanging to the frames on strings, and all have slate-pencils fastened to the frames. Happy gives out the slates as the others march by.*)

HAPPY: Come along, boys—git your slates.

TRINIDAD: Whoop!

GIRL: Trin, you're out of step, there. Git in step, Happy. (*The boys all march forward in the manner of school children. As each one gets his slate, he takes his seat. The Girl sits back of her desk on the platform. With a sickly laugh, trying to take interest in the scholars.*) Now, boys: what books have we left over from last year?

HAPPY: (*Rising.*) Why, we scared up jest one whole book left—and the name of it is—

SONORA: (*Taking the book out of his pocket, and reading the title.*) "Old Joe Miller's Jokes."

GIRL: That will do nicely.

SONORA: (*Rising.*) Now, boys, before we begin, I propose no drawin' of weppings, drinkin' or swearin' in school hours. The conduct of certain members wore on teacher last term. I don't want to mention no names—but I want Handsome and Happy to hear what I'm sayin'. Is that straight?

ALL: You bet it is!

GIRL: (*Timidly.*) Last year you led off with an openin' address, Jack. (*She looks at him timidly.*)

ALL: Yes! Yes! Yes! Yes! Go on, Sheriff!

TRINIDAD: Let her go, Jack. (*There is a pause. Rance looks at the Girl, then turns away.*)

RANCE: I pass.

GIRL: (*Quickly and with anxiety.*) Then Sonora?

SONORA: (*Embarrassed at being called upon to make a speech.*) Oh, Hell! I—

ALL: Sh! Sh! Sh! Go on! Go on! Go on!

SONORA: (*Abashed.*) I didn't mean that, of course. (*As he rises, he shifts his tobacco and unconsciously spits on Bucking Billy's new boots. Bucking Billy moves away.*) I look upon this place as somethin' more than a place to set around an' spit on the stove. I claim they's culture in the air of California—an' we're here to buck up again' it an' hook on.

ALL: Hear! Hear! Hear! (*Several of the men pound upon the desks enthusiastically.*)

SONORA: With these few remarks, I—I set.

GIRL: (*With deep feeling.*) Once more we meet together. There's been a lot happened of late that has learned me that—(*Rance turns slightly in his seat. Nick looks at Rance, Rance at the Girl.*) perhaps—I don't know so much as I thought I did—and I can't learn you much more. But if you're willin' to take me for what I am,—jest a woman who wants everybody to be all they ought to be,—why I'm willin' to rise up with you, an' help reach out (*Handsome raises his hand.*) an'—What is it, Handsome?

HANDSOME: Whiskey, teacher. I want it so bad! Just one drink 'fore we start.

(*The boys all stand up, raising their hands and calling: "Teacher." The Girl puts her fingers in her ears.*)

GIRL: No! . . . And now jest a few words on the subject of not settin' in judgment on the errin'—(*The boys all sit down again.*) a subjeck near my heart.

(*The Sidney Duck opens the door. The card is still pinned on his coat.*)

ALL: (*At the sight of the Sidney Duck.*) Git! Git! (*Sid is about to retreat.*)

GIRL: Boys! Boys! I was jest gittin' to you, Sid, as I promised. Come in. (*Sid enters.*)

SONORA: What—here? Among gentlemen? Git!

ALL: Eh? What? Git! Git!

TRINIDAD: Why, this fellow's a—

GIRL: I know—I know . . . but of late a man in trouble has been on my mind—

ALL: Eh?

GIRL: (*Catching Rance's eye.*) Sid—of course, Sid—

ALL: Oh . . .

GIRL: —and I fell to thinkin' of the Prodigal Son—he done better at last, didn't he?

SONORA: I never heard that he was a card sharp.

TRINIDAD: No.

GIRL: (*Overcome with guilt—swallowing nervously.*) But suppose there was a moment in Sid's life when he felt called upon to find an extra ace. (*There is a slight pause.*) Can't we forgive him? He says he's sorry. Sid?

SID: Oh, yes, Miss, I'm sorry. Course if I 'adn't got caught, things would 'a been different. I'm sorry.

GIRL: Sid, you git your chance. (*The boys mutter. The Girl takes the card off Sid's coat.*) Now go and set down. (*The Girl sits.*)

(*Happy strikes Sid as he attempts to sit.*)

HAPPY: Git out of here!

GIRL: Happy! Happy! (*Sonora, as Sid passes him, puts out his foot and trips him.*) Sonora!

(*Sid sits on a stool in a corner. Everyone moves away as far as possible.*)

TRINIDAD: (*Rises.*) Say, Girl: you mean to say that honesty ain't the best policy? Supposin' my watch had no works, an' I was to sell it to the Sheriff for one hundred dollars. Would you have much respect for me?

GIRL: If you could do it, I'd have more respect for you than for the Sheriff.

(*The two Indians, Billy Jackrabbit and Wowkle, enter quietly and sit on the bench by the wall under the blackboard. They take no part, but listen stupidly. Wowkle has the papoose on her back.*)

RANCE: (*Rising.*) Well, being Sheriff, I'm careful about the company I keep. I'll sit in the bar. Cheats—(*Looking at Sid.*) or road-agents aren't jest in my line. (*He turns and starts to go.*) I walk in the open road, with my head up—(*The Girl looks down.*) and my face to the sun; and wherever I've pulled up, you'll remark I've always played square and stood by the cyards. (*He pauses in the doorway.*)

GIRL: (*Sitting.*) I know—I know—an' that's the way to travel—in the straight road. But if ever I don't travel that road—or—you—

NICK: You always will, you bet!

ALL: You bet she will! You bet!

GIRL: But if I don't—I hope there'll be someone to lead me back to the right road. Cause remember. Rance: some of us are lucky enough to be born good—others have to be elected. (*Rance goes out.*)

SONORA: (*Touched.*) That's eloquence.

(*Sid sobs. Happy takes out a bottle of whiskey and puts it to his lips. The boys all reach for it. The Girl takes the bottle away.*)

GIRL: Give me that and set down. (*The boys sit down obediently. The Girl goes back to her desk, hands the bottle to Nick and sits. Nick puts the bottle on the shelf of the desk.*) Now, if somebody can sing "My Country 'Tis"—Academy's opened. Sonora?

SONORA: No—I can't sing.

(*The boys all try to make each other sing. While they are chafing each other, Wowkle and Billy Jackrabbit rise and sing.*)

BILLY JACKRABBIT *and* WOWKLE:
"My country 'tis of thee,
Sweet land of liberty,
Of thee I sing!"

SONORA: Well, if that ain't sarkism!

BILLY JACKRABBIT *and* WOWKLE:
"Land where our fathers died" . . .

SONORA: (*Quickly during the pause between the two lines.*) You bet they died hard!

INDIANS:
"Land of the Pilgrim's pride,
From every mountain-side
Let freedom ring!"

(*When the song is ended, the Indians sit down again.*)

GIRL: Thank you, Billy and Wowkle. Now, them that can read, read.

TRINIDAD: This is us! Old Joe Miller!

SONORA: (*Reading from the book.*) "Can Feb-u-ary March? No, but—A-pril May."

GIRL: Now, Trin. (*As Trinidad laboriously reads the ancient joke, Sid, who has noticed Bucking Billy's dinner-pail, reaches out with his feet, pulls the pail over to him, helps himself to food and a small flask of whiskey. He pushes the pail back and starts to eat and drink, glancing at the others furtively to see if he has been caught.*) Now, then, boys, we mustn't forget out general infla—information. Trin, who killed Abel?

TRINIDAD: (*In a surprised tone—thinking of some local character.*) Why, I didn't know he was dead.

GIRL: Bucking Billy: you count up to ten.

BUCKING BILLY: (*Rising.*) 1, 2, 3, 4—

SONORA: Pretty good! I didn't think he knowed that much.

BUCKING BILLY: 5, 6, 7, 8, 9, 10, Jack, Queen—(*Everybody laughs. Bucking Billy suddenly discovers that his pail has been opened.*) Somebody stole my lunch!

SONORA: (*Rising.*) Who?

BUCKING BILLY: Him! (*Pointing to Sid.*)

ALL: Put him out! Git out! Put him out!

GIRL: Boys! Boys!

(*Sonora, Trinidad and Handsome throw Sid out and return to their seats. The Girl looks out through the window for a moment, then turns and opens a book.*)

GIRL: I will read you a little verse from a book of pomes.
"No star is ever lost we once have seen,
We always may be what we might have been."

(*She rests her hand on the desk and breaks down, sobbing quietly. Nick rises and goes to her.*)

SONORA: Why, what's the—
ALL: Why—what's—
GIRL: Nothin' . . . Nothin' . . . Only it jest came over me that we mustn't be hard on sinners and . . . (*Breaking down completely.*) Oh, boys . . . I'll be leavin' you soon—how can I do it? How can I do it?
SONORA: What?
TRINIDAD: What did she say?
SONORA: What'd you say? (*Going to her.*) Why, what's the matter?
GIRL: (*Raising her head.*) Nothin'—nothin'—only I jest remembered I've promised to leave Cloudy soon, an' perhaps we—might never be together again—you an' me an' the Polka. Oh, it took me jest like that—when I seen your dear old faces—your dear, plucky old faces—an' reelized that—(*She drops her head on the desk again.*)

(*Rance enters.*)

SONORA: (*After a pause.*) What! You leavin' us?
HAPPY: Leavin' us?
NICK: (*Softly, that the others do not hear.*) Careful, Girl, careful!
GIRL: It's bound to happen soon.
SONORA: Why, I don't quite understand. Great Gilead! We done anythin' to offend you?
GIRL: Oh, no, no!
SONORA: Tired of us? Ain't we got—(*Casting about for a word.*) style enough for you?
HAPPY: (*Rising.*) Be you goin' to show them Ridge boys we're petered out an' culture's a dead dog here?
TRINIDAD: Ain't we your boys no more?
SONORA: (*With sentiment, looking like a large, fat cherub.*) Ain't I your boy? Why, what is it, Girl? Has anybody—tell me—perhaps—
GIRL: (*Raising her head and drying her eyes.*) We won't say no more about it. Let's forgit it. Only—when I go away—I want to leave the key of my cabin with old Sonora here. And I want you all to come up sometimes, an' to think of me as the Girl who loved you all, an' somewhere wishin' you well—an'—I want to think of little Nick here runnin' my bar, an' not givin' the boys too much whiskey. (*Putting her hand on Nick's shoulder.*)
SONORA: Hold on! They's jest one reason for a girl to leave her home an' friends . . . only one. Some other fellow away from here—that she—she likes better than she does any of us. Is that it?
GIRL: (*Raising her head again.*) Likes in a different way,—yes.
HAPPY: Well, so help me!

(*Sonora goes sadly back to his seat. The boys form a pathetic picture.*)

TRINIDAD: Sure you ain't makin' a mistake?

GIRL: Mistake? No, no, boys—no mistake. Oh, boys: if you knew—(*She rises, hesitates a moment, then goes to them.*) Trin . . . (*Putting hands on Trinidad's shoulder.*) Ah, Sonora . . . (*She kisses Sonora on the cheek, turns and exits into the bar-room, sobbing.*)

SONORA: Boys, Academy's busted . . .

(*There is a pause.*)

RANCE: (*Sitting down in front of the stove.*) Ha! Ha! Ha! Well, the right man has come at last. Take your medicine, gentlemen.

SONORA: Rance, who's the man?

RANCE: (*Casually.*) Oh,—Johnson.

TRINIDAD: Holy—!

SONORA: Great—!

TRINIDAD *and* SONORA: You lie!

(*During the following speeches, some of the boys move the benches and desks back against the walls. Bucking Billy and the Miner leave.*)

RANCE: Ask Nick.

(*Trinidad and Sonora look at Nick.*)

SONORA: Why, you told me I had the first chance.

TRINIDAD: He told me the same thing.

SONORA: Well, for a first class liar!

TRINIDAD: You bet!

SONORA: But Johnson's dead. (*Suddenly, after a short pause.*) He got away . . .

RANCE: (*Shaking the ashes from his cigar.*) Yes, he got away . . .

(*There is a pause as they realize the situation. Sonora comes to Rance, followed by Trinidad and Happy.*)

SONORA: Jack Rance: I call on you, as Sheriff, for Johnson. He was in your county.

HAPPY: You hustle up an' run a bridle through your pinto's teeth, or your boom for re-election's over, you lily-fingered gambler!

TRINIDAD: (*Shaking his fist at Rance.*) You bet!

RANCE: (*Coolly.*) Oh—I—don't know as I give a—

TRINIDAD: No talk! We want—

ALL: (*Save Rance and Nick.*) Johnson!

(*Ashby's voice is heard outside.*)

ASHBY: Boys!

NICK: Why, that's—

RANCE: That's Ashby! Oh, if—(*In his face is the hope of Johnson's capture. To Ashby, who is still outside.*) You've got him?

(*Ashby enters, his face cool, triumphant. He stands near the door. The Deputy hastens out. This entire scene is played easily and naturally—no suggestion of dramatic emphasis.*)

ASHBY: Yes—we've got him!
SONORA: Not—
ASHBY: Johnson.

(*All look at each other with meaning glances. Nick alone is sorry that Johnson is caught.*)

TRINIDAD: Alive?
ASHBY: You bet!
RANCE: (*With a short, brutal laugh—the veneer of the gambler disappearing.*) Well, I didn't do it. I didn't do it. Now he be damned! (*Johnson enters, his arms bound, pale, but with the courage of a man who is accustomed to risking his life. He is followed by the Deputy.*) There's an end of him. How do you do, Mr. Johnson? I think, Mr. Johnson, about five minutes will do for you.

(*Trinidad takes out his watch.*)

JOHNSON: I think so.
SONORA: (*Sarcastically.*) So this is the gentleman the girl loves?
RANCE: That's the gentleman.

(*The Girl's voice is heard outside.*)

GIRL: Nick? Boys? (*Nick holds the door open. The Girl appears on the threshold of the bar-room. Ashby steps between the Girl and Johnson, so that the Girl does not see him.*) I forgot . . . it's recess. They can have a drink now. (*She moves away from the door.*)
JOHNSON: Lock that door, Nick. (*Nick shuts the door to the bar and locks it.*)
RANCE: Why the hell—
JOHNSON: Please!
SONORA: (*Threateningly.*) Why, you—
RANCE: (*To Sonora.*) You keep out of this. I handle the rope—I pick the tree.
SONORA: Then hurry.
TRINIDAD: You bet!

(*Ashby nods in approval.*)

SONORA: Come on.

(*There is a general movement towards the door leading to the trail.*)

RANCE: Deputy? (*The Deputy comes forward.*)
JOHNSON: One minute . . .
RANCE: Be quick, then.
JOHNSON: It's true . . . I love the Girl.
RANCE: (*Brutally.*) Well—you won't in a minute. You—(*He makes a movement to strike him.*)

JOHNSON: Oh, I don't care what you do to me. I'm prepared for death. That's nothing new. The man who travels my path faces death every day—for a drink of water or ten minutes' sleep. You've got me, and I wouldn't care . . . but for the Girl.

TRINIDAD: You've jest got three minutes.

SONORA: Yes.

JOHNSON: I don't want her to know my end. That would be an awful thought—that I died out there, close at hand. She couldn't stay here after that—she couldn't, boys, she couldn't.

RANCE: (*Briefly.*) That's understood.

JOHNSON: I'd like her to think that I got away—went East—and changed my way of living. So you jest drag me a long way from here before you . . . and when she grows tired of looking for letters that never come, she will say: "He has forgotten me," and that will be about enough for her to remember. She loved me before she knew what I was . . . and you can't change love in a minute.

RANCE: (*Striking him in the face.*) Why, you . . .

JOHNSON: I don't blame you! Strike me again—strike me! Hanging is too good for me. Damn me, body and soul—damn me! Why couldn't I have let her pass? Oh, by God, I'm sorry I came her way; but it's too late now—it's too late! (*He bows his head.*)

(*There is a pause.*)

RANCE: Is that your last word? (*Johnson does not answer.*) That your last word? (*Trinidad snaps his fingers to indicate that time is up.*) Dep. (*The Deputy comes to Johnson, Rance moves away, but Nick steps to Johnson's side.*)

NICK: Good-bye, sir . . .

JOHNSON: Good-bye, Nick. You tell the Girl—no, don't say anything.

HAPPY: Come on, you!

(*They start to go.*)

NICK: (*His voice trembling.*) Boys: when Alliger was hanged, Rance let him see his sweetheart. I think—considerin' as how she ain't goin' to see no more of Mr. Johnson here—an' knowin' the Girl's feelin's,—I think she ought to have a chance to—

ALL: No! No! No!

RANCE: No!

JOHNSON: I've had my chance—inside of ten minutes I'll be dead, and it will be all your way. Couldn't you let me? I thought I'd have the courage not to ask, but—Oh, couldn't you?

(*Nick goes to the door as though hearing some sound.*)

NICK: Here's the Girl, boys.

RANCE: No!

JOHNSON: All right. Thank you, Nick.

NICK: You must excuse Rance for bein' so small a man as to deny the usual courtesies, but he ain't quite himself.

JOHNSON: Come, boys, come.

(He starts for the door left. Sonora pushes him back. The Deputy and one of the miners step between Johnson and the door.)

RANCE: Wait a minute. *(There is a pause. Johnson slowly turns to face Rance.)* I don't know that I'm so small a man as to deny the usual courtesies, since you put it that way. I always have extended them. But we'll hear what you have to say—that's our protection; and it might interest some of us to hear what the Girl will have to say to you, Mr. Johnson. After a week in her cabin, there may be more to know than—

JOHNSON: *(In a low voice.)* Why, you damned—

(Nick moves towards Rance.)

NICK: Rance, you—

(The boys all look at Rance angrily, showing that they resent his words.)

SONORA: Now, Rance, you stop that!
RANCE: We'll hear every word he has to say.
SONORA: You bet! He puts up nothin' noo on us.
ASHBY: *(Looking at his watch.)* Well, boys, you've got him safe—I can't wait. I'm off. *(He goes off.)*

(The Girl's voice is heard outside the bar-room door.)

GIRL: Nick? Nick?
NICK: Here's the Girl, boys.
RANCE: Deputy . . . *(He unties Johnson.)* Circle around to the bar, boys. Trin, put a man at that door. Sonora, put a couple of men at those windows. *(Happy, Sonora, the Deputy and the Gambler go outside. Handsome and Trinidad go into the lean-to. Nick stands at the bar-room door.)* Johnson, if you can't think of something pleasant to tell the Girl, lie to her.
JOHNSON: I'll let her think I came back to see her again. She needn't know it's the last time.

(The Girl's voice is heard outside.)

GIRL: Nick? Nick?

(Rance leaves the room. Trinidad, Handsome and Rance can be seen to pass the windows. Johnson steps behind the door. Nick unbars the bar-room door and the Girl enters.)

GIRL: What you got the door barred for, Nick? *(Looking around.)* Where are the boys?
NICK: Well, you see, the boys—the boys—has—has—
GIRL: Has what?
NICK: *(As though struck by a bright idea.)* Has gone.
GIRL: Gone where?
NICK: Why, to the Palmetter. Oh, say, Girl—*(He crosses over to her and puts his*

hand on her shoulders.) I like you. You've been my religion—the bar an' you. You don't never want to leave us. Why, I'd drop dead for you!

GIRL: (*Somewhat surprised and touched.*) Nick! (*She goes up to her desk as Johnson knocks on the door.*)

JOHNSON: (*Appearing.*) Girl! (*He holds out his arms to her.*)

GIRL: You? You? Look outside and—

(*Nick closes the door, bars and holds it.*)

JOHNSON: Don't say a word.

GIRL: (*In Johnson's arms.*) You shouldn't have come back.

JOHNSON: I had to—to say good-bye once more.

NICK: (*Lying with effort.*) It's all right—it's all right. (*During Nick's speech, the Girl draws the curtains.*) The boys—why, the boys—they are good for quite a little bit yet. Don't git nervous. I'll give you warning. (*Nick steps into the bar.*)

JOHNSON: Don't be afraid, Girl.

GIRL: But you can't go now without being seen.

JOHNSON: (*With a smile.*) Yes—there's one way out of Cloudy—and I'm going to take it.

GIRL: (*Attempting to move from him.*) Then go! Go!

JOHNSON: Just remember that I am sorry for the past—and don't forget me.

GIRL: Forgit you? How could—

JOHNSON: I mean . . . till we meet.

GIRL: (*Apprehensively.*) Did he call?

JOHNSON: No. He will—he'll warn me . . . don't forget me.

GIRL: Every day that dawns I'll wait for a message from you. I'll feel you wanting me. Every night, I'll say: "Tomorrow"—and every to-morow I'll say: "To-day!" For you've changed the whole world for me. I can't let you go . . . but I must. Dick—Oh, I'm afraid! (*She hides her head on Johnson's shoulder.*)

JOHNSON: You mustn't be afraid. In a few minutes, I shall be quite free.

GIRL: And you'll make a little home for me where you're goin'—soon—with you? (*She is overcome. Johnson merely nods.*) A strange feelin' has come over me. A feelin' to hold you, to cling to you—not to let you go. Somethin' in my heart says, "Don't let him go."

JOHNSON: Girl, it's been worth life just to know you. You've brought me nearer Heaven. You—to love a man like me! (*He covers his face with his hands, breaks down and sobs.*)

GIRL: Don't say that. Don't! Suppose you was only a road-agent—an' I was a saloon-keeper:we both came out of nothin' an' we met, but, through loving, we're goin' to reach things now—that's us! We had to be lifted up like this, to be saved.

(*Nick enters. As he opens the door, the boys are seen outside, but the Girl has her back to them.*)

NICK: It's all clear now. (*Nick backs off, closing the door again.*)

JOHNSON: Good-bye.

GIRL: (*In Johnson's arms.*) You act as though we was never goin' to meet again, an' we are, ain't we?

JOHNSON: Why, surely—we are.

GIRL: I want you to think of me here jes' waitin'. You was the first . . . there'll never be anyone but you. All that mother was to father, *I'm* goin' to be to you. You're the man I'd want settin' across the table, if they was a little kid like I was, playin' under it. I can't say more than that! Only—you—you will—you must get through safe—and, well, think of me here jes' waitin' . . . jes' waitin' . . . jes' waitin' . . .

(He stands looking at her. After a little pause, she puts her face in his arm and weeps.)

JOHNSON: Oh, Girl, Girl! That first night I went to your cabin—I saw you kneeling—praying. Say that in your heart again for me—now. Perhaps I believe it—perhaps I don't. I hope I do. I want to. But say it—say it, Girl—just for the luck of it. Say it. *(He kneels at her feet, his head bowed. The Girl prays silently, crossing herself before she begins, and, at the end of the prayer, they embrace. Sonora opens the door quietly.)* God bless you! Good-bye . . . Good-bye, Girl!

(Sonora is followed by the rest of the boys, Rance being the last to enter. Johnson, looking over the Girl's shoulder, sees the boys. He kisses her hands affectionately.)

GIRL: Good-bye . . .
JOHNSON: Girl! Girl! *(He goes off left.)*
GIRL: He's gone—Nick. *(Sobbing, she makes a movement to follow Johnson, then goes to Nick and sobs in his arms. Suddenly she sees the men.)*
NICK: *(Soothingly.)* Girl! Girl!
GIRL: *(In alarm.)* You—you knew . . . You all knew . . . You had him—you had him all the time . . . An' you're goin' to kill him—but you shan't. *(Running over to the door, she throws herself against it—her back to it, then sobs convulsively.)* No! You sha'n't kill him—you sha'n't—you sha'n't!
SONORA: *(Advances.)* Girl . . . the boys an' me ain't perhaps reelized jest what Johnson stood for to you, Girl—an', hearin' what you said, an' seein' you prayin' over the cuss—
RANCE: Damned cuss!
SONORA: Yes, the damned cuss, I got an idee maybe God's back of this here game.
GIRL: *(With much anxiety.)* You're not goin' to pull the rope on him?
RANCE: *(To the men.)* You mean I am to set him free?
GIRL: *(With a gleam of hope in her heart.)* You set him free?
RANCE: I let him go?
SONORA: That's our verdict, an' we're prepared to back it up.
GIRL: Dick—Dick—you're free! *(She rushes out and her voice is heard outside.)* You're free! You're free!

(There is a pause. The men stand silently looking at each other.)

NICK: The Polka won't never be the same, boys—the Girl's gone.

Curtain.

END OF ACT III

ACT IV

The boundless prairies of the West. On the way East, at the dawn of a day about a week later.

"Oh, my beautiful West!
Oh, my California!"

The scene is a great stretch of prairie. In the far background are foothills with here and there a suggestion of a winding trail leading to the West. The foliage is the pale green of sage brush,—the hills the deeper green of pine and hemlock. In the foreground is a little tepee made of two blankets on crossed sticks. The tepee is built against a grass mound and is apparently only a rude shelter for the night. Back of the tent is an old tree stump which stands out distinctly against the horizon. Here and there are little clumps of grass, bushes and small mounds of earth and rocks. A log fire is burning to the left of the tepee, a Mexican saddle lies beside the fire.

As the curtain rises, the stage is in darkness. Johnson is lying on the grass, leaning against his saddle, smoking a cigarette. The Girl is inside the tepee. Gradually the dawn begins to break. As the scene becomes visible, the Girl pushes aside the blanket and appears in the opening.

GIRL: Dick, are you awake?
JOHNSON: (*Turning to her.*) Another day . . . the dawn is breaking.
GIRL: (*Looking towards the unseen hills in the distance.*) Another day . . . Look back . . . the foothills are growing fainter—every dawn—farther away. Some night when I am going to sleep, I'll turn—and they won't be there—red and shining. That was the promised land.
JOHNSON: (*Rising.*) We must look ahead, Girl, not backwards. The promised land is always ahead.

(*A glimmer of the rising sun is seen on the foliage of the foothills.*)

GIRL: Always ahead . . . Yes, it must be. (*She comes out of the tepee and goes up the path.*) Dick: all the people there in Cloudy—how far off they seem now—like shadows in a dream. Only a few days ago, I clasped their hands; I saw their faces—their dear faces! And now they are fading. In this little, little while, I've lost them . . . I've lost them. (*There are tears in her voice.*)

JOHNSON: Through you, all my old life has faded away. *I* have lost that.

GIRL: Look! (*Pointing to the left as she notices the sunrise.*) The dawn is breaking in the East—far away—fair and clear.

JOHNSON: A new day . . . Trust me. (*Stretching out his hands to her.*) Trust me . . . A new life!

GIRL: A new life. (*Putting her hands in his.*) Oh, my mountains—I'm leaving you—Oh, my California, I'm leaving you—Oh, my lovely West—my Sierras!—I'm leaving you!—Oh, my—(*Turning to Johnson, going to him and resting in his arms.*)—my home.

Curtain.

END